IF YOU ARE ~~~
THESE EXCI~~~

- **American Airlines** — Now he~~~ ~~~ and African American employee ~~~ ~~~ groups that meet each month. The sky is the limit where employees receive guidance from a formal mentoring program.
- **Anheuser-Busch** — With three minority board members, it's no wonder this company has a policy that enables African Americans, Asians and Hispanics to reach the very highest line and staff positions. They hold such top jobs as Division President, Senior Vice President of Market Development and Vice President of Finance.
- **Sara Lee** — Sara Lee has it all: an aggressive diversity training steering committee; two African American board members; strong recruitment programs; more than $11 million annually to charitable organizations; and 20% of its total purchasing budget spent on minority contractors.
- **The Clorox Company** — A corporation that encourages risk-taking, especially for its scientists, this Oakland, California, company has long been committed to minority advancement, the opportunity to cross-train in different departments and the moving of minorities into high-ranking management positions.

Plus great news about UPS, General Motors, Pepsico, American Express, MCI, Polaroid, US West, General Mills, Philip Morris and more!

LAWRENCE OTIS GRAHAM is a graduate of Princeton University and Harvard Law School. The author of ten other books and numerous articles on race relations, business and diversity issues, Graham appeared on the covers of *New York* magazine and *Ebony Man* magazine for his first-person investigative story on discrimination at country clubs in America. His story is being turned into a feature film by Warner Brothers. Having worked as a corporate attorney in New York for five years, Graham is an adjunct professor at Fordham University and has worked at The White House and Ford Foundation. A popular lecturer and consultant to companies throughout the U.S. and Japan, Graham has been profiled by *Fortune* and *The New York Times*. He is president of the consulting firm Progressive Management Associates in White Plains, N.Y.

ROSABETH MOSS KANTER holds the Class of 1960 Chair as Professor of Business Administration at Harvard Business School. A former editor of the *Harvard Business Review,* Dr. Kanter has authored many books and articles on business issues and organizational change.

LAWRENCE OTIS GRAHAM

THE BEST
COMPANIES FOR
MINORITIES

A PLUME BOOK

PLUME

Published by the Penguin Group
Penguin Books USA Inc., 375 Hudson Street, New York, New York 10014, U.S.A.
Penguin Books Ltd, 27 Wrights Lane, London W8 5TZ, England
Penguin Books Australia Ltd, Ringwood, Victoria, Australia
Penguin Books Canada Ltd, 10 Alcorn Avenue, Toronto, Ontario, Canada M4V 3B2
Penguin Books (N.Z.) Ltd, 182–190 Wairau Road, Auckland 10, New Zealand

Penguin Books Ltd, Registered Offices:
Harmondsworth, Middlesex, England

First published by Plume, an imprint of Dutton Signet,
a division of Penguin Books USA Inc.

First Printing, October, 1993
3 5 7 9 10 8 6 4 2

LIBRARY OF CONGRESS CATALOGING IN PUBLICATION DATA:
Graham, Lawrence.
The best companies for minorities / Lawrence Otis Graham;
foreword by Rosabeth Moss Kanter.
p.   cm.
Includes index.
ISBN 0-452-26844-3
1. Minorities—Employment—United States.   I. Title.
HD8081.A5G73   1993
331.13'3—dc20   93–1465   CIP

Printed in the United States of America
Set in Goudy, Industria and Trade Gothic

Designed by Steven N. Stathakis

BOOKS ARE AVAILABLE AT QUANTITY DISCOUNTS WHEN USED TO PROMOTE PRODUCTS OR SERVICES. FOR INFORMATION PLEASE WRITE TO PREMIUM MARKETING DIVISION, PENGUIN BOOKS USA INC., 375 HUDSON STREET, NEW YORK, NEW YORK 10014.

To my wife, Pamela,
and in memory of my friend and mentor
Reginald F. Lewis

CONTENTS

CONTENTS

ACKNOWLEDGMENTS

During the past twenty-two months, a great number of people have contributed to the research for this book. Most of these individuals are managers who agreed to be interviewed or provided me with information on companies.

To begin with, I would like to thank those leaders of associations who agreed to speak with me about the issues that affect minority success and failure in America's corporate settings: John Jacob, Executive Director, National Urban League; Dr. William F. Gibson, President, NAACP; Hazel Dukes, President, New York State Conference of NAACP Branches; Louis Nuñez, President, National Puerto Rican Coalition, Inc.; Ernest Prince, President, Urban League of Westchester; Dr. Setsuko Matsunaga Nishi, President, Asian American Federation of New York; Conrad Harper, President, Association of the Bar of the City of New York; Cau O, Executive Director, Asian American Federation of New York; Sharon McPhail, President, National Bar Association; José Niño, President, U.S. Hispanic Chamber of Commerce; Derryl Reed, President, National Black MBA Association; Howard Mills, Director of Conferences, National Urban League; Faith Williams, Assistant Director of Communications, National Urban League; and Henry Der, Executive Director, Chinese for Affirmative Action.

And I would like to thank those individuals who provided me with information on the companies profiled:

Teo Diaz, Moses Hardy, Ken Marques, Larry Collingwood and Ned Kyle of Allstate Insurance Company; Cindy Findlay, Luther Brewster, Don McQuilkin and Robert Hosey of American Airlines (AMR Corporation); Steve Kumagai, Waltrine Cooke, Randy McVane and Jean Fraser of American Express

Company; Georgiana Jackson, Stephen Chen, Keith Miller, Harriet Kass, Michael Jacobs, Maureen Lynch and Donna Cunningham of American Telephone & Telegraph Company; Brenda Lane, Sharyn Taylor, Neil Kulick, Robert Hurst, Robert Knowling and Loren Lehnen of Ameritech (American Information Technologies Corporation);

Cassandra Singleton and Norris Overton of Amtrak (National Railroad Passenger Corporation); Wayman Smith, Thelma Cook and Dan Williams of Anheuser-Busch Companies; William Holland, Cindy Conover, Edgar Twine, O. D. Harris and Jane Crane of Atlantic Richfield Company; Carol Riley, Allene Weathers and Karen Wong of Avis Rent-A-Car System, Inc.; José Agosto, Jr., Elaine Benvenuto, Alvin Smith, Vickey Cintron and Shirley Dong of Avon Products, Inc.;

Sandra Deeble, Suellen Farrington, Terri Ferguson and Bruce Gordon of Bell Atlantic Corporation; Frank Voigt, Ronald Cosey and Essex Mitchell of Borden, Inc.; Lionel Stevens, Tony Carter and Milton Goggins of Bristol-Myers Squibb Company; Rachelle Hood Phillips, Terri Giles and Marianela Aran of Burger King Corporation; Wally Petersen of Leo Burnett Company, Inc.; Deborah Pierce, Megan McNichols and Scott Rombach of Campbell Soup Company; Tom O'Brien and John Parker of Champion International Corporation;

Jeet Bindra, Angela Knight, George Marich, Brian McCarthy and Gregory Redmond of Chevron Corporation; Machelle McAdory, George Ferrell and William Beebe of Chrysler Corporation; Vincent Alvarez and Rianne O'Reilly of Clorox Company; Shirley Dilsworth, Verona Smith, Linda Peek and Leigh Sweney of Coca-Cola Company; Randi Bergman, Gregory Andrews and Ronald Martin of Colgate-Palmolive Company; Joseph Fuentes, Anita Russell and Carlos Soto of Adolph Coors Company; Sandra Mitchell, Robert Pavlick, Michelle Cox, Karen Martin and Ajita Rajendra of Corning Incorporated; Edwin Wingate, Nancy Kimura Fuller and Michael Hyter of Dayton Hudson Corporation; Louise Reid Ritchie, Neal Shine and Larry Olmsted of *The Detroit Free Press*;

Scot Wheeler, Stan Land and Rita Shellenberger of Dow Chemical Company; Lori Folts of E. I. Dupont de Nemours and Company; Darwin Davis, Mary Mannarino and Michael Rush of The Equitable Life Assurance Society; Charles Eldridge, Paul Ostling, John Warren, Anthony Anderson and Cynthia Woltemath of Ernst & Young; R. W. Gentry, Ava Washington, Gerald McElvy and William Wigglesworth of Exxon Corporation; Suey Coleman, Carolyn Freeman, Shirley Finley, Sybille Noble and Al Alexander of Federal Express Corporation; Madelyn Jennings and Jose Berrios of Gannett Co., Inc.;

Gene Skogg, Carla Fischer and Eugene Andrews of General Electric Company; Jean Spence and Cheryl Adkins-Green of General Foods USA; Luis Rubi, James Moody, Sherri Hall, Reatha Clark King and Chuck Chakrabarti of General Mills, Inc.; Jerry Florence, William Powell, Mark Tanner, Tom Pyden and John Maciarz of General Motors Corporation; Adrienne Lallo, Paul Quick, Tom Wright and Vincent Eades of Hallmark Cards Incorporated; Nettie Calamia of Hewlett-Packard Company;

Richard Ramirez, Jane McBunch and Cora Drewry of Hoechst Celanese Corporation; Vincent Cohen of Hogan & Hartson; Thomas Lawrence, Barbara Jerich and Reed Welke of Honeywell Inc.; Patricia Stinson, Jim Keller, Ted Childs and Maria Magana of International Business Machines Corporation; Jim Rose and Marion HochbergSmith of Johnson & Johnson; Annette Zalner, Tim Knowlton and Joseph Stewart of Kellogg Company;

Mee Wing, Leonard Redon, Mary Harrington and Al Brackoniecki of Eastman Kodak Company; Joyce Bustinduy and Michael Giannini of Levi Strauss & Co.; Stephanie Skurdy, Robert Beavers and Mel Hopson of McDonald's Corporation; Maruiel Perkins-Chavis and Curtis Dean of Marriott Corporation; Carlton Stockton, Nate Davis, Timothy Harris and Walter Sanderson of MCI Communications Corporation; Kevin Colgan, Lawrence Branch and Timothy Proctor of Merck & Co., Inc.; Margaret Ingate, Rudley Anthony, Valerie Johnson and Bobbie Collins of Merrill Lynch & Co., Inc.;

Gus Gomez, Robert Eaton and Myra Pilson of Metropolitan Life Insurance Company; Jane Cooperman, Keith Wetmore and Stephen Dunham of Morrison & Foerster; Roberta Gutman of Motorola, Inc.; Colette Ragin, Anna Jones, Janet Humdy, Joseph Anderson and Colin Watson of NYNEX Corporation; Alex Coleman, Lena Williams, Sharon Yakata and June Clarke Doar of The New York Times Company; Cheryl Newton, Richard Jones, Kendall Bishop and Eric Richards of O'Melveny & Myers;

Bunnie Brown of Pacific Gas & Electric Company; George Krock and Bert Birdsall of PPG Industries, Inc.; Douglas Wolsieffer and Grace Alcala of J. C. Penney Company, Inc.; Ronnie Miller, Maurice Cox and Ed Adams of PepsiCo, Inc.; Robert Brown and Marilyn Budzanoski of Pfizer Inc.; Clotilde Dillon, Edward Van Dyke, Mary Herbert, Allene Roberts and Victor Han of Philip Morris Companies; Eloise Adamson, Michael LeBlanc and John Carrington of Polaroid Corporation; Linda Ulrey, David Clark and Lynwood Battle of The Procter & Gamble Company; Ignace Conic, Dennis Alvarado, Alyce Nicosia and Joe Vecchione of The Prudential Insurance Company of America;

Kristine Martinez and Joan Green of The Quaker Oats Company; James Champion, George Perera, Gerri Rocker and Art Stone of Ryder System, Inc.; Eva Chess, Janice Fenn and Denise Stovell of Sara Lee Corporation; Thomas Cole, Geraldine Alexis and Linzey Jones of Sidley & Austin; Richard Beattie, John Carr and Dee Pifer of Simpson Thacher & Bartlett;

Donna Pedro Bradford and Adrian White of Sony Music Entertainment Inc.; Charles Pinto and Kay Brown of US Sprint

Communications Company; Claudia Cortole and John Muilenberg of 3M (Minnesota Mining and Manufacturing Company); Isaac Brooks and Laura Colflesh of TRW Inc.; Alvin Washington and Ed Robinson of Time Warner Inc.; Xernona Clayton, Allan DeNiro and Hope Allen of Turner Broadcasting System, Inc.;

Fred Fernandez, Tom Binder, Henry Short and Luis Hernandez of United Parcel Service; Leon Clark, Jr., Dianne Nightingale, Beverly Fowles and Denise Todd of The Upjohn Company; Angela Brooks and Darlene Siedschlaw of US West, Inc.; Maria Gagnier and Lawana Dumas of Warner-Lambert Company; Leonade Jones, Beth Landon and Barbara Reising of The Washington Post Company; Madeline Lacovara, Mary Jean Potenzone and Stephen Dannhauser of Weil, Gotshal & Manges; and Beatriz Vidal, Judd Everhart, Joseph Cahalan, Al Martins and Mignon Williams of Xerox Corporation.

I wish to thank my editors Deborah Brody and Arnold Dolin, as well as my friends Barbara Lowenstein and Madeleine Morel, who helped shape this project at its very beginning.

I thank the friends who have provided me with information, conversation and a greater insight into minority life in America: Naoko Fuji, Elisabeth Radow, Steven Price, Jay Ward, Derrick Bell, Un Suk Ko, Dauna Williams, Lawrence Hamdan, Letitia Noble, Adam Cohen, Mirian Hinds, Leona Farrington, Diane Faber, Yvonne Jones, Barbara Nichols, Sarah Johnson, Randall Kennedy, Steve Emanuel, James Benerofe, Susan Kennedy, Jamin Raskin, Yvonne Ashley, David Schwartzbaum, Marguerite Gritenas, Bruce Wilson, Jordan Horvath, Brad Roth, James Grasfield, Rosabeth Moss Kanter and Barry Stein.

I would also like to thank my lawyer friends Stephen Dannhauser, Stephen Jacobs, Marsha Simms, Howard Chatzinoff and Lois Rubin, who stood up for me and made sure that my career in corporate America was going in the right direction.

I thank Sarah Weddington, my very first boss, who brought

me to the White House and gave me the chance to meet and work with many of the women and minorities who were changing America in the 1970s and 1980s.

I thank Margaret Morton, Annie Ohayan, Nancy Marx Better, Elliot Hoffman and the brilliant David Garth for providing me with political and business savvy at a crucial time.

For the research on this and my prior books, I am grateful to have utilized the resources of five of the best library systems that a writer has ever encountered. They are the libraries of Harvard University; Princeton University; Beverly Hills, California; Scarsdale, New York; and White Plains, New York.

Very special thanks go to Andrea Heyward, who, as a friend and a secretary, has contributed more to this book and my career than I could ever ask.

I thank Ron Brown for inviting me to Washington and bringing me into a presidential campaign that introduced me to many of the women and minorities who are continuing to change America today.

As always, I give thanks to my wonderfully supportive family, Betty, Richard and Richard Jr., who have always inspired me.

I thank my wife, Pamela, whose intellect, creativity and integrity have made me challenge my own biases.

My final thanks go to Ira Millstein, a business and civic leader who saw the importance of this project and helped make it a reality.

—Lawrence Otis Graham, Esq.
February 1993

FOREWORD

BY ROSABETH MOSS KANTER

Malcolm S. Forbes, the third generation of the Forbes family to serve as publisher of *Forbes* magazine, once commented that the secret of his career success was choosing the right grandparents. Since that option is not available to most minorities in American business, they have to do the next best thing: choose the right company.

The "right" company is one that appreciates and uses the contributions of all its people in pursuit of an intelligent strategy that provides value to customers and employees. This is a place where there is an opportunity for workers to succeed and grow.

In my twenty-five years as a consultant to major companies, I have watched—and guided—the careers of many business leaders moving up the corporate ladder. That ladder is often shorter and less steady today because of restructuring, the flattening of hierarchies, the downsizing of corporate giants, and the increasing number of people who are moving into smaller companies or out on their own as entrepreneurs. Still, a number of lessons endure.

The right company provides the employee with opportunity for growth and development: well-trodden career paths, special assignments to open new vistas, participation on teams outside the department, formal education and informal training. The best companies also offer employees power: to participate in decisions; to gain access to resources, information and political support that ensure that their voices are heard and that they can get things done. Both of these are functions of the company's structure and culture. Without opportunity and power, even the most talented people can find themselves stuck in dead-end jobs. Unfortunately, companies have traditionally denied opportunity and power to many members of minority groups.

Another principal issue that minorities face is simply that they are "different." In my videotape "A Tale of 'O': On Being Different," I describe these dynamics in terms of a corporate fable—the saga of what happens to the lone "O" in a work team with seven "X's." For example:

- The "O's" competence is hard to notice because people are too busy just staring at it.
- The "O's" are put in behind-the-scenes support jobs rather than in up-front leadership roles.
- The "O's" have to do twice as much to get half as far.
- The "X's" have lots of other "X's" behind them, to encourage, support and mentor them; the "O's" must often stand alone.

The best companies recognize that having just a few minorities makes those minorities into "O's." These companies look actively for enough members of minority groups to provide a critical mass. They go beyond tokenism to develop a truly multicultural environment. But why?

Consider four common arguments for increasing the skills of managers in managing diversity effectively. Each of them gives minorities a boost. But each also represents a potential trap that the minority job hunter must consider as he or she goes forward.

1. *The Talent Pool Argument.* One oft-quoted statistic says that by the year 2000, up to 80% of all new entrants to the work force will be minorities and women. Human resources departments are already working with their Joe Goodoldboys—their white male managers—to ready them for this change by urging them to hire and develop more minorities. This sounds great, but unfortunately, what the raw statistic doesn't reveal is that white males who are already employed at their companies will

still dominate the upper ends of professional and managerial pyramids.

So, when the Joe Goodoldboy manager is filling positions, he chooses someone he feels comfortable with for his best job, as his second-in-command. He picks someone he can relate to. Someone who reminds him of himself. Someone who looks just like him. In most cases, the person he selects is the one white male in the pool. Joe Goodoldboy then fills his other jobs—the more technical ones, the lower-end jobs—with minorities. And he gives these "other" jobs impressive titles so that his EEO reports will look just fine.

In short, minorities move in, but they do not necessarily move up, and thus they get stuck in jobs without much power or growth opportunity. And even if minorities come with the best credentials of the pool, such as an engineering Ph.D. from MIT or an MBA from Harvard, they are not guaranteed access to the best opportunities. Not surprisingly, if the company still stigmatizes minorities—even the most qualified minorities—as being too different to fit in well, these individuals can be kept out of the power circles. There are plenty of ways to use talent without sharing power. The bottom line: *Demographics are on the side of minorities. But demographics will not ensure the minority employee's success.*

2. *The Creative-Thinking Argument.* To remain competitive in a tough economy, American companies need to get rid of suffocating bureaucracies that stress conformity and stifle innovation and creativity. Companies that maintain a work force which is too homogeneous find themselves with employees who think alike, who get settled into routines and who fail to act on the need for change until it is too late.

Examples of projects that have benefited from nontraditional or creative perspectives include IBM's Silverlake project team, developers of IBM's highly successful minicomputer, the AS-400. The project was headed by a group of engineers with international experience, including managers of Asian American background.

But, of course, racial diversity alone is not likely to result in fresh new perspectives. For instance, "O's" with nontraditional backgrounds are often concerned about fitting in and will, therefore, play it safe and overconform. They may try to be more like the "X's" than any "X" would naturally be. And there is a reason that these "O's" conform. They understand the corporate mentality. They realize that when companies ask for innovation, they don't want *too much* innovation. They realize that companies frequently make comments like, "We want more innovation, but let's not be the first company to enter this area."

Organizations want to be understood before they are changed; they welcome change from someone who seems like an insider more than someone who is totally different. Thus, the search for creative new perspectives is more likely to lead companies to hire consultants than to increase their minority populations.

So, companies should realize that minority employees can bring new points of view, but employers should not expect these same people, who are struggling so hard to fit in, to also carry the burden of converting an entire staff to a different perspective.

Therefore: *The reason to court minorities is that they can do the job, and not just that they are "different."*

3. *The Cultural Assets Argument.* In a global economy, one in which ethnic identities are stronger than ever before, minorities can bring relationship benefits.

For example, if Joe Goodoldboy heads the marketing department for a company based in Miami, he would be just plain foolish not to have Hispanics and blacks—a large segment of the Miami consumer base—on his team. If he is transferred to San Francisco, he should have Asian employees working with him. IBM certainly knows this. To get into China, a notoriously closed and relationship-oriented economy whose members are suspicious of foreigners, IBM tapped a group of American ethnic Chinese Mandarin-speakers from around the company.

Ethnic or racial status can be an asset in a few circumstances, a trap in others. Hispanics might want to rise at headquarters in Detroit, not be exiled to the parts plant in Mexico. Blacks might find that their very success in developing a pharmaceutical product oriented toward the needs of the black community undermines their credibility in using the same talents for a general-purpose health care product; they are tagged as specialists. And as for the global economy, the market growth opportunities in places with large black populations, such as Nigeria, are not nearly as great as those in northern Europe.

The important thing to remember: *Presumed cultural assets could be good for the company, but not necessarily good for the career of the minority person who has been tagged with the "cultural label."*

4. *The Social Costs Argument.* When opportunity for minorities is blocked and they are removed from the mainstream economy, poverty and unrest can ensue. The resulting social turmoil raises the costs for companies operating in urban areas with large underclasses: expenditures for security or drug testing; higher salaries to attract managers to decaying communities; higher taxes to pay for government welfare programs. Opening employment opportunities for minorities helps reduce these costs.

The desire for companies to "do good" in their communities has led to minority hiring programs. And government pressure has led others to seek minorities. But creating employment opportunities this way is likely to be almost entirely at the lower ends, and while it certainly can diffuse community tensions, it does not necessarily benefit career mobility. Furthermore, employees hired because of an employer's "do-good" motivation can set minorities apart from their non-minority counterparts. It can lead to the frequently voiced assumption that the minority person's position is due only to affirmative action, not to competence.

Therefore: *As long as the door is open, minorities should go on in. But they must watch which door they enter, and if it's the wrong one, their performance has to be so good that it erases all memory of the entry route.*

The "Talent Pool," "Creative-Thinking," "Cultural Assets" and "Social Costs" propositions are all reasonably good arguments for increasing diversity in the work force, but minority job hunters should want to work for companies that have a completely different reason for placing a value on diversity. Minority job hunters should look for companies that appear to have more compelling reasons to value diversity. They should want to work for companies that realize that diversity is a part of an entire mode of business practice. That mode could be called "The Best Practices Argument." Companies which fall into this category (and which are listed in this book) realize that minority employee concerns are just as important as employee medical benefits, child care, occupational safety and other concerns of the progressive, employee-sensitive company.

Quite simply, companies which make the best employers for minorities are usually also the most progressive in terms of other business practices. Companies that have run themselves like a meritocracy, that work with fewer levels of hierarchy, that use employee-friendly evaluation and grievance procedures, that encourage cross-functional teamwork, that value quality and customer service, that encourage and reward constant experimentation, that show interest in results rather than tradition or procedures—these are the companies that will be the best for minorities. These are companies that have found the best business practices and realize that valuing diversity is one of them.

The companies described in Lawrence Graham's book recognize that valuing diversity is one of the many business practices that will allow them to continue as competitive organizations in the global economy.

—ROSABETH MOSS KANTER
Harvard Business School

INTRODUCTION

Before I graduated from Harvard Law School in 1988, I interviewed at a group of large New York law firms which, at first glance, seemed almost indistinguishable: they were all large, well known, extremely successful, mostly white and well respected. Moreover, each of them was paying the same entry-level salary of $72,000 per year—an astronomical figure for anyone, especially for a black twenty-five-year-old student who had never before held a full-time job.

As I went through interview after interview with attorneys at each of the firms, I found myself raising the same law-related questions that my classmates were asking. I asked about the history of the firm, the breadth of its practice, the assignment and review process, the types of clients, the route to partnership, the salary scale, the vacation benefits. I even asked about my eventual office space: "Will I have to share my office, and if so, for how long?"

While walking through the beautifully appointed hallways, offices and libraries in those Wall Street and Park Avenue skyscrapers, I persevered with these questions—the same career-driven questions that my white peers were asking during the interview process.

As I sat, focused on the answers given to me by the conscientious law partners and associates, I knew I was conning myself. For each question I raised, there was another that I considered, but dared not ask. The information I was desperate for—but was too intimidated to address—centered around one simple issue: "Would a minority person like me be accepted and be treated fairly by this company and its coworkers?"

Even as a confident twenty-five-year-old law student, I was unwilling to raise the "minority issue."

Instead, during my job search, I was ready to rely on guesswork. I was ready to make a crapshoot of my career and take a gamble on an employer without even asking the questions that really mattered. During the last days of my law firm job search, a partner at a well-respected Wall Street firm made me an offer while I was seated on a long, comfortable couch against the wall of his brightly lit office.

After I described how impressed I was with his firm's recent corporate transactions, the partner began to explain how his firm differed from certain other New York firms that I might be considering. In the space of a few minutes, he made what I took to be more than one or two anti-Semitic remarks. I am not Jewish, but a red light went on in my head that suggested that this guy—this future employer of mine—might have some equally offensive views about black people.

Finally I felt compelled to ask the question that I had wanted to ask all along.

"Mr. Smith, I was wondering, would it be possible for a black person to become a partner at this firm?" My query was met with a blank stare. I quickly offered an easier question: "Well, I mean, how many of your attorneys are black?"

The partner's final answer shocked me into a reality that I had somehow avoided during the entire job-hunting process. He first allowed his eyes to linger on *The Wall Street Journal* that lay folded on the coffee table between us, and then he looked up and responded pointedly, "Why should that matter?"

I don't know what I was expecting to hear, but this was clearly the wrong answer. It was 1986. The firm had more than 250 attorneys. I was about to make a career decision that would shape the next several years of my life. The partner's peculiar response to my query suddenly made my question more important than anything else I had asked all day.

After thanking the partner, I returned to my school dormitory, made some phone calls to some older minority attorneys in New York and quickly learned why the partner had been so reticent about discussing the status of minorities at his firm. But worse than learning that the firm had only one black in its office was discovering that the subject of minority treatment and ethnic diversity was simply not open for discussion.

This incident inspired me to write this book.

Minority composition, minority promotion and minority treatment are all relevant issues when one is selecting a workplace. While pay scales, benefits, training opportunities and office environments are important factors in anyone's job decisions, the minority person has additional concerns.

Because there are many minority job hunters like me who are either unable to gain the necessary information or too intimidated to ask the crucial minority-specific questions of an employer, I have collected that information in this book and selected the employers who have the best records in hiring and promoting minority professionals and creating an environment in which minority workers will advance and enjoy their careers.

In 1987, when the Indianapolis-based Hudson Institute released its report *Workforce 2000*, it suddenly became clear to employers and labor experts that the subject of ethnic diversity had to be addressed in corporate America. The report noted that by the year 2010—less than twenty years from now—white males will make up less than 40% of the U.S. work force. Minorities and women will have become the largest group of workers in the country. According to the report, which has become the seminal document on the topic of corporate diversity, women and minorities will account for 85% of all new job entrants by the year 2000. Looking at these statistics, it becomes obvious that employers need to address the concerns of minority job hunters. But even more obvious is that we, as minorities, must face the real numbers and concerns that relate to us as minority employees. We must look at the company executives who consider our points of view and who want to create an environment hospitable to workers from different racial and ethnic backgrounds.

Yes, we could walk through the hallways during our job interviews and surreptitiously count the number of faces that appear to be Hispanic, black, Asian or Native American. We could try to gauge the company's overall attitude about minority hiring, retention and promotion by looking at the percentage of minority persons who appear in the photos of the company's slickly produced annual report. We could ask our relatives or friends whether they've ever heard any bad rumors about the way minority professionals are treated at Company X.

But counting the nonwhite faces in random hallways and flipping through the photos of an annual report are nothing more than guesswork. That's an unscientific approach toward making a decision that can affect our careers and our lives.

This book is written for young or mature professionals who want to learn about those companies with a top track record not only for hiring ethnic minorities, but also for retaining and promoting them into top management positions and for addressing such issues as diversity and sensitivity training. The book talks about those companies that have established minority mentoring programs, created minority employee organizations and contributed to important minority causes.

The book also provides details on how these companies have established minority recruiting programs at colleges and professional schools, implemented minority vendor programs and contributed to minority issues through targeted scholarships and through such organizations as the NAACP, the Urban League, the National Council of La Raza, the Mexican American Legal Defense and Education Fund, the Japanese-American Citizens League, Chinese for Affirmative Action and the American Indian College Fund.

HOW THE BOOK WAS RESEARCHED

This book is the result of research that took place over a two-year period. It began with the surveying of 625 public companies and private firms with a detailed three-page questionnaire which asked employers to provide information on the following:

Annual revenues

Percentage of minorities in the company's overall work force

Percentage of minorities within the management pool

Salary scale

Minority members on the board of directors

Minority recruiting programs at colleges, graduate schools and job fairs

Contributions to minority organizations or causes

Company-sanctioned minority employee groups

Diversity training programs and sensitivity training workshops

Company-sponsored minority supplier-vendor programs

Minority mentoring programs

Management training for minority employees

Minority internship programs

Highest-ranking minority executives

With the results from the surveys, the group of companies was further narrowed by focusing on those companies that had not only succeeded in hiring and promoting large numbers of minority professionals, but had also dedicated time and resources to developing various minority support systems. Among these support systems were mentoring programs, employee networks, affirmative action task forces and diversity workshops which sensitized and trained nonminority managers in ways to remove their biases and appreciate differences among a multicultural employee pool.

The group of firms was yet again narrowed after interviews with minority business and civic leaders, as well as with current and former minority employees who spoke candidly about their personal experiences. Minority managers were interviewed to gain personal insight into the work environment, as well as to identify special programs offered by companies on minority issues. It should also be noted that one of the companies profiled in this book (Weil, Gotshal, & Manges) was a previous employer of the author.

The eighty-five companies that are profiled in the book represent a cross-section of industries including aviation, automotive, retailing, computer, financial services, food products, insurance, pharmaceuticals, law, accounting, consumer products, chemical, publishing, entertainment, petroleum, cosmetics and telecommunications.

COMPANIES THAT WERE NOT INCLUDED

Several factors explain the absence of certain companies from this book. In spite of a conscientious effort on the part of the author to gain information on the hiring and retention of minority managers and professionals, a number of companies were unusually reticent about revealing this data. This was often the case for privately held firms that have few public reporting requirements and public companies unwilling to publicize the fact that while many minority employees work on their support staff, they have virtually no minority managers in their executive offices.

And while minority employee statistics were, by no means, the sole basis for selecting companies as finalists to be interviewed, the lack of numerical data logically precluded a company from consideration.

It should also be stated here that while the minority-owned company should probably rank high on the minority job hunter's list of desired workplaces, most of those employers that were contacted were too regional in scope and had too few management positions to justify being included in a list that is intended to offer job opportunities across the United States and abroad. The few remaining minority-owned companies that did qualify turned down the opportunity to respond to the surveys.

Occasionally the surveys uncovered a company that had a marvelous record for hiring and promoting minorities but an overwhelmingly negative record in minority retention, minority board composition, sensitivity training among nonminorities and contributions to the minority community. (See the section "Eleven Principles for Responsible Corporate Diversity" on page 436.) These companies were not listed. Similarly, I found companies that contribute generously to minority organizations, run groundbreaking diversity training workshops for employees and have well-established recruiting programs at predominantly black or Hispanic universities, yet somehow have not managed to promote a single minority person to the rank of vice president or senior manager. These companies were also omitted.

ADVICE TO THE EMPLOYER

As many of the company profiles in this book indicate, there are simple reasons that explain why employers have decided to address the issue of ethnic and racial diversity in their companies. Many of the reasons are purely economic:

■ Since the percentage of minority consumers is growing faster than the percentage of nonminority consumers, it is likely that minority managers will have a better sense of the type of new products that this group wants as well as the most effective way of marketing to this new consumer base.

■ As the *Workforce 2000* study has demonstrated, minorities are quickly becoming a majority of the work force. In order to make these minority employees productive people, both minority and nonminority managers must be trained and sensitized to issues that relate to cultural differences.

■ By creating a work environment that is nonhostile to the minority employee, employers will retain satisfied employees and avoid the expense of rehiring and retraining.

These few reasons should give impetus to those company executives who perceive the "minority issue" as one that needs to be addressed only in the corporate affairs office, where financial contributions are made to local minority groups and scholarship funds. The "minority issue" is a business issue, and it is one that touches on more than corporate moral responsibility. It is a reality that companies will have to address if they want to compete in an increasingly global economy with an increasingly global and nonwhite, nonmale work force and consumer.

So whether you hire a diversity training consultant, organize a task force on minority issues, create company-sanctioned minority support groups, design a diversity issues workshop, sensitize your managers by getting them to review instructional videos like *A Tale of "O"* or minority business publications like *Black Enterprise, Transpacific* and *Hispanic Business* or simply attend business conferences sponsored by groups like the National Urban League, the National Black MBA Association and the Council of La Raza, you will see the positive results resonate throughout the company.

ADVICE TO THE MINORITY JOB HUNTER

Black, Asian, Hispanic or Native American—whatever your racial or ethnic background, you have probably experienced some form of discrimination at one point or another in an academic, business or social setting. The benefits of finding an employer who is enthusiastic about fairly hiring, retaining and promoting minorities are obvious. This book is meant to send you in the direction of companies that are making an effort at creating an hospitable and diverse workplace.

But more than merely providing you with eighty-five profiles of progressive, employee-sensitive companies, this book is meant to give you the courage to address the issues that are important to you as a minority person. Recognizing that there are many companies out there that are interested in these issues, you should begin to assert yourself whether you are a job changer or a first-time job hunter. Ask employers about the percentage of minority managers, request the opportunity to meet other minority employees, find out whether the company has ever held sensitivity workshops to teach employees how to manage and get along with workers from different cultures.

And as you take a closer look at potential employers, try to take a closer look at yourself. Are you joining the minority business groups, attending the minority business conferences and subscribing to the minority business publications that will keep you informed? In a perfect world—a world where race and ethnicity did not affect the way people judged one another—you might not need to raise so many questions for yourself and your future employers. But in the world of business, you must be a realist. After all, this is your career. This is your future. Make the most of it.

COMPANY
PROFILES

ALLSTATE INSURANCE COMPANY

Allstate is one of the nation's largest insurance companies. A wholly owned subsidiary of Sears, the company is part of the Sears Financial Network, which includes Dean Witter Financial Services and Coldwell Banker Real Estate.

Allstate has three major business divisions: Personal Property and Casualty (PP&C), Allstate Life, and Business Insurance. PP&C is Allstate's largest division, offering auto, personal liability, and homeowners' insurance products to consumers.

Allstate Life Insurance Company offers personal life, disability, annuity and pension products sold by Allstate agents, Dean Witter account executives and settlement brokers. The Business Insurance division handles property and liability coverages for businesses, as well as reinsurance for other insurers.

Besides the three major divisions, Allstate has several other operations, including Allstate Enterprises Inc., the holding company for the Direct Marketing Center; the Allstate Motor Club; the Allstate Research and Planning Center; and the Allstate Reinsurance Company, Ltd.

1990 revenues: $18,532,000,000
1991 revenues: $19,531,000,000
1992 revenues: $20,230,000,000

Number of full-time U.S. employees: 54,444

Percentage of these employees who are minorities: 22.8
    Black: 14.1
    Hispanic: 5.5

Asian/Pacific Islander: 2.8
Native American: 0.4

Number of people in the total management pool: 6,684

Percentage of minorities in the total management pool: 19.7

Percentage of minority managers who comprise each managerial level:

Officer: 6.7
Director: 8.2
Bonus manager: 15.8
Non-bonus manager/professional: 17.9

Salary information:

Entry-level (40 different jobs)	$24,050–$39,740
Professional/non-bonus manager	$27,840–$86,830
Bonus manager and director	$60,770–$128,230
Officers	$107,000–$430,000

Founded in 1931 when the president of Sears, Roebuck was persuaded to found a new enterprise for selling insurance coverage through the Sears catalog, Allstate Insurance Company has long been dedicated to equal employment opportunity. Under CEO Wayne Heiden, Allstate has continued to pursue several methods for recruiting minority graduates and professionals. The company recruits at universities and colleges with high black and Hispanic enrollment, such as Morehouse College, Dillard University, Trinity College, St. Mary's College and the University of Texas. Allstate advertises in publications aimed at minorities, including *Hispanic Business*, *Black Enterprise* and *Emerge*. A recent ad campaign showed rows of employees of different ages and ethnic groups under the words, "When you're in the business of solving problems, you want as many points of view as you can get." The company also sends representatives to minority-oriented job fairs and conferences, and provides summer internships. Allstate uses these programs to interest candidates in employment and to place individuals in the areas that best match their skills.

The Allstate Internship Program is a vital part of the company's minority outreach efforts. The program is targeted at college students, and special emphasis is placed on campuses with high black and Hispanic enrollment. Internships are offered in most of the twenty-eight regional offices and at the Northbrook, Illinois, home office. For interns who have chosen a site away from home, the company provides transportation to the office to begin the internship, help in finding living arrangements, subsidies for up to half of monthly rent, and a competitive salary. In the years 1988–90, Allstate placed 502 interns. Of these, 19.6% were black, 13% Hispanic and 4.3% Asian or Pacific Islanders. At Florida A&M University, Allstate offers internships during the school year, and funds a scholarship in actuarial science. The company also supports INROADS, a national high school internship program designed to interest minority youth in business careers.

The impact of these efforts is reflected in Allstate's impressive numbers of minority employees and the degree to which these employees are spread throughout the company's operations. The claims division is 24.5% minority; sales, 17.5%; human resources, 27.9%; underwriting, 25%; and finance/all other, 21.6%.

The company's culture is based upon four "basic values": integrity, caring, initiative and innovation. In the area of equal employment opportunity, these values have translated into diversity training for all employees, and establishing diversity as one of six key business issues for the company. Since 1988, the company has used the "Valuing Diversity" videotapes developed by Copeland Griggs Productions in San Francisco, followed by discussions within departments on diversity issues. A Cultural Diversity Action Team, with twenty managers, officers and directors from several Allstate offices, meets every six weeks to surface and discuss issues related to diversity, help develop policies and report back to senior management. Tom Tewksbury, Senior Vice President for Corporate Human Resources, is actively involved in the U.S. Senate Republican Conference Task Force on Hispanic Affairs. Established in 1987, the task force is charged with ensuring that the concerns of the Hispanic community are considered in legislation, improved government policy and private/public partnerships. Tewksbury is also on the board of directors of the Urban League and SER—Jobs for Progress.

The Hispanic Cultural Committee at Allstate was founded by Tewksbury in 1983. Teo Diaz, Allstate's Diversity Manager, is a committee member. "The committee was originally founded to help recruit more minorities into the company," says Diaz. "We've evolved into discussing a broad range of professional issues. But the committee also serves as a resource for incoming employees. For example, I moved [to the Chicago area] from New Jersey. I had a lot of questions about where I, as a Hispanic person, would feel comfortable buying a house. I discovered this great network of people who could answer all my questions. It's become a group where you can go professionally if you're working on a project and need information; it's also a place to find role models and mentors, since there is no formal mentoring program." The committee meets once a month, more often if necessary. Recently the group brought students from a Hispanic neighborhood in Chicago into headquarters to introduce them to jobs in the insurance industry.

Because of these and other efforts, Allstate has been successful in promoting minority managers through the company. Minorities hold such positions as Senior Vice President, Corporate Relations, and Vice President, Human Resources. Four regional vice presidents—in San Francisco, Wisconsin, Southern California and Valley Forge, Pennsylvania—are minorities. The

Assistant Vice President for Human Resources and the Assistant Vice President for Field Claims are also minorities. Rita Wilson, a black woman who is Executive Vice President for Corporate Relations, serves on the board of directors.

Allstate's Minority Vendor Opportunity Program is designed to assist minority vendors in becoming competitive. In 1992, the company spent $49 million with minority suppliers. Larry Collingwood is Vendor Development Manager. "Human resources is only one arm of a strong affirmative action program," Collingwood says. "Our efforts help build the economic base in the minority community. We have a range of minority vendors, from people who provide office equipment and furniture, to printing and paper products, to personalized premiums and incentives for awards programs. Most of the program money is spent in the claims area, where we have minority attorneys, doctors, auto body shops and home repairmen." The company is a member of the Chicago Regional Purchasing Council, and purchasing managers have incentives written into their annual performance reviews to ensure that the company reaches its goals.

In 1992, the Allstate Foundation, the company's philanthropic arm, contributed $314,000 to organizations such as the NAACP, the Urban League, the Hispanic Association of Colleges and Universities (HACU), the National Council of La Raza and SER—Jobs for Progress. The company sends representatives to the annual conferences of all these organizations. An additional $1.2 million assisted other minority organizations in health and human services. The Hispanic Cultural Committee is one of the ways that Allstate reaches out to the community. Says Diaz, "We raise money for the Boys and Girls Clubs of Chicago, and provide Saturday tutoring of seventh- and eighth-graders. We're raising money to repair old buildings in many neighborhoods in Chicago."

The Good Hands People have succeeded in creating an environment in which minorities can prosper and develop their careers. "It's more than lip service," says Diaz. "We're very serious about making things happen."

Office locations: The company's headquarters are in suburban Chicago. Allstate has 1,000 claim service offices nationwide, and 8,800 sales offices in twenty-eight regions. The firm has international operations in Canada, England and Switzerland, and participates in joint ventures in Japan and Korea.

Allstate Plaza
Northbrook, Illinois 60062
(708) 402–5000

AMERICAN AIRLINES
[AMR CORPORATION]

AMR Corporation is a holding company whose principal subsidiary is American Airlines, Inc. American is the second-largest airline carrier in the world and provides scheduled jet service to 118 destinations on the U.S. mainland and Hawaii, 16 destinations in the Caribbean and 48 destinations in other countries. The company operates charter services and a freight and mail service, as well as SAABRE, a computerized airline reservation system. American Airlines accounts for about 94% of the parent company's assets and revenues.

1990 revenues: $11,719,600,000
1991 revenues: $12,887,000,000
1992 revenues: $14,396,000,000

Number of full-time U.S. employees: 88,500

Percentage of these employees who are minorities: 19.8
  Black: 8.6
  Hispanic: 8.1
  Asian/Pacific Islander: 2.7
  Native American: 0.4

Number of people in the total management pool: 11,875

Percentage of minorities in the total management pool: 12.5

Percentage of minority managers who comprise each managerial level:
  Upper management: 6.3

Early on the morning of April 15, 1926, Charles Lindbergh took off from Chicago for St. Louis in a DH-4 biplane with a bag of mail. It was the first regularly scheduled flight for what was to become American Airlines. Lindbergh's employer, Robertson Aircraft, combined with several small aviation companies during the next few years to form American Airways, later renamed American Airlines. Under the leadership of chairman and president Robert L. Crandall, AMR has established itself as an airline industry leader in attracting and developing minority managers.

American Airlines' minority recruiting program involves several initiatives, including financial support for the Consortium for Graduate Study in Management, which recognized the company for its participation for the years 1989 through 1992. American is an active participant in the National Black MBA Association's annual conference, and contributes to the Dallas chapter's scholarship program. The corporation has close ties with black, Asian and Hispanic student organizations at several business schools, including Wharton, Kellogg (Northwestern), Cornell University, the University of Chicago, the University of Michigan, Indiana University and the University of Texas at Austin. Activities with these organizations include formal and informal presentations, receptions, and breakfasts and luncheons.

AMR also participates in INROADS, the national high school internship program for minorities. American Airlines places several interns each year under the program.

Since the late 1970s, AMR has had Affirmative Action Task Forces which meet at its Tulsa and Chicago offices. The task forces are meant to be a forum in which employees and management discuss minority-related issues. Each one has about fifteen members, with representatives from the rank-and-file to the vice president of the region. The groups meet once a month, or more often if needed. Luther Brewster, a black manager who is American Airlines' Division Managing Director, Aircraft

Maintenance, is a member of the Chicago task force. An American Airlines employee since 1978, Brewster started as a mechanic and worked as a supervisor, a Maintenance Manager at Boston's Logan Airport and an Area Manager at New York's LaGuardia Airport before assuming his current position at O'Hare. He is now responsible for all aircraft maintenance at the facility, and manages 515 mechanics, 30 managers and 20 agents/clerical staff. "The task force is a good way for us to surface diversity issues," Brewster notes. "We've also started a mentorship program, which is one of the most important things we've ever done. I was lucky enough to find mentors during my career here, so I know how important they can be. One of my mentors told me that promotions are like circles rotating within circles; each one has an opening, but you need someone to help you see just the moment when they align, so you can jump to the next biggest one. Now we're making it easier to find people who can help young minorities see those overlaps."

Since 1989, AMR has also had minority employee organizations at its Dallas headquarters. The Asian Cultural Association and the Organization of African Americans at AMR are open to employees at all levels. According to Robert Hosey, a black man who serves as Manager of Affirmative Action, each organization meets monthly and functions as a support system for minority employees who want to network to discuss ideas that affect their group. "In addition to planning training seminars and workshops for members, the groups also sponsor fundraisers for minority organizations in the Dallas community," Hosey says.

While there is currently no overall diversity training program, Hosey says the company has met with several diversity consultants to assess performance and discuss possible programs. "Most recently," he says, "we met with Roosevelt Thomas of the American Institute for Managing Diversity. He visited our facilities, interviewed employees and performed a cultural audit." In the interim, the company is conducting mini-workshops in selected locations during which tapes from the Copeland Griggs "Valuing Diversity" video series are viewed and discussed. Additional diversity-related training programs are under consideration for the near future.

AMR has instituted several innovative programs meant to encourage minority employee development. The Career Development Program is a self-nominating system that requires the employee to nominate himself or herself for a position. The program provides employees with a systematic method of establishing career goals and receiving guidance in choosing career paths. Employees interested in a particular position within the corporation are also encouraged to use the Walk-a-Mile Program. Employees work for a day in the position in which they are interested with a person who currently holds that position.

AMR offers a comprehensive listing of employee development programs and independent study programs which enable employees to enhance their skills, and American Airlines offers English as a Second Language for minority employees. Technical jobs, such as mechanics, have apprenticeship programs at American Airlines, and employees throughout the company can apply for them. AMR also worked with Richard J. Daly College to open the American Airlines Maintenance Academy in Chicago to help train and recruit female and minority aircraft mechanics.

As a result of these efforts, minorities have moved into several high-ranking management positions. Minorities hold such positions as Senior Vice President, Field Services; Vice President, Aircraft Maintenance; Division Managing Director, Passenger Sales; Regional Managing Director, Operations; Managing Director, Crew Resources/Scheduling; Managing Director, Data Processing; Area Director, Aircraft Maintenance; and Regional Manager, Communications. AMR Corporation has two minorities on its board of directors: Christopher F. Edley, former president of the United Negro College Fund, and Antonio Luis Ferre, publisher of the newspaper El Nuevo Día.

AMR's minority vendor program is headed by Don McQuilkin, Coordinator for Minority Vendor Development. "Our program began in 1989," he notes, "and last year we spent $155 million with minority- and women-owned businesses. Our major suppliers include vendors of aircraft parts, construction services, printing, office supplies, vending services, uniforms, and architectural and design services." AMR also participates in the American Bar Association's Minority Counsel Demonstration Program, which exposes minority-owned law firms to various *Fortune* 500 companies that are looking for legal counsel.

AMR supports minority organizations in a variety of ways: money, airline tickets, matching employee gifts and memberships. In 1992, the company contributed to several minority organizations, including the NAACP, the Boys' Choir of Harlem, the National Urban League, the U.S. Hispanic Chamber of Commerce, the National Association of Black Accountants, the Organization of Black Airline Pilots and the Dallas/Fort Worth Association of Black Communicators.

Black Collegian and *Black Enterprise* have recognized American Airlines as a top employer for blacks. Luther Brewster agrees with those accolades. "The best thing about American Airlines is that if you're willing to work hard, you can go as far as your abilities allow. The place is not perfect—there are always going to be some people around who will try to slow you down. But the company has policies and procedures in place to help you navigate around those people and come out on top."

Office locations: Headquarters are at the Dallas/Fort Worth Airport in Texas; there are facilities in Tulsa, Chicago and most other major U.S. cities.

P.O. Box 619616
Dallas/Fort Worth Airport, Texas 75261
(817) 963-1234

AMERICAN EXPRESS COMPANY

American Express Company competes in three industries: financial services, travel and lifestyle services and information services. It comprises five operating companies: Travel Related Services, IDS Financial Services, American Express Bank, Information Services Corporation and Shearson Lehman Brothers.

1990 revenues: $24,332,000,000
1991 revenues: $25,763,000,000
1992 revenues: $26,961,000,000

Number of full-time U.S. employees: 84,000

Percentage of these employees who are minorities: 22.3
    Black: 12.6
    Hispanic: 6.3
    Asian/Pacific Islander: 2.9
    Native American: .5

Number of people in the total management pool: 12,357

Percentage of minorities in the total management pool: 12.9

American Express was founded in 1850 as an express freight company. Although it is primarily known for its charge cards and travelers' checks, the company has five major divisions. Travel Related Services manages the charge cards, travel agencies and certain personal services such as insurance and direct-mail merchandising. The president of this division is Kenneth

Chenault, a black graduate of Harvard Law School and one of the most influential executives in corporate America.

IDS Financial Services provides financial planning for investors and offers investment and insurance products; American Express Bank offers financial services for high-net-worth individuals and their businesses; Information Services Corporation processes bank card transactions, cable television billings, hospital information and mutual fund transfers; and Shearson Lehman Brothers offers retail brokerage, asset management and investment banking services.

Minorities at American Express hold such positions as President of the Consumer Card and Financial Services Group at Travel Related Services, Senior Vice President and Deputy Controller, Vice President of Risk Financing, Managing Director of Corporate Bond Trading at Shearson, Vice President of Industry Marketing at Travel Related Services, Deputy President of American Express Bank Ltd., Senior Vice President and Associate General Sales Manager at IDS, and Vice President of Vacation and Leisure at Travel Related Services.

There is one minority member on the board of directors: Vernon E. Jordan, former head of the National Urban League and a partner at the law firm Akin, Gump, Strauss, Hauer & Feld.

According to Waltrine Cooke, Vice President of Organization Diversity for the parent company, each of the American Express companies carries out its own diversity initiatives. IDS, which is based in Minneapolis, seems to have the most active minority employee organizations and diversity programs. "At IDS, there are several minority employee networks," Cooke says. "The Black Employee Network and the East-West Exchange, an Asian employee network that was begun in 1990, act as support groups to aid in networking and self-help programs. The organizations bring in speakers and sponsor events around Black History Month and other special holidays. Recently the division held a company-wide Diversity Week."

Steve Kumagai speaks highly of the diversity efforts made by IDS. A Senior Vice President and Associate General Sales Manager with a master's degree in industrial relations, Kumagai has been with IDS in Minneapolis since 1983. He had spent several years at Control Data Corporation, also in Minneapolis, before arriving at IDS—just weeks before it was acquired by American Express. "I think we have some of the strongest networking organizations," Kumagai says. "I am already mentoring several Asian employees, but our East-West Exchange helps to teach Asian values to the rest of the company so that others will understand our culture as well." Kumagai says the organization meets once a month and allows Asian employees to network, sponsor seminars on business issues and learn skills that will aid their careers.

"We have a Hispanic Employee Network and a Black Employee Network," adds Kumagai, who acknowledges that there are many less progressive companies who fear the creation of these types of organizations. "These groups, along with our field organization's Diversity Council, bring us business benefits as well," he adds. "With our Diversity Council, we talk about such bottom-line issues as how to explain our financial planning services to consumers from different racial and ethnic backgrounds. At a recent meeting, we had a Chinese manager from Forest Hills, New York, contrasting his methods with a Hispanic manager who was dealing with clients in Miami, Florida, and with a black manager from another part of the country. Dealing with diversity issues is practical for all of us."

The IDS division has worked with such diversity consultants as Merlin Pope & Associates and has sent all of its regional vice presidents through training sessions.

"At the American Express Bank," says Cooke, "there is a black employee network which was created in order to address promotional efforts. The group helped to hire a diversity consultant for the division, which then led to a survey of employees on diversity issues."

In 1989, the Travel Related Services division spoke to outside consultants about developing a diversity training program, but no formal program has been established. The division is, however, forming a Diversity Board which includes senior executives. The board is supported by the Human Resources Department and currently has some pilot diversity projects. There are currently no minority employee organizations at Shearson.

Having spent seven years in the Travel Related Services division, Randy R. J. McVane says American Express is an international company that wants to be more diverse in its ideas and its people because it serves more than just an American market. A Senior Director of Travelers Check Marketing, McVane holds a bachelor's degree in economics from Johns Hopkins and an MBA from the University of Chicago. "I was working in marketing at Procter & Gamble before coming to AmEx," says McVane, "and once I got here, I realized that this was a company that wanted people to exercise their own creativity and to use their own special backgrounds and perspectives to solve problems. As an African American, I bring an additional perspective to marketing. Minority employees can help any company better understand the minority consumer."

McVane, who has been active in the National Black MBA Association and the Urban League's Black Executive Exchange Program, says, "Before I got to American Express, it was well known that blacks and other minorities were moving into the higher positions here. The banking industry, overall, has few minorities, but American Express has an excellent record." Steve Kumagai agrees, and says, "It is inspirational to walk into a senior executive meeting with the highest-ranking people at the company and to see other minorities like Ken Chenault."

In recruiting, the parent company operates a significant program to attract minority MBA students which involves working with the National Black MBA Association, placing prominent minority American Express executives on panels at business schools and sponsoring a minority fellowship program which was begun in 1988 at the Wharton School of Business and the University of Chicago's MBA program. Cooke has helped create special recruiting events on campuses. "At Harvard Business School recently," she says, "we brought minority employees for a separate event on campus and asked them to tell students what it's like to be a minority at American Express. We're trying to share minority role models with the students who are looking at us. Because our CEO sent out an edict several years ago that we need to work hard at recruiting and retaining minority employees, we know we have the kind of support that will make our programs effective."

The IDS division has an active minority recruiting program which interviews at such predominantly black schools as Florida A&M University and Clark-Atlanta University. That division also offers a four-year actuarial fellowship for students at Howard University. There is a strong targeting of Asian and Hispanic students as well. Shearson recruits at Morgan State, Morehouse College and Howard. Although a great number of American Express jobs are in New York, IDS is based in Minneapolis, and has the challenge of attracting students who might not naturally be drawn to a city with such a cold climate.

For recruits from business school, the typical path moves through such positions as assistant manager, entry-level manager, midlevel manager, senior manager, entry-level director, midlevel director, senior director, entry-level vice president, midlevel vice president, senior vice president and executive vice president. McVane advises minority and other recruits that mentors are helpful not only in the early career positions, but also in more senior positions. "Minority professionals especially need mentors in order to collect information on the corporate culture here," McVane says. "And expect to have several mentors as you progress because one mentor may give you personal support while another mentor advises you on career strategy. I've found it very easy to find mentors throughout my career here."

One of American Express's greatest contributions to the minority community was its launch, in 1982, of the Academies of Finance, a two-year program in which inner-city high school students combine classroom instruction with on-the-job experience in preparation for careers in the financial services industries. The students are also provided with summer internships in the financial area.

American Express also supports the National Puerto Rican Forum, the National Urban League's Black Executive Exchange Program, the NAACP, the National Council of La Raza and many other minority organizations and programs. In 1992, the company's charitable contributions exceeded $22 million.

The American Express Minority Business Program works with minority vendors who wish to sell to any of the five businesses at the company. The company is also a member of the National Minority Supplier Development Council.

Office locations: American Express Company is based in New York City's Wall Street area. Its five operating units have offices across the United States and in many other countries.

American Express Tower
World Financial Center
New York, New York 10285
(212) 640-2000

AMERICAN TELEPHONE AND TELEGRAPH

AT&T is known to most consumers as "the phone company." AT&T's primary business is still providing basic telephone service to residential customers and businesses across the United States and around the world. However, with the deregulation of the telecommunications industry, the company has expanded its mission to the broader realm of information management. This means that AT&T provides systems, products and services that combine computers and communication to solve a wide variety of business problems. The company's Worldwide Intelligent Network carries voice, data, image and facsimile messages around the world. The telecommunications and computer products, which can be networked into integrated systems, provide global access to information. In addition, with the Universal card, the company has entered the general-purpose credit card business, and also provides value-added financial and leasing services for AT&T and other products.

1990 revenues: $62,191,000,000
1991 revenues: $63,089,000,000
1992 revenues: $64,904,000,000

Number of full-time U.S. employees: 238,535

Percentage of these employees who are minorities: 23.3
    Black: 15.0
    Hispanic: 4.3
    Asian/Pacific Islander: 3.7
    Native American: 0.3

Number of people in the total management pool: 109,087

Percentage of minorities in the total management pool: 17.6

AT&T was incorporated in 1885 but traces its lineage to Alexander Graham Bell and his invention of the telephone in 1876. The company has achieved several firsts: commercial transatlantic telephone service in 1927; an electric digital computer in 1937, and the communications satellite Telstar in 1962. It was also one of the first major corporations to begin addressing the issue of equal employment opportunity, and has long been known for its commitment to a diverse work force. Under the stewardship of CEO Robert Allen, AT&T has developed several initiatives to ensure that the company continues to attract and develop talented minority managers.

AT&T recruits at all major colleges and universities, including such predominantly black colleges and universities as Jackson State, Tuskegee and Tennessee State, and universities with high Hispanic enrollment like the University of Miami, the University of Puerto Rico and Texas A&M. The company looks for candidates for positions in sales and marketing, business applications/systems programming, manufacturing/operations engineering and research and development. Keith Miller, Assistant Staff Manager for College Recruiting and University Relations, helps develop relationships on campus that will lead to successful recruiting. "One of our important efforts is the Historically Black Colleges and Universities (HBCU) program," says Miller. "We send our staff into the university, or we bring the faculty to AT&T, so that they can better introduce students to current developments in the telecommunications industry." The company also donates computers and other technical equipment.

The company makes a concerted effort to ensure that minority candidates have an opportunity to build skills and develop into managers. AT&T has a Corporate Diversity Officer, Ann Fritz, who oversees all efforts, and there is a Corporate Diversity Team with representatives from each of the major minority employee organizations to surface and discuss diversity issues and bring them to the attention of senior management. The corporate Diversity Center provides resources for managers who wish to develop their own initiatives, including a library of training videotapes. There is a company-wide effort to tie diversity into business planning and traditional development programs. Georgiana Jackson, a black manager who is Staff Director for Operations Business Network Sales, became involved with Horizons, a yearlong program to accelerate the development of entry-level managers. "I was working in the Consumer Services Business Unit at the time, and served as an adviser for a group of entry-level people," Jackson says. "I served as a mentor whom they could bounce ideas off, and even now I maintain a network with them. We help each other out."

There are several minority employee organizations within AT&T. Stephen Chen, department head of Global Network and Switched Services Planning for Bell Laboratories, founded the "4As"—Asian Americans for Affirmative Action—in 1981. "We have over three thousand members, and there are chapters at various AT&T locations across the country," says Chen. "The chapters meet once a month, and there is also a national conference every May to commemorate Asian American Heritage Month. The national conference has had speakers like former New Jersey governor Tom Keane and TV anchorperson Kaity Tong." The 4As receives funding from corporate headquarters for its events, and all functions are open to all employees. "The goal," says Chen, "is to introduce diversity issues to everyone, as well as to provide a support system for Asian employees." Chen's activities don't end with the 4As. "I also have bimonthly meetings where we work on the diversity module with thirty to forty other people in my department; it's a chance to discuss minority issues in an open forum."

There are employee organizations for other minorities as well. The Alliance of Black Telecommunications Employees supports African Americans within AT&T. The group has twenty-eight chapters across the country and provides opportunities for professional development, community action, networking, affirmative action advocacy and spiritual development. Senior AT&T managers participate in some seminars and the semiannual professional development conferences to provide the group with a forum for discussing issues and concerns. *Newslink*, the group's quarterly newsletter, keeps members informed about chapter activities. Each February, several events are held to commemorate Black History Month. HISPA, the Hispanic Association for AT&T Employees, has more than 1,500 members and a Public Relations Special Markets office that keeps AT&T management informed about the concerns of Hispanic employees. The group coordinates seminars, conferences and the September observance of National Hispanic Heritage Month. In the *Bell Lab News* recently, Millie Castillo, International Market Manager for Latin America, discussed why the group is vitally important both to Hispanic employees and to AT&T. "We provide information and networking opportunities that have enabled many Hispanic employees to further their careers. We have also been instrumental in helping AT&T achieve success in the Hispanic consumer market in the United States, and have opened doors in Latin America."

Minorities hold such positions at AT&T as Vice President and Chief Financial Officer, Communications Products; Vice President, Information Management Services, Planning; Vice President, International Market Management; Vice President, Network Systems; Vice President, Law; and Sales Vice President, Consumer Operations. Curtis J. Crawford, Vice President of AT&T's Microelectronics Division, was named one of the Top 50 Black Executives in Corporate America by *Ebony* magazine in 1992. In 1991, *Black Enterprise* named Martina L. Bradford one of the 21 Most Influential Women in Corporate

America. Bradford is Vice President of Federal Government Affairs and an attorney for the company. AT&T has two minority board members: Donald F. McHenry, former U.S. Ambassador to the United Nations, and Franklin A. Thomas, president of the Ford Foundation.

The company's Minority and Women's Business Enterprise program awarded $208 million in contracts to such firms in 1992.

The company pursues philanthropic efforts within the minority community. Working with several minority organizations, the company developed the Summer Science Program, a successful summer intern program that provides minority high school students with employment and training at AT&T facilities across the country. The program has three components: Basic, High Achiever, and High Step, which students can work through over the course of three summers. By the end, they can perform jobs such as lab assistant that expose them to life as a professional engineer. Project View is targeted at minority college students. Each year, a select group of engineering majors is brought to AT&T for a week during winter break to learn about the range of research going on at Bell Labs. The exposure usually leads to summer jobs. The Cooperative Research Fellowship Program provides tuition, fees, books and an annual stipend of $13,200 to minority Ph.D. candidates. The Engineering Scholarship Program, targeted at minorities and women pursuing undergraduate engineering degrees, provides tuition, books, fees, room and board and a summer job for four years. The Summer Research Program provides an opportunity for minorities and women to work at Bell Laboratories for the summer before their senior year in college. The program provides housing, transportation and a research scientist as a mentor. Other educational activities in the minority community include career awareness programs to introduce minority youths to career options in science and engineering; a tutoring program for elementary school children; science fairs; and a Saturday-morning lecture series on science topics aimed at high school students and teachers.

The AT&T Foundation contributes to a variety of minority civic and charitable organizations, including the United Negro College Fund, the American Indian Science and Engineering Society, the Hispanic Association of Colleges and Universities, the Asia Society, the Cuban American National Council, the National Council of La Raza and the Interracial Council for Business Opportunity.

Focusing on building a diverse work force and managing it successfully has been an AT&T hallmark for many years, and commitment to the principle runs deep, perhaps because of the success it has brought AT&T in the marketplace. "Our customers are diverse, so we want to be diverse," says Stephen Chen. "We can't expect our customers to spend money with us if we don't respect their diversity, too."

Office locations: Domestically, AT&T has about 3,000 locations in the fifty states, including factories in seventeen states. The company's primary locations are in New Jersey. Internationally, AT&T has a direct presence in more than thirty-five countries.

550 Madison Avenue
New York, New York 10022
(212) 605-5500

AMERITECH
(AMERICAN INFORMATION
TECHNOLOGIES CORPORATION)

Ameritech is the parent of five Bell telephone companies serving the Great Lakes region: Illinois Bell, Indiana Bell, Michigan Bell, Ohio Bell and Wisconsin Bell. These companies provide advanced communication services for residential and business customers.

1990 revenues: $10,662,500,000
1991 revenues: $10,818,400,000
1992 revenues: $11,153,000,000

Number of full-time employees: 75,395

Percentage of these employees who are minorities: 22.6
    Black: 19.8
    Hispanic: 2.1
    Asian/Pacific Islander: .5
    Native American: .2

Number of people in the total management pool: 23,474

Percentage of minorities in the total management pool: 17.2

Percentage of minority managers who comprise each managerial level:
    Vice president: 5.0
    Assistant vice president: 5.3
    General manager: 8.4

District manager: 9.3
Staff manager: 11.5
Supervisor: 19.7

Salary information:

Level 5 assistant vice president:	$86,500–$169,300
Level 4 general manager:	$65,000–$111,800
Level 3 district manager:	$50,900–$84,500
Level 2 staff manager:	$40,900–$69,100
Level 1 supervisor:	$27,200–$54,100

Besides the five Great Lakes Bell companies, Ameritech also consists of several subsidiaries, among them Ameritech Mobile Communications, which provides wireless communication including mobile phones and paging services; Ameritech Publishing, which produces phone directories; and American Credit, which provides financing and leasing of computer hardware.

Minorities at Ameritech hold such positions as President of the Ameritech Information Systems division, President of the Ameritech International division, President of Michigan Bell, General Manager of Business Customer Support at Indiana Bell, Senior Attorney at Illinois Bell and Vice President of Sales and Services at Michigan Bell. There are, however, no minorities on the board of directors.

The company recruits at such schools as Atlanta University, Southern University and Purdue University. The company is also involved in a variety of job fairs and other recruitment events that target minorities, held at the University of Illinois, Ohio State University, the University of Wisconsin and Cleveland State University.

According to Brenda K. Lane, Manager of Affirmative Action, "We have twenty-four minority employee organizations at the company. Some of them have been active for more than ten years. Among these organizations are business-unit–based panels and advocacy groups." Employees are beginning to form regional groups in the smaller offices as well. Lane says these groups help employees in the area of networking and mentoring, as well as in keeping the company's attention focused on using the diverse talents of the work force.

Robert Knowling, General Manager at Ameritech's Indiana Bell division in Indianapolis, was a founding member of the Indiana Bell Black Managers Association. "When we started the organization in 1989," Knowling says, "we had eighty people. Our goal was to create an environment where black managers could network and discuss business and political issues as well as create community programs." Knowling, who came directly to the company after graduating from Wabash College, says it took almost a year before he knew of other minorities at Indiana Bell. With the networking organizations that now exist at the company, new hires can tap directly into the working community. "Our association meets monthly," says Knowling, "and we sponsor minority scholarships for graduating high school students."

Besides the various business unit efforts, Ameritech recently formed a corporate-level Diversity Forum, designed to serve as a vehicle for sustaining attention to diversity issues on the part of corporate leadership, to establish a forum for testing proposed new policies and to provide a conduit for sharing successful approaches across businesses. "In the broadest terms," says Martha Thornton, Ameritech's Senior Vice President of Human Resources, "management sees the Diversity Forum as a laboratory, or a research center, for uncovering issues and for subjecting solutions to review by those most affected." Thornton chairs the Forum; the membership is made up of representatives from each of the business units.

In 1988, Ameritech officially sanctioned the Ameritech Regional Black Advisory Panel, a group that deals with pay, retention and promotions. Knowling, a founder of this group, says the panel deals directly with Ameritech senior management and the company chairman. "We have influenced hiring practices and have advised the human resources department," says Knowling. "Because of our own group's success, we have had the opportunity to advise the Hispanic group and women's group as they have organized themselves into an advisory panel."

Ameritech's various panels sometimes hire their own diversity consultants and run mentoring and career planning programs. One advisory panel at Michigan Bell recently raised $60,000 for the United Negro College Fund.

A diversity training program at Ameritech uses special seminars and workshops created by such diversity consultants as J. Howard & Associates, Copeland Griggs and Kochman Communications Consultants, Ltd. The company has made a strong commitment to addressing diversity issues through training its managers. The company's overall management training programs have 17% minority enrollment. Some of the most popular workshops are "Managing Development and Diversity," "Efficacy for Women" and "Efficacy for Minority Corporate Professionals," which gives special advice to minority managers and professionals.

Robert Knowling says the diversity training the company has provided for him has been extremely valuable. "Through the workshops I have taken, I have seen that it is too easy for all of us to feel comfortable around people who are identical to us. Minority and nonminority employees teach all of us to appreciate the different cultures that are represented here."

The "Managing Development and Diversity" seminar focuses on the importance of sharing responsibility for solving problems in a diverse population. The seminar teaches managers the importance of structuring an intergroup climate which minimizes race and gender-related tensions. It also discusses the process of improving productivity among minority employees. The "Managing Differences" workshop teaches managers that certain people from different backgrounds may not be motivated by the same incentives.

A course called "African-American/Anglo Culturally

Based Patterns of Difference" deals with the etiquette of interaction. In addition, the company furthers its diversity efforts by tying senior management compensation to the company's affirmative action/EEO goals.

The company's philanthropic efforts include contributions to the National Urban League, the National Council of La Raza, the National Black MBA Association, the NAACP, INROADS, the National Action Council for Minorities in Engineering, the United Negro College Fund, the Congress of National Black Churches and Latino Family Services.

Ameritech is particularly involved in minority scholarship and internship programs. Besides sponsoring minority students for internships in the INROADS program, the company supports or underwrites several other programs. The Illinois Minority Precollege Internship Program identifies minority students who demonstrate promise and an interest in studying engineering or computer science. It places them in a work environment related to their studies. The President's Leadership Program targets Hispanic, Native American and African American students at the University of Illinois. Operation 1993 is an annual program in which minority public high school students are placed in part-time jobs in various departments at Ameritech. The University of Wisconsin at Madison Minority Engineering Program allows minority students to work at Ameritech during the summer and then to receive $1,000 stipends for the following semester.

On a local level, in the Chicago area Ameritech sponsors Junior Achievement, Adopt-a-School programs and festivals celebrating Puerto Rican Friendly Day and Black History Month.

A minority supplier-vendor program at the company, called the Minority and Woman's Business Enterprise Program, encourages employees to identify minority-owned businesses and to use those suppliers whenever possible. In 1992, the program spent $127 million with minority vendors. The program also sponsors seminars, scholarships and conferences to promote continued growth and development of minorities in business.

Office locations: The company's headquarters are in Chicago. Ameritech has offices in other parts of Illinois and in Indiana, Michigan, Ohio, Wisconsin and Texas.

30 South Wacker Drive
Chicago, Illinois 60606
(312) 750-5000

AMTRAK
[NATIONAL RAILROAD
PASSENGER CORPORATION]

Amtrak is the provider of America's coast-to-coast rail passenger service. Its 24,000-mile national system serves more than 500 destinations with a fleet of more than 2,000 cars and locomotives.

1990 revenues: $1,308,000,000
1991 revenues: $1,359,000,000
1992 revenues: $1,324,800,000

Number of full-time employees: 23,952

Percentage of these employees who are minorities: 32.9
    Black: 27.0
    Hispanic: 4.0
    Asian/Pacific Islander: 1.5
    Native American: .4

Number of people in the total management pool: 1,830

Percentage of minorities in the total management pool: 19.8

Founded on May 1, 1971, with federal funding, Amtrak began its operations with a mismatched fleet of passenger cars and locomotives. Today it carries 40 million passengers a year on its trains, which offer such luxury services as private conference rooms, telephones, dining rooms and videotape players.

Minorities at Amtrak hold such positions as Executive Vice President and Member of the Management Committee, Vice President of Information Systems, Assistant General Counsel, Senior Director of Policy, Senior Director of Data Center Operations, Director of Passenger Services and Sales Accounting, Director of Operating Budget, Director of Environmental Control, Director of Contract Audit, Director of User Services and Support, Director of Minority Business Development, Director of Human Resources Field Operations and Director of Employee Assistance Programs. There are, however, no minorities on the board of directors.

Norris W. Overton, a black vice president who is responsible for Information Systems, has been with the company since 1982 and is a top-ranking officer. He says he was extremely impressed by a "No Punches Pulled" program that Amtrak offered when many minority employees were just entering the company. "It was a great opportunity for minorities who were in entry-level positions," says Overton, "because it paired them with a seasoned employee who was usually at the vice president level. That vice president would 'adopt' the new employee, answer the difficult questions, give suggestions on how to understand and fit into the corporate culture, take the employee out to lunch twice a month and act as a type of role model."

Several years ago, Overton acted as a mentor for two years to a young black female keypunch operator. Now she is a mid-level manager. Overton believes that this type of program was important several years ago when there were only a handful of minority managers. "Now," he says, "we have a much greater representation of minority managers, and because of this, natural mentoring and networking relationships are created."

Overton's department has 311 employees, 40% minority. He says the employees' ethnic and religious sensitivity is heightened by international celebrations and other events that focus on the different cultures of the department's personnel.

Today Amtrak promotes a large number of minority employees into management positions through its Management Associate Program and its Apprentice Program.

According to Casandra Singleton, Manager of Affirmative Employment Programs, the Management Associate Program, which has a 32% minority makeup, is a twelve-month training program which combines classroom training with practical supervisory and management skills. "Each associate," says Singleton, "is assigned to a mentor and sponsor who guide the associate through the program and help him or her make the transition to professional manager." After the program is completed, the Management Associate is assigned to an entry-level management position.

Singleton says the Apprentice Program creates a foundation for many management jobs in the company's Mechanical Department. It is a three-year training program and has a 28% minority makeup.

The company recruits many Hispanic and black students from such schools as New Mexico State University; California State University at Los Angeles; Southern University and A&M College in Baton Rouge, Louisiana; North Carolina A&T State University; South Carolina State University; Morgan State University and Howard University.

Amtrak takes several avenues in recruiting minority candidates. The company works with a number of city-sponsored youth employment programs to hire minority summer and after-school interns from junior high and high schools. Members of the office also serve as volunteers for school career days and other activities. For more senior positions, the company sends representatives to career fairs, recruits on campuses and encourages employee referrals.

According to Singleton, there is no diversity training program yet, but Amtrak is currently meeting with consultants and talking to other *Fortune* 500 companies such as Corning to see what programs have been most successful in training employees on diversity issues.

One of the most important ways in which Amtrak demonstrates its commitment to the minority community is through its Minority Business Development Program, which was founded in 1971, shortly after the creation of Amtrak itself. In working with minority vendors, its goal is to award at least 15% of its total dollar volume in the procurement program to minority- and women-owned businesses. The company has exceeded the goal for several years, awarding more than $80 million each year since 1989.

President and CEO W. Graham Claytor, Jr., says the vendor program continues "to be a vital part of Amtrak's business effort in which the cooperation of the entire company will be essential." The company's development office advertises to solicit minority-owned businesses in such publications as *Minority Business Engineer*, *Hispanic Business* and *Black Enterprise*. The company also takes part in more than thirty annual trade fairs, seminars and conferences that help it reach minority contractors.

Since Amtrak is supported by federal tax funds, its policy is not to contribute financially to special causes or programs. The company is, however, an active member of the Conference on Minority Transportation Officials and the National Minority Supplier Development Council.

Office locations: Amtrak's headquarters are in Washington, D.C. It also has offices in New York, Chicago, Los Angeles, San Francisco, Orlando, New Orleans and other cities.

60 Massachusetts Avenue
Washington, D.C. 20002
(202) 906-3000

ANHEUSER-BUSCH COMPANIES, INC.

Anheuser-Busch, founded in 1852, is a diversified corporation with subsidiaries that include the world's largest brewing company, the country's second-largest producer of baked goods and the country's second-largest theme park operation. It also has interests in container manufacturing and recycling, malt production, international brewing and beer marketing, snack foods, refrigerated and frozen foods, real estate development, major-league baseball, stadium ownership, railcar repair and transportation services.

1990 revenues: $11,600,000,000
1991 revenues: $12,630,000,000
1992 revenues: $13,062,300,000

Number of full-time employees: 44,836

Percentage of these employees who are minorities: 22.5

Number of people in the total management pool: 7,266

Percentage of minorities in the total management pool: 11.5

Percentage of minority managers who comprise each managerial level:
    Officers: 4.8
    Directors: 5.0
    Managers: 12.2

While Anheuser-Busch is best known for Budweiser and Michelob, its 100-year-old brands of beer, the company actually runs three major business operations. Grouped under Beer and Beer-related Operations are the breweries that produce the fifteen beer brands, as well as the various rice mills, malt plants, licensing offices, trucking services and railcar repair facilities. Food Products Operations includes Eagle Snacks, Inc., which markets peanuts, pretzels and potato chips, as well as Campbell Taggart, Inc., a baker of breads and desserts. Grouped under Entertainment Operations are the St. Louis Cardinals baseball team, Busch Stadium and Busch Entertainment Corporation, which runs Sea World and the Busch Gardens entertainment parks.

It would be almost impossible to match Anheuser Busch's record on minority issues. Not only does the company give a staggering amount of money to minority causes and organizations, but it also has some of the most powerful and influential minority executives in corporate America. Its board of directors has more minority members than just about any other board in the *Fortune* 500, and the company has made sure that blacks, Asians and Hispanics can reach the very highest line and staff positions. Minorities at Anheuser hold such jobs as Senior Vice President of Market Development, Vice President of Corporate Affairs, President and Managing Director, Vice President and General Manager, Vice President of Finance, Vice President of Corporate Relations and Vice President of Human Resources.

The company has three minority board members: John E. Jacob, president of the National Urban League; Vilma Martinez, a partner at the California law firm of Munger, Tolles & Olson; and Sybil C. Mobley, dean of the School of Business and Industry at Florida A&M University.

Wayman F. Smith, Vice President of Corporate Affairs, is probably one of the most influential minority executives in the beer and beverage industry, and is certainly the reason that Anheuser's name appears as the primary sponsor of so many minority-related programs and fund-raisers, like Lou Rawls's annually televised Parade of Stars telethon for the United Negro College

Fund. A graduate of Howard University Law School and chairman of the university's board of trustees, Smith was also named, in 1992, by *Ebony* magazine one of the 50 Top Black Executives in Corporate America. "I was hired as a vice president in 1980," says Smith, "but my first contact with the company was in 1969 when the chairman, August Busch, asked me to help the firm with a labor dispute."

Smith, who had been running his own small labor law firm, was impressed with the interest the company's chairman showed when seeking out minority talent. He was ecstatic when the company asked him to act as outside labor counsel, and later to join the company and deal with these and many other issues. Besides serving on the board of the subsidiary that manufactures the beer, Anheuser-Busch, Inc., Smith is also in charge of one of the country's largest minority vendor programs. The program, called Partners in Economic Progress, seeks out, helps develop and purchases products and services from minority contractors. "When I first came to the company," says Smith, "we were spending approximately $800,000 annually with minority vendors. Today, because of our own networking and development of vendors, we spend almost $100 million with minority contractors."

The first recipient of the NAACP's corporate citizen award, Smith is a tireless cheerleader, whether he is recruiting vendors at the economic development seminars that the company sponsors at various hotels around the country, or selling the company to minority graduates looking for employment. Smith says, "This is a company that is truly dedicated to giving opportunities to everyone. It is hard not to be excited when you're working in a place where people rise to the top regardless of race, sex or ethnicity."

Dan Williams, Anheuser's Director of Diversity, agrees with that description of the company. He runs a two-day diversity training program which helps minorities and others remain productive in the company's multicultural work force.

"In 1990," says Williams, "we worked with the consulting firm Pope & Associates and developed a program that trains a cross-section of our employees. We don't want a feeling of 'them' and 'us' to pervade the staff, and this is what diversity workshops can eliminate. The world is more diverse. Our consumers are more diverse. These are issues that have to be addressed." Williams explains that discussion groups are formed after the training in which the employees discuss how to apply the diversity principles.

Other diversity programs used by the company are leadership forums, which invite speakers to address diversity issues; a diversity calendar, which displays the many holidays celebrated by different ethnic and religious groups; and the *Corporate Affairs News Monitor*, a publication which discusses diversity topics and employment issues.

While there are no formal minority employee organizations, informal networks of full-time employees have formed around such minority programs as INROADS, through which Anheuser-Busch hires many of its minority interns.

The company recruits from many colleges and universities with large minority enrollments, such as Howard and Florida A&M universities.

Anheuser has also formed strong relationships with minority financial institutions. It maintains investments in twelve-month certificates of deposit, has established lines of credit and has set up payroll accounts with many minority banks. The company's payroll taxes are paid through minority-owned banks. In addition, the company has established a reinsurance program with a minority life insurance company to provide life insurance protection for its 45,000 employees.

Anheuser-Busch contributes to many minority organizations including the National Organization of Chinese Americans, the American Indian Science and Engineering Society, the Japanese-American Citizens League, the American Indian Center and the National Asian-American Bar Association.

Since 1980, the company has sponsored the Lou Rawls Parade of Stars Telethon for the United Negro College Fund and helped raise $100 million for UNCF, which educates more than 51,000 students.

Recently the company paid tribute to Rosa Parks, the black woman who became a civil rights leader when she helped launch the historic Montgomery bus boycott. During Black History Month, the company donated a bronze statue of Parks to the National Portrait Gallery in Washington, D.C.

The company is also the leading corporate sponsor of the largest educational support program for Hispanics in the United States, the National Hispanic Scholarship Fund. Since 1983, the organization has worked with Anheuser-Busch to raise several million dollars in direct scholarship aid for students.

Through its relationship with the Mexican-American Legal Defense and Education Fund (MALDEF), the company has given more than $1 million and helped create a public analyst internship program for Hispanic students who have an interest in law and political science. The two-year internship teaches students about the legislative process and helps them monitor Hispanic issues such as voting rights, immigration, education and employment law.

Another program sponsored by Smith's Corporate Affairs office is the Anheuser-Busch/Urban League Scholars Program, designed to give older adults a second chance at a college education. Students in the program, primarily single, female minority parents, attend a junior college with the goal of earning an associate's degree and continuing to a college and better employment. The company funds the program in St. Louis, Chicago, Houston, Newark and Columbus, Ohio.

The company has for many years manufactured and distributed free posters and calendars that celebrate the history of different ethnic and racial groups. Posters are created to celebrate Asian-Pacific American Heritage Month, as well as Black History Month.

As board member John Jacob says, "This company has a phenomenal record with regard to minorities both in the work force and in the community. And things happen here because the people at the top care about these issues."

Office locations: The company is headquartered in St. Louis and has breweries, offices and other operations in almost every state in the United States. There are overseas operations in Japan, Spain, England, Hong Kong, Singapore, Taiwan and Puerto Rico.

One Busch Place
St. Louis, Missouri 63118
(314) 577-2000

ATLANTIC RICHFIELD COMPANY [ARCO]

ARCO is the sixth-largest oil company in the United States. Its operations encompass all aspects of the oil and gas business: exploration and production of crude oil, natural gas and natural gas liquids, and refining, marketing and transportation of petroleum products. ARCO also mines and markets coal and has interests in two companies that produce and market petrochemical products.

1990 revenues: $19,896,000,000
1991 revenues: $18,922,000,000
1992 revenues: $19,300,000,000

Number of full-time U.S. employees: 21,561

Percentage of these employees who are minorities: 19.6
    Black: 8.3
    Hispanic: 6.0
    Asian/Pacific Islander: 3.9
    Native American/Alaskan Native: 1.4

Number of people in the total management pool: 4,768

Percentage of minorities in the total management pool: 10.7

Under the stewardship of chairman and CEO Lod Cook, ARCO has proved itself deeply committed to equal employment opportunity. Cook, well known for his philanthropic efforts, says, "I believe that the future of this country depends on our support of programs that unite youth, minorities, and education." The company's activities reflect this commitment.

ARCO recruits on college and university campuses and in the community at large, primarily for candidates in engineering and the sciences, and makes a special effort to attract minority candidates. Edgar H. Twine, a black attorney who received his law degree from the University of Illinois and an MBA from MIT's Sloan School of Management, is Associate General Counsel for ARCO. Twine has been actively involved in minority recruiting. "We visit schools with high minority enrollment," he says, "like Texas Southern University in Houston and Alcorn University in Mississippi. I talk about my experience at ARCO and what the work of a corporate attorney involves. I think it makes a big difference if they can meet a person of color from the company; I hope it makes them more willing to ask the tough questions of us." ARCO recruits at several other schools with high minority enrollment, including the University of Michigan, the University of Indiana, Florida A&M, the University of Texas—El Paso, Texas A&M, Prairie View A&M, California State University at Northridge and Central State University in Ohio.

Besides several operating-company–specific summer intern programs for college students, Corporate Personnel Relations sponsors a minority internship program in the Los Angeles area that doubled in size in 1992. The program includes separate high school, college and MBA programs, and involves a total of fifty-three students throughout the various operating companies. The program encompasses luncheons, seminars and tours, as well as the opportunity to meet key managers throughout the company.

These recruiting efforts bolster ARCO's overall affirmative action plans. ARCO policy requires each facility to have a current affirmative action policy in place, regardless of size and whether or not the unit does business with the federal government. The corporate EEO department conducts periodic internal audits to review progress toward affirmative action goals and to identify and resolve obstacles to minority employees. The

EEO policy is renewed annually and is posted on bulletin boards throughout the company's offices. In addition, each operating company distributes and posts its own such policy. EEO is discussed with each new hire during orientation, and periodic training sessions are conducted. All six ARCO operating companies have an EEO component in their annual business plans, and several operating companies have also developed strategic long-range EEO plans.

ARCO takes several steps to create an atmosphere that will foster the development of minority managers. Each operating company conducts its own work force diversity training for management. Jane Crane, Manager of Diversity for the Transportation Division, has been helping to develop a diversity training program for her division. "We are starting a pilot program with a training firm called Advanced Research Management Consultants," says Crane. "They have done several training programs for other ARCO divisions, and we believe they could have great impact here. We would start the program with middle management, then 'cascade' it down throughout the organization."

In addition, ARCO's corporate headquarters and several operating companies have recently begun offering specialized training courses for the self-development of minority employees. Cynthia Conover, Advisor on Equal Opportunity Affairs, described the program. "Six to seven sessions consisting of twenty-five people were conducted over the past two years; each session lasted three days. We recently conducted a pilot training program for twenty-five managers to refine the course curriculum. If deemed successful, it will be rolled out to each operating company."

There is no formal minority employee organization at ARCO, but Edgar Twine believes that there is a strong informal network. "I always introduce myself to new minority professionals, and I try to serve as a mentor and role model whenever I can," he says. "I think it would be helpful to have a formal network, like the one at Xerox, but in the meantime,

I think we do a pretty good job of supporting each other." ARCO also encourages employees to participate in outside organizations that can lead to building a network of minority professionals. For example, through the National Urban League, employees participate in the Black Executive Exchange Program (BEEP). BEEP sends black professionals to historically black colleges for two weeks to teach seminars on how to succeed in corporate America. The program allows students to build relationships with the executives and to identify role models. William A. Holland, Manager of Equal Opportunity Affairs and Minority Business Development, publishes a quarterly newsletter, *Opportunity!*, which reports on issues related to the equal employment opportunity responsibilities of ARCO supervisors and managers, and which also includes news of the accomplishments of minority employees.

ARCO has also taken a stand on membership in private social clubs. The company will pay fees and other business-related expenses for managerial private club memberships only if the club has no membership policies or practices that exclude minority or female members. "Lod Cook instituted that policy," notes Twine, "and I think it says a lot about his sensitivity to issues that women and minorities face in the workplace."

ARCO offers an Employee Problem Resolution Procedure through which employees can present EEO-related and other problems for resolution without fear of retaliation. ARCO also offers an Employee Assistance Program, a confidential counseling and referral service for employees and their families. Finally, ARCO's Educational Reimbursement Program reimburses employees for tuition, textbook and related expenses for approved courses and degree programs.

ARCO is known for its commitment to community service. The company's philanthropic efforts include support of several minority organizations through the ARCO Foundation, including the National Black MBA Association, the National Society of Black Engineers, the National Society of Hispanic

MBA's, the Hispanic Association of Colleges, the American Indian College Fund and the Consortium for Graduate Studies in Management Scholarship. The company also funds a National Merit Scholarship and provides scholarships to minority students in California and Texas through the LULAC National Education Service Centers. In addition, the company's Volunteer Service Program features a unique award and recognition system in which outstanding volunteers can receive up to $2,500 for the nonprofit agencies they support. The Matching Gifts Program encourages employees and retirees to give personal financial support to qualifying nonprofits by matching all qualifying gifts ranging from $25 to $20,000 in a calendar year. Finally, ARCO donated $1 million to United Way of Los Angeles to provide emergency aid to victims of the riot in the spring of 1992.

ARCO has a Minority Business Development department charged with developing minority- and female-owned businesses so that they can provide the goods and services the company needs. The MBD Coordinator helps expand the directory of minority suppliers and contractors, directs these companies to ARCO buyers and makes technical and business assistance available to vendors who require it. In 1992, ARCO committed 5% of its purchasing budget to minority- and female-owned businesses, which represented more than $200 million worth of business.

Minorities have achieved several high-ranking management positions within ARCO, including Associate General Counsel; Vice President, National Accounting Management; President, Four Corners Pipe Line Company; and President, ARCO Transportation Company Alaska, Inc. John B. Slaughter, president of Occidental College, is a member of the board of directors. Their success is a testament to ARCO's commitment to achieving a diverse work force at all levels of the company. "Is there still a glass ceiling?" asks Twine. "I'd say in just about every major company in this country, yes, there is. But this is an open place where race and ethnicity can be discussed. Our EEO head is very vocal about where we stand and where we need to be as an employer of minorities. Our CEO has to be one of the best in the country when it comes to awareness of these issues. I'd say that makes this an excellent company in which to build a career."

Office locations: The company's domestic operations are based in California, Texas, Colorado, Pennsylvania and Alaska. ARCO has operations in Indonesia, Australia, the United Kingdom, Italy, France, Singapore, Hong Kong, Taiwan and Korea.

515 South Flower Street
Los Angeles, California 90051
(213) 486-3511

AVIS RENT-A-CAR SYSTEM, INC.

Avis is the second-largest car rental and leasing company in the United States. It operates rental offices at airports, hotels, convention centers and downtown office areas.

1990 revenues: $1,200,000,000
1991 revenues: $1,220,000,000

Number of full-time employees: 13,425

Percentage of these employees who are minorities: 33.6
    Black: 20.0
    Hispanic: 9.5
    Asian/Pacific Islander: 3.6
    Native American: .5

Number of people in the total management pool: 1,013

Percentage of minorities in the total management pool: 12.5

Percentage of minority managers who comprise each managerial level:
    Senior executives: 3.3
    Managers: 7.6
    Middle managers: 14.5

Founded in 1946 by Warren Avis, a former Army Air Corps flyer who was also a Detroit car dealer, Avis was the first auto rental company based at airports. Originally called Avis Airlines Rent-A-Car System, the company surpassed other auto rental companies because of its unique convenience for air travelers. In 1948, Avis began opening offices in downtown areas near hotels and office buildings.

The company has had a series of owners including ITT Corporation, Norton Simon, Inc., and Lazard Freres and Co.; in 1987, Avis was purchased on behalf of its 11,500 U.S. employees for $1.75 billion. The company operates with two divisions, Avis, Inc., and Avis Europe.

Minorities at Avis hold such positions as Director of International Marketing, District Manager in Miami Office, Director of Voice Operations and District Manager of Washington, D.C., Office.

Karen Wong, Director of International Marketing for Avis Europe, has been with the company since 1981. She has advanced through seven positions and believes there is a great opportunity for minority advancement at the company. As an Asian woman, she was concerned about finding a company that would treat her as it would treat any other young manager. "Ever since I came to Avis, I have never had a problem asking for additional responsibilities," Wong says, "and my bosses have always had the confidence to challenge me with larger and more complex duties."

Wong says that because the company has operations around the United States and abroad, she has traveled a great deal as she has advanced. "I began as an account executive in San Francisco, then moved to regional management, then to national accounts," she says. "Then I was promoted to sales manager, then to marketing manager and finally to my current position with Avis Europe." Wong says that her work requires her to deal with managers in both the auto industry and the travel industry, where minorities are also very visible on most levels. "There really need to be more minorities in upper management at some of the auto companies, and this is the group I'm dealing with much of the time," Wong says, "but all of this presents a challenge to me."

The company recruits many minority college students from Adelphi University, Hofstra University, New York Institute of Technology and C. W. Post College, all of which are near the corporate headquarters.

According to Carol Riley, Director of Equal Opportunity, Avis has had a diversity training program since 1990. The Bridges program uses interactive video and covers cultural diversity issues. "I travel to our different locations throughout the country and teach our managers how to incorporate diversity into every aspect of our business—from hiring, to evaluating, to disciplining, to promoting," says Riley. Her half-day workshops on appreciating other cultures have elicited some interesting and productive responses from managers.

"I recently performed a training program for our Information Services Group on how to give a performance review of employees," says Riley, "and while I was speaking about the cultural differences between traditional Asian and traditional American cultures, I was explaining that some Asian employees might be quite offended by the American business tradition of giving tough but honest performance evaluations. In some Asian cultures whose people work for businesses outside of the United States, an employee who is doing top-quality work is never told that he has specific weaknesses and that he can strengthen certain areas. In American business, however, the American employee accepts this as constructive criticism. In certain Asian cultures, this type of criticism would bring shame to an employee and possibly cause him to quit because he would feel that he has let down his team."

Ironically, Riley discovered a manager in her audience who admitted that two talented Asian employees had quit soon after receiving their performance evaluations. "And these evaluations were not meant to be negative indictments," says Riley. "This is why we all need to understand cultural differences. At Avis, we are proud to see that our training is giving us the best possible work force."

Allene Weathers, a black District Manager in the Washington, D.C., office, joined the company in 1966 as a rental sales agent in San Francisco. "It probably comes as no surprise," says Weathers, "but when I first joined this company, I had to look to older white male bosses in order to find my mentors." Weathers moved quickly into management, and she says she was encouraged by enthusiastic white senior managers. By the time she became Station Manager in San Francisco, District Manager and Operations Manager in Oakland, she said she had absolutely no fears about being a black manager at Avis.

"I have mentored many minority employees," says Weathers, whose location brings in $16 million annually. "But this is a company that is now very accustomed to hiring and promoting minorities into important positions."

While there are no formal minority employee organizations at Avis, the company supports such organizations as the NAACP and keeps in close contact with groups like the Urban League to notify them of job openings. The company also participates in minority job fairs sponsored by National Career Centers in the New York area and other cities.

The company's Disadvantaged and Minority Business Enterprise Program has been working with minority suppliers since 1986.

Office locations: The corporate headquarters are in Garden City (Long Island), New York. There are offices across the United States and operations in 137 other countries in Europe, Africa and the Middle East.

900 Old Country Road
Garden City, New York 11530
(516) 222-3000

AVON PRODUCTS, INC.

Avon manufactures and markets a line of cosmetics, toiletries, fragrances and jewelry through more than 1.5 million part-time direct sales representatives in the United States and abroad. The company also owns the Giorgio Beverly Hills line of products, which includes *Giorgio* and *Red*, sold through retail channels.

1990 revenues: $3,453,800,000
1991 revenues: $3,600,000,000
1992 revenues: $3,809,900,000

Number of full-time U.S. employees: 6,809

Percentage of these employees who are minorities: 21.5
    Black: 13
    Hispanic: 6
    Asian/Pacific Islander: 2
    Native American: .5

Number of people in the total management pool: 610

Percentage of minorities in the total management pool: 16

Percentage of minority managers who comprise each managerial level:
    Vice president: 11
    Director: 12
    Manager: 16

Founded in 1886, Avon has grown into one of the largest cosmetics companies in the world. Besides being one of the first major employers of women, it is renowned for its unique minority employee organizations.

Minorities have gained important positions at the company. Ernesta Procope, the well-known black Wall Street entrepreneur and president of the insurance brokerage firm E. G. Bowman Co., Inc., is on Avon's board of directors. Also on the board is Remedios Diaz-Oliver, president and CEO of All-American Containers, Inc. Another high-powered minority executive at Avon is Joyce Roche, Vice President of Brand Marketing. Minorities hold such other positions as Regional Vice President of Sales and Customer Service, Vice President of Sales Contemporization, Vice President of Human Resources and General Manager of Organization Development.

Avon recruits on campuses, placing special emphasis on high-potential minority candidates; the company also advertises in publications aimed at minorities and sends representatives to minority-oriented job fairs and conferences. It also solicits professional organizations for potential candidates. In addition, the Avon Career Advancement Program allows interested representatives to advance by compensating them for recruiting, training and managing other representatives. They are compensated not only for their own sales, but also for the performance of the representatives they recruit.

All senior managers of the company have a diversity goal against which they are measured. The company has also developed a three-week residence program for high-potential managers at Morehouse College in conjunction with the American Institute for Managing Diversity. Participants receive management, leadership and diversity training.

Avon is well known for its minority employee organizations, which include the Black Professionals of Avon, the Asian Network and the Hispanic Network. Each group offers networking, mentoring and cultural activities.

Alvin Smith, Manager of Organization Development, was a founder of Black Professionals of Avon and currently serves as the group's chairman. "Employee organizations like this are extremely important to new minority employees," says Smith. "When we first began the group, it consisted of twenty-five coworkers and was primarily focused on helping the members network and discuss certain professional or social concerns." Smith says minorities succeed in a company by understanding that it takes more than just hard work. "You have to understand the corporate culture. You have to know who to call and where to go to get certain information. An employee network can teach you all these things much faster than trial and error can."

Smith's organization has served as a model for many companies that have established minority employee groups. Black Professionals at Avon offers mentoring, publishes a newsletter, presents social events, raises money for such organizations as the United Negro College Fund, keeps track of services available in the black community and meets once every three months at different offices. What is particularly interesting about groups like this is that they can also support the marketing strategies of the company. Smith realizes that his organization and the other two minority organizations at Avon serve as good sounding boards for Avon marketing executives who are launching new cosmetics and other products aimed at the minority market.

Having been at the company since 1987, Shirley Dong is as enthusiastic and as excited as Smith. A Senior Product Counselor in Brand Marketing, Dong serves as chairperson of the Avon Asian Network. "I had worked for two retailers and an investment bank before coming to Avon," says Dong. "And it took only three months for me to discover that this was a company with a truly diverse culture. Before coming here, I had never heard of a company that sanctioned minority networks. It was a dream come true."

Dong's group meets every quarter, during lunchtime. She

says CEO Jim Preston asks for updates on what the Asian Network is doing and thinking. "It's not just lip service," Dong says. "These people really support us and care about our opinions. Management has funded us so that we could give professional seminars to our members. Recently we hired Herbert Wong Consultants in San Francisco to train our members on management issues. We had told the company that we wanted to find an Asian management trainer, and the human resources office went out there and got us the right people."

Like the black professionals' group, the Asian Network sponsors cultural events at the corporate headquarters for all employees. "In May," says Dong, "we celebrated Asian Heritage Month and offered Japanese origami, Chinese dough sculpture, how to drape saris, and a Korean costume exhibit."

The Hispanic Network also received company funding to hire an outside consultant. José Agosto is Avon's Manager of Telemarketing Services and president of its Hispanic Network. He says the network recently sponsored a four-day management enhancement seminar for Hispanic employees. "We wanted to invite someone who understood that Hispanic professionals face a glass ceiling in corporate America," says Agosto, who has worked with Avon since 1972. "So we found a Hispanic-owned consulting firm, Armistad Associates, in California, and focused on issues that are particular to us."

Like Smith and Dong, Agosto is impressed by the environment Avon has fostered for minority and nonminority professionals. "No one gets penalized at this company for saying what needs to be said." The network has given suggestions to marketing executives on products that targeted the Hispanic population, in addition to giving career advice to its members. The organization has been in existence since 1987, meets monthly and actively supports an elementary school in the Bronx by introducing the students to the office environment and by presenting Hispanic cultural performances.

There is a minority supplier-vendor program at Avon which spends nearly $50 million each year with minority contractors.

Avon is extremely generous in charitable giving. Recently the company gave $500,000 to the Schomburg Center for Research in Black Culture, a branch of the New York Public Library. The company is also a major donor to the NAACP, the National Council of LaRaza, the Anti-Defamation League, the National Puerto Rican Coalition, SER—Jobs for Progress, the National Black MBA Association, the Cuban National Planning Council and other groups.

Most recently, the company has sponsored minority high school students through the YouthEmPact Program, whereby students are paid to work during the summer at such organizations as the Hispanic Federation of New York.

Office locations: Corporate headquarters are in New York City. There are offices across the United States and in the United Kingdom, Germany, Taiwan, Thailand, Japan, Mexico and Brazil.

9 West 57th Street
New York, New York 10019
(212) 546-6015

BELL ATLANTIC CORPORATION

Bell Atlantic is the parent of seven regional Bell telephone companies: New Jersey Bell, Bell of Pennsylvania, Diamond State Telephone Company, and the Chesapeake and Potomac (C&P) Telephone Companies of Washington, D.C., Maryland, Virginia and West Virginia. These companies provide voice and data communications to residential and business customers. In addition, Bell Atlantic provides cellular and paging service and equipment through its Mobile Systems and Paging subsidiaries; hardware, software and support for business systems through its Business Systems Services subsidiary; and diversified financial services through the Bell Atlantic Capital Corporation.

1990 revenues: $12,298,000,000
1991 revenues: $12,279,000,000

Number of full-time U.S. employees: 72,241

Percentage of these employees who are minorities: 24.3
    Black: 22.1
    Hispanic: 1.6
    Asian/Pacific Islander: .5
    Native American: .1

Number of people in the total management pool: 20,176

Percentage of minorities in the total management pool: 17.7

Percentage of minority managers who comprise each managerial level:

Executive: 3.7
Director: 7.1
Manager: 12.0
Supervisor: 20.8

Salary information:

Executive:	not released
Director:	not released
Manager:	$42,400–$69,800
Supervisor:	$26,300–$57,700

Bell Atlantic was created after the 1984 divestiture by the former national Bell System. Minorities at Bell Atlantic hold many top positions, including President and CEO of the Chesapeake & Potomac Telephone Company; Vice President of Marketing and Sales; Vice President and General Counsel of New Jersey Bell Telephone Company; Vice President and General Counsel of Bell of Pennsylvania; and Vice President and General Counsel of the Chesapeake & Potomac Telephone Company.

There are also two minority members on the company's board of directors: Shirley Young, Vice President of Consumer Market Development at General Motors Corporation, and James H. Gilliam, Executive Vice President and General Counsel of Beneficial Corporation.

The company targets selected colleges and universities annually in order to recruit top graduates. It is actively implementing a minority recruiting strategy which includes contacting minority organizations and clubs at each of its eighteen primary targeted schools (among them Spelman and Morehouse colleges) to maximize the company's ability to identify and attract high-potential candidates.

Bell Atlantic also participates in numerous minority job fairs and career conferences, including the Whitney M. Young Conference at the Wharton School of Business, the Hispanic

Engineer conferences and the National Black MBA Association conferences.

Employee referrals are encouraged, and referrals from the Black Telecommunications Managers organization, CITE, are also pursued. The company also uses a summer internship program to identify potential full-time hires. The program is open to all college students, with the company targeting minorities. In addition, Bell Atlantic works through the INROADS internship program as a recruiting channel, and recruits students as early as high school graduation for a four-summer internship.

Bell Atlantic is committed to providing all employees with the opportunity to advance in the company. According to Bruce Gordon, Vice President of Marketing and Sales in Arlington, Virginia, affirmative action is not new at the company. As a black executive who has been with the company since 1968, he has always been aware of the company's efforts. "As early as 1968," Gordon recalls, "Bell was conducting seminars on racial sensitivity. When I was working as a manager at the division Bell of Pennsylvania, I helped found the group Action Alliance of Black Managers."

Gordon says the company's top managers support minority employee organizations because they realize that minorities want to develop additional networks and create even greater access to career information. "Our chairman, Ray Smith," says Gordon, "attends CITE's annual event, which is a three-day weekend that offers seminars and workshops on issues of interest to minority employees."

Career resource centers, career management workshops and other career development tools are available to all employees, and supervisors are encouraged to discuss these programs with their subordinates. Progress of minorities is tracked annually and reported to higher management, and succession planning is routinely analyzed to determine the representation of minority candidates at all levels. A wide variety of tuition assistance and after-work education programs are also available; more than $6.2 million was spent on these programs in 1991.

Bell Atlantic conducts a number of programs that address issues of diversity and the specific training of minority managers. The Black Managers' Workshop has been offered every year since 1978. There are three offerings a year, with an enrollment of approximately 150 managers annually. More than 2,000 black managers have attended the workshop. The six-day residential workshop serves as a developmental tool enabling black managers to increase awareness of and confidence in their abilities, and learn how to use them in the corporate culture. The workshop focuses on accountability in relationships and enhancing one's impact in the corporate setting; career development strategies; effective managerial styles; race-related stress and coping strategies.

The company also conducts awareness sessions which include a presentation by managers from the EEO/Diversity Management organization who use the Copeland Griggs videotapes called "Valuing Diversity." There are plans to expand these sessions to include diversity management and related issues.

Bell Atlantic provides an EEO/Diversity Hotline, available to all employees, that supplements the regular lines of organization in explaining the company's policies, handling questions and looking into problems.

The company has pursued numerous philanthropic efforts in support of the minority community. One example is the C&P Telephone Company's work-study program. Recently fourteen students from inner-city high schools were engaged as part-time C&P operators after completing a six-week tutorial. Upon graduation from high school, the students were offered full-time jobs. C&P also has employees volunteering in seven schools in minority neighborhoods of the District of Columbia. Services provided by these volunteers include support of programs to motivate students; career awareness/shadowing experiences; role models; health awareness; mentoring and tutoring. Each Bell company has numerous efforts under way in its community, including work in homeless shelters, scholarship programs and funding of inner-city youth programs.

In 1993, *Hispanic* magazine recognized the company as one of the 100 best in providing opportunities to Hispanics. The Links, Inc., the national black women's organization, recognized Bell Atlantic recently for featuring prominent black men and women as spokespersons for the company's services, among them the actor James Earl Jones, the singer Roberta Flack and the late author of *Roots*, Alex Haley.

There is a minority supplier-vendor program at the company which spends more than $100 million each year with minority contractors.

Office locations: Bell Atlantic's corporate headquarters are in Philadelphia. It has major domestic operations in Delaware, Washington, D.C., Maryland, New Jersey, Pennsylvania, Virginia and West Virginia. The company has international operations in Austria, France, Italy, Czechoslovakia, the Netherlands, Spain, Switzerland and the United Kingdom.

1600 Market Street
Philadelphia, Pennsylvania 19103
(215) 963-6000

BORDEN, INC.

Borden is a worldwide producer of foods, nonfood consumer products, and packaging and industrial products. Among its food products are Creamette pasta, Prince spaghetti sauces, Cheez Doodles, Wise brand salty snacks, Cracker Jacks and a full line of dairy products. The company also produces Elmer's glue, a variety of wallcoverings and a line of films and adhesives.

1990 revenues: $7,632,800,000
1991 revenues: $7,235,100,000

Number of full-time U.S. employees: 46,000

Percentage of these employees who are minorities: 24

In 1851, Gail Borden, a newspaper publisher and inventor, discovered the formula for condensed milk. Six years later, after developing other milk products, Borden founded a dairy company in Ohio. Today the company is the largest dairy operator and largest pasta manufacturer in the United States.

Borden's commitment to equal employment opportunity earned it the highest ranking in *Shopping for a Better World*, the consumer guide to socially responsible corporations.

Borden sets affirmative action hiring and promotion goals at each of its offices and plants, and for the company as a whole. Performance reviews of all supervisors and managers include an evaluation of their ability to reach EEO goals in hiring and promotion.

Minorities at Borden hold such positions as Corporate Vice

President and President of the Borden Foundation, General Manager of Refrigerated Products, General Manager of International Business, Group Counsel, General Manager of the Vernon Plastics Group and Corporate Vice President of Health and Environmental Affairs. There is one minority person on the board of directors: Wilbert J. LeMelle, President of the Phelps-Stokes Fund.

Essex Mitchell, Manager of Borden's Corporate Equal Employment Office, says the company has an active recruiting program that is aimed at getting more Hispanics, blacks, Asians and Native Americans into line positions. "Our recruiting goal," says Mitchell, "is to put more high-potential minority employees into engineering, marketing, sales and other line jobs so they can eventually run whole divisions."

The company advertises in publications aimed at minority job hunters and sends representatives to numerous minority-oriented job fairs and conferences like those sponsored by the U.S. Hispanic Chamber of Commerce and the National Urban League.

Since Borden has a reputation for hiring experienced managers who have already been trained by the other large consumer products companies like Procter & Gamble, it does not have an aggressive college recruiting program. The company does, however, offer a co-op program aimed at college students who want to work at the company for alternating semesters. According to Mitchell, the co-op program has hired many minority students from such universities as Fisk, Florida A&M, Central State, Wilberforce and Jackson State. "We can attract more minority employees to the company," says Mitchell, "when we can offer minority students good experiences early in their careers."

Mitchell says the company is launching its Associates Mentor Program in order to match new employees with more experienced Borden executives, who will act as career advisers. Although a primary goal of the program is to improve retention and advancement of minority professionals, Borden's style is to avoid creating formal "minority" programs. This is why the company has no minority employee organizations.

According to Mitchell, the company has been able to advance many minority employees' career goals through a Career Options Program, established in 1988, which allows employees in one department to request an introduction to additional training in other departments. "This opportunity," says Mitchell, "can broaden one's potential in the company because the employee learns greater skills."

Management training is available to all employees, and the company has also developed a Minority and Recruiting and Development Program for high-potential minority candidates. There is an Executive EEO Incentive Program, whereby each key manager's compensation includes a bonus tied to the hiring and promotion of minority professionals and managers. The company also sponsors black entrepreneurs for various executive programs at the Tuck School of Business at Dartmouth College.

Borden also participates in the Urban League's Black Executive Exchange Program by sending black managers to historically black colleges to introduce students to the corporate world and the minority executives who work there. One such executive is Ronald Cosey, who has visited such universities as Central State, Prairie View A&M, Johnson C. Smith and Norfolk State since coming to the company in 1976. "Students need to see that there are black managers in corporate America," says Cosey. "We give them insights that they might not learn in the classroom, and we also serve as mentors." As Manager of Minority Purchasing at Borden, Cosey has taught college seminars as an exchange executive on such topics as the globalization of corporate America.

Because of his work in the company's Equal Employment Opportunity office, Mitchell is well aware of the importance of diversity training for all employees. The company uses lectures, as well as the videotape series "Affirmative Action: The Next

Phase," created by Harbridge House. Borden offers an EEO and Affirmative Action Training Program to all managers. "We want our employees to know," says Mitchell, "that issues of diversity are not just for minority employees. They are for everyone. We offer three versions of our training program. One is for the senior core management group, and there is also an hour-long session and a three-and-a-half-hour presentation."

Borden was a pioneer and continues to lead in minority purchasing, having established a volunteer minority purchasing program in the early 1970s. In 1992, Borden's purchases of goods and services from minority suppliers totaled more than $70 million. The company is a charter member of the National Minority Supplier Development Council and has a seat on the Council's board of directors.

The company has taken extra steps to make certain that minority suppliers have an opportunity to win contracts. Minority firms were involved early in the bidding process for the construction of the Borden plants in Jackson, Mississippi, and St. Louis, Missouri, and more than $1 million has been spent with local minority firms on these projects.

Borden also made major purchases of wheat for its pasta business and potatoes for its snack business from Native American farmers, of plant equipment from Hispanic-owned firms and of raw milk from minority-owned producers.

Recently Borden introduced almost 700 additional minority-owned firms to its minority purchasing program through participation in trade shows, and was a sponsor of *Try Us*, a national minority business directory. The company also uses minority-owned banks by making more than $50 million of its tax payments through such institutions. The amount represented more than 25% of Borden's tax payments for 1992.

The company's charitable contributions are handled by the Borden Foundation, headed by Judy Barker, a black executive who is also Corporate Vice President. The foundation, established in 1944, supports such minority organizations as the Hispanic Association of Colleges and Universities, the United Negro College Fund, the Links and the National Urban League. In 1991, Borden assisted ASPIRA Association, the national Hispanic organization, in launching an educational program for disadvantaged elementary school children in the United States and Puerto Rico.

Office locations: Although the company's administrative head-quarters are in Columbus, Ohio, the executive offices are in New York City. There are operations in thirty-four other states including Illinois, Alabama, Arizona, California, Missouri, Pennsylvania and Massachusetts. There are also plants and of-fices in Latin America, Western Europe and Canada.

180 East Broad Street
Columbus, Ohio 43215
(614) 225-4000

BRISTOL-MYERS SQUIBB COMPANY

Bristol-Myers Squibb is a global pharmaceutical and consumer products company. The Pharmaceutical division is the company's largest. It manufactures and markets such products as Capoten, Questran and Isovue. The Medical Devices division markets a wide variety of prosthetic devices. The Nonprescription Health Product division is responsible for such well-known consumer brands as Excedrin, Nuprin, Bufferin, Gerber Baby Formula and Enfamil. The Toiletries, Beauty Aids, and Household Products division includes the Clairol line of beauty products, Windex glass cleaner and Renuzit air fresheners.

1991 revenues: $10,500,000,000
1992 revenues: $11,159,000,000

Number of full-time employees: 28,139

Percentage of these employees who are minorities: 18.4
    Black: 11.0
    Hispanic: 4.1
    Asian/Pacific Islander: 3.0
    Native American: 0.3

Number of people in the total management pool: 4,249

Percentage of minorities in the total management pool: 10.6

Percentage of minority managers who comprise each management level:
    Officers and management: 10.3
    Professional   14.5

| Technical | 20.4 |
| Sales | 17.1 |

Long known for its commitment to improving human health, Bristol-Myers Squibb has also made a serious commitment to recruiting, developing and promoting minority employees. All Bristol-Myers Squibb divisions have affirmative action objectives, and managers and supervisors are evaluated on their success in applying the company's EEO policy.

A corporate advertising review committee, with minority and women representatives, monitors the company's U.S. advertising to ensure that women and minorities are presented positively and fairly. Several Bristol-Myers ad campaigns feature minority spokespersons. Recently Gerber Baby Formula received two CEBA (Communications Excellence to Black Audiences) Awards from the World Institute of Black Communications.

Bristol-Myers Squibb hires in such areas as marketing, finance, research and operations.

The company has developed a unique recruiting vehicle in its Minority Recruitment Program. Begun in 1987, the program functions as an in-house executive search firm. "Most companies wedge their search for minority candidates in among other human resource functions," says Lionel Stevens, Corporate Director, Recruiting and Equal Opportunity Affairs. "Bristol-Myers Squibb has a group of people devoted solely to finding the best minority candidates and placing them in positions where their talents are needed."

Company recruiters have built a data base of qualified candidates, and are frequently on campus at colleges with large minority enrollments. In 1992 the Mead Johnson Nutritional division recruited at Clark-Atlanta University, Central State University and Tuskegee University. The Clairol division recruited at Hampton University. The Bristol-Myers Products division interviewed students at Florida A&M and Howard universities. The company's pharmaceutical research division recruited at Tennessee State and North Carolina State universities.

As a result of these efforts, the company has increased representation of minorities among its managers and professionals by 36% since 1982. Minorities hold such positions as Vice President and Associate General Counsel, Vice President of Employee Relations, Vice President of Corporate Security, Vice President of Marketing, Vice President of Manufacturing Accounting, Vice President of Engineering and Vice President of Media Operations.

Gilroye A. Griffin, Jr., Vice President of Corporate Employee Relations, was named one of *Ebony* magazine's 50 Top Black Executives in corporate America in 1992. However, the company has no minority board members.

Milton E. Goggans, Vice President of Sales for the company's Princeton Pharmaceutical Products division, is convinced that Bristol-Myers Squibb is a place where minority managers can advance at the same rate as nonminority executives. Goggans, who has been with the company since 1987, manages 460 sales representatives, 52 district managers and 6 regional sales directors. He spent seventeen years in sales and marketing positions at a major pharmaceuticals company that competes with Bristol-Myers Squibb. "At my prior employer," says Goggans, "I got a clear message that there was an old-boys' network which determined who got promoted. I had always known that Bristol-Myers was a company that was more bottom-line oriented—more focused on promoting based on an employee's performance. As a black executive, I can never be a member of the old-boys' club, so it makes a lot more sense to work with a company that will promote me and recognize me because of my accomplishments, and not because of who I know."

The company conducts specialized recruitment and affirmative action support programs with community and national organizations. The Pharmaceutical Group is a sponsor of the annual Wharton African American MBA Association's Whitney M. Young, Jr., Conference. Other divisions recruit through the Native American Manpower Center and the Puerto Rican American Community Association, the National Black MBA Association and the National Institute of Medical Sciences Minority Program.

At several divisions, minority MBA candidates are hired as summer interns for professional-level assignments. Several divisions also participate in INROADS, the national minority internship program for high school students. The company also employs minority high school students for professional and other assignments through a number of summer employment programs.

It is important to note that college recruits represent a small fraction of the new hires at Bristol-Myers Squibb. Stevens, who has been with the company since 1985, says fewer than seventy students are hired directly out of college each year. "Most of our new people," he says, "are experienced hires who are coming from other companies." The fact that most new employees join the company after spending several years at other firms might explain why neither the company nor its minority employees have ever established minority mentoring programs.

Stevens does, however, point to the Corporate Associates Program, designed to mentor minority employees into management positions. "We hire minority students who are graduating from U.S. military programs like Annapolis or West Point," says Stevens, "and we place them in a division where they rotate for two years in different positions. During this time, we provide each of the employees with a mentor who can give them career planning advice. After the two years of work, we send each of the corporate associates to get his or her MBA. We pay for their schooling and hope that they will return upon graduation."

Bristol-Myers Squibb has no minority employee organizations, but there are some programs that foster upward mobility for minority employees. All divisions train managers in applying the company's EEO policy to meet its affirmative action plans. Division presidents participate in formal reviews of steps being taken to support the company's EEO goals. A variety of tuition aid programs offers employees the opportunity to complete their education or undertake advanced study. Squibb College, part of the Pharmaceutical Group, offers sixty-five courses that help all employees increase their proficiency and prepare for advancement. There is no formal diversity training program.

The company supports a variety of scholarship programs. In 1991, Bristol-Myers Squibb provided four fellowships under the Minority MBA Fellowships Program for black and Hispanic marketing majors at Northwestern and Columbia universities. The company sponsors these same fellowships at Cornell, Duke, Harvard and the University of Virginia. The Bristol-Myers Squibb Foundation joined the Commonwealth Fund in supporting the National Medical Fellowship Program, which helps academically gifted minority medical students prepare for careers in academic medicine and biomedical research. In 1993, Clairol was a key sponsor of the Essence Awards, which recognizes outstanding achievements by black women.

The Mead Johnson Nutritional Group provides scholarships to minority high school students seeking degrees in engineering, science or computer science. Recipients are employed the summer after they graduate from high school and become eligible for the company's cooperative education program upon completion of their freshman year in college. Westwood Pharmaceuticals offered a minority graduate fellowship in 1992, including part-time employment at the company for two years, for an MBA student at the State University of New York at Buffalo.

Bristol-Myers Squibb Pharmaceutical Group provided minority fellowships to MBA students at the University of Pennsylvania, MIT, Columbia University and Northwestern University. The group also gave financial support to Meharry Medical College, the Fomento Scholarship Fund, the Cornell University Medical College Minority Student Scholarship

Fund, the Puerto Rican-Latin American Scholarship Fund, Navajo Community College and other minority programs and institutions.

Financial support is provided directly to a variety of minority educational institutions, including the Howard University College of Medicine, the National Hispanic Scholarship Fund, the Society of Hispanic Professional Engineers and the United Negro College Fund. Bristol-Myers Squibb actively supports community cultural organizations, such as Dance Theater of Harlem, the Spanish Repertory Theater and the American Indian Archaeological Institute. The company supports the National Urban League's Black Executive Exchange role model program and sponsors black professionals and managers as guest lecturers in business courses at predominantly black colleges.

Bristol-Myers Squibb's policy is to seek out minority-owned suppliers wherever possible and to encourage them to make their services known to the company. Purchasing representatives throughout the company participate in minority purchasing councils, and divisions have programs designed to identify businesses owned by women and minorities, with the goal of increasing purchases from these sources. Most of the company's divisions belong to the New York/New Jersey Minority Purchasing Council, an affiliate of the National Minority Supplier Development Council.

Bristol-Myers Squibb has maintained a presence in South Africa despite continuing apartheid. However, the company is a signatory of the Sullivan Principles, which outline an ethical means of conducting business in a country which continues to discriminate against blacks. In 1992, for the fifth consecutive year, the company received the highest rating possible from the independent consulting firm that monitors signatories. All South African Bristol-Myers facilities are fully integrated, and the company encourages black employees to live in white areas. The company's loan assistance program helps make this possible. Bristol-Myers supports the Katlehong Health Center and cosponsors a satellite clinic. It also provides legal funds for victims of apartheid.

Office locations: The company is headquartered in New York City. It has operations across the United States, Puerto Rico, Canada, Western Europe, Asia, South and Central America, Australia, Africa and the Middle East.

345 Park Avenue
New York, New York 10154
(212) 546-4000

BURGER KING CORPORATION

Burger King is the world's second-largest hamburger restaurant chain, with more than 6,400 franchised and managed restaurants in forty-one countries. Burger King currently has a 17% market share in the United States.

1990 revenues: $6,100,000,000
1991 revenues: $6,100,000,000
1992 revenues: $6,400,000,000

Number of full-time employees: 5,238

Percentage of these employees who are minorities: 26.0
    Black: 16.2
    Hispanic: 7.5
    Asian/Pacific Islander: 2.1
    Native American: 0.2

Number of people in the total management pool: 553

Percentage of minorities in the total management pool: 4.5

Percentage of minority managers who comprise each managerial level:
    Officers: 3
    Directors: 17
    Managers: 18

Salary information:
    Director: $77,000–$120,000
    Manager: $50,000–$77,000

| Supervisor/analyst: | $30,000–$50,000 |
| Secretary/clerk: | $20,000–$30,000 |

Founded in 1954, Burger King is owned by the British conglom-erate Grand Metropolitan PLC, which also owns several other U.S. food, beverage and retailing companies, including Pills-bury, Häagen Dazs Ice Cream, Green Giant, Absolut Vodka and Pearle Vision Centers.

Since acquiring the company, Grand Met has made in-creased awareness of diversity issues a priority. Marianela Aran is Director of Operations Standards and has worked for Burger King since 1981. "Since we were bought by Grand Metropoli-tan," says Aran, "the company feels particularly international, with a greater appreciation for different languages and ethnic backgrounds. People are much more aware of the need to value diversity."

The company's recruiting program encompasses a broad range of colleges and universities, including seven historically black institutions: Florida A&M University, Bennett College, North Carolina Agricultural and Technical State University, Howard University, Clark-Atlanta University, Norfolk State University and Elizabeth City State University. Burger King donated $50,000 to each of these schools in 1991. The company also targets universities with large Hispanic enrollments such as the University of Texas at El Paso and at San Antonio, Florida International, California State and the National Hispanic Uni-versity at San Diego.

To help retain and develop minority managers, Burger King has formed a Diversity Resource Group with twenty-two members to provide a forum for discussing minority issues. The group meets at least monthly, formally and informally. In the near future, the company will establish a formal People of Color Network. "Currently there is a lot of informal networking," says Aran.

In addition, the company hired an independent consulting firm to conduct a one-day diversity awareness workshop at each regional office and at headquarters. Rachelle Hood-Phillips, Vice President of Diversity and Corporate Human Resources, believes "people were really awakened by the diversity training. It's had a tremendous impact." Hood-Phillips heads the Diversity Affairs department and publishes a quarterly newsletter called *Alliance* filled with statistics and news about minority issues; a supplement called *Alianza* reports on the Hispanic community.

The company provides attractive benefits for all employees: paid management and public speaking courses both inside and outside the company.

The company has been successful at moving minorities into high-ranking management positions. Rafael Levin, a Cuban American employee, is Vice President of Operations in Europe, and Esau Simms, an African American employee, is Vice President of Franchise Sales and Service. Burger King has no board of directors, but its executive committee includes an Asian American manager, Sam Yong. There are no minorities on the Grand Metropolitan board.

Minorities are building a presence within the company's franchises as well. Burger King added 77 minority-owned restaurants to the system in 1991, bringing the total to 565. This was an 18% increase over the previous year.

Black and Hispanic consumers are crucial to Burger King's success, and in 1992 the corporation spent more than $34 million in the development, execution and delivery of advertising and promotion programs to African Americans and Hispanics. In conjunction with UniWorld Group, the company's African American advertising agency, Burger King launched the successful Black Music Month Celebration promotion in June. Sosa & Associates, the Hispanic advertising agency, developed the Baila Con Burger King promotion.

Burger King donates approximately $3 million annually

to minority charitable organizations. The company has established Burger King Academies in partnership with the Cities in Schools program to promote education for high school dropouts and at-risk students. Terri Giles, a black woman who is Burger King's Manager of Consumer Relations, served as a mentor for the program. "These are high-risk students," says Giles. "I was paired off with a black sixteen-year-old woman who lives in a neighborhood similar to the one I grew up in. We talked about college- and career-related issues. I brought her to the company to see what we do here, and attended a college fair with her. Now she's attending Grambling State University—my own alma mater." In 1991, the Academies program won the National Society of Hispanic MBA's Brillante Award, given annually to "a company which has contributed to making the future of Hispanics brighter."

Burger King has a minority vendor program to help build entrepreneurship in minority communities. The company spent more than $60 million with minority suppliers in 1992, a 33% increase over the previous fiscal year. About 75% was spent with African American suppliers; spending with Hispanic suppliers was $12 million, with Asian American $3 million. Most of the spending was concentrated in food and paper products, travel, construction, printing, external consultants and legal services.

The company's location makes it particularly hospitable for minority managers. As Aran notes, "Miami has a large Hispanic population, and is filled with Hispanic and many other cultures. Many colleagues understand those cultures, and it adds to their comfort in dealing with a diverse work force." Perhaps as a result, Burger King has succeeded in creating an environment in which minorities feel free to express their ethnicity in the workplace. Says Giles, "Once I get to the door, I can still be a black woman at work."

Office locations: Corporate headquarters are in Miami, Florida. There are regional offices across the country, and franchises and managed stores in all fifty states and abroad.

17777 Old Cutler Road
Miami, Florida 33157
(305) 378-7011

LEO BURNETT ADVERTISING COMPANY

Leo Burnett is one of the country's leading advertising agencies. It has represented and helped build such products as Kellogg's Corn Flakes, Star Kist tuna and Pert shampoo. It has a long history with such corporate clients as Allstate, Heinz, Keebler, Maytag, Philip Morris, Pillsbury, Procter & Gamble and United Airlines.

1991 billings: $2,500,000,000

Number of full-time employees: 2,200

Founded in 1935 in Chicago, Leo Burnett is run quite differently from many of the other advertising agencies that got their start on New York's Madison Avenue. While many of the other agencies have become divisions of large corporate media conglomerates, Burnett is privately held and its stockholders are employees of the company.

Minority managers are hardly visible in many large agencies; Burnett is clearly the best of the group. In spite of its position as a leading supporter of minority employees and minority causes, the company was reluctant to release numerical data. Burnett is being cited here for reasons that go beyond numerical records for minority hiring.

Minorities at Leo Burnett hold such positions as Senior Vice President and Director of Resource Development; Senior Vice President and Director of Information Services; Media Director; Vice President of Real Estate Services; Direct Marketing Account Director; and Vice President and Account Director.

To ensure a focus on minority representation within the agency, black ad executive and senior vice president Don Richards was made Director of Resource Development, responsible for increasing the involvement of individuals from all minority communities.

Richards's efforts include recruiting minority students from schools like Spelman and Morehouse colleges, and attending minority career fairs like the National Black MBA Association annual conference. Burnett also holds seminars and workshops with minority students throughout the Chicago area, and offers a full scholarship each year to an outstanding minority art student at the University of Texas.

Once hired, each employee is assigned an adviser who provides coaching and perspective on Burnett. Because most training at the agency is on-the-job, the focus is on helping minorities develop relationships with more senior employees who can give encouragement and suggestions.

According to Burnett vice president Wally Petersen, the agency has recruiting programs in each of its four major departments—client service, creative, research and media services. Sixty-seven percent of the students being hired are undergraduates. Thirty-three percent are graduate students.

Since 1970, Burnett has offered minority internships through the INROADS program. The agency also works with the Consortium for Graduate Study to provide fellowships and summer internships for minority business school students.

Within the minority community, the agency contributes to the NAACP, the Mexican American Legal Defense and Education Fund, the United Negro College Fund and the Urban League. The agency also sponsors many gallery exhibitions which display graphic design pieces by young minority artists in the Chicago area.

Office locations: Corporate headquarters are in Chicago. There are a total of fifty-six offices in the United States and more than forty-eight other countries.

35 West Wacker Drive
Chicago, Illinois 60601
(312) 220-5959

CAMPBELL SOUP COMPANY

Campbell's is one of the country's largest food companies, manufacturing and marketing such well-known products as Campbell's Soup, Vlasic pickles, Swanson frozen dinners and entrees, Prego spaghetti sauce, V8 vegetable juice, Godiva chocolates and Pepperidge Farm baked goods.

1990 revenues: $6,205,800,000
1991 revenues: $6,204,100,000
1992 revenues: $6,263,200,000

Number of full-time U.S. employees: 28,815

Percentage of these employees who are minorities: 30.3
    Black: 16.4
    Hispanic: 10.0
    Asian/Pacific Islander: 2.8
    Native American: 1.1

Number of people in the total management pool: 4,004

Percentage of minorities in the total management pool: 8.4

Campbell was founded by Dr. John T. Dorrance, the inventor of condensed soup. The company has long been committed to a policy of employing and promoting qualified minority candidates. Each business sector has an affirmative action plan, and each facility tries to reflect in its work force the availability of qualified minorities in its labor area.

During 1990, the restructuring of the business prompted a

reduction of the work force. Total employment fell by about 8%. However, for minorities there was a 1% increase in the proportion of total work force, and minority representation in the white-collar groups increased from 10% to 13%.

Campbell's recruiting efforts extend to predominantly minority schools like Howard University and Morehouse College, and minority-oriented job fairs and conferences like the National Black MBA Association's annual conference. The company offers several programs to ensure an environment conducive to minority progress through the company. Deborah R. Pierce, Director of Affirmative Action and Government Compliance and a graduate of the University of Pennsylvania Law School, describes some of them. "We have EEO coordinators to help divisions achieve their goals, and each coordinator goes through a training program to make him or her more effective at accomplishing this task. At headquarters, we hold programs on understanding EEO compliance regulations for all managers." The company is also planning to conduct work force diversity training. "Diversity training is connected to our core values," Pierce comments. "There will be a separate program for executives, and another for managers. We are meeting with diversity consultants now in order to design a program. The plan is to begin a program during 1993."

There are also many opportunities for training and self-development. In 800 Quality Circles and 750 Quality Improvement Teams in the United States, employees can sharpen work-related and personal skills. The company offers many other training programs to all employees to help with speaking, writing and supervisory skills. The emphasis on personal and professional development includes a Tuition Aid Plan for which all employees are eligible. The company also awards twenty-one four-year academic scholarships to children of employees.

There are no formal minority employee organizations at Campbell, but there is an Affirmative Action Council. Pierce sits on the council. "The group has about twelve members," she notes, "and focuses on Campbell's progress in hiring, promoting and training." In 1990 the company formed a Hispanic Marketing Council at corporate headquarters to increase its responsiveness to the Hispanic community. The council includes managers from Human Resources, Procurement and Corporate Relations. Although it was originally created for consumer research and community relations, it has expanded to include trying to attract more Hispanic line managers.

Campbell has three minority officers, including Alfred Poe, a black manager who is Vice President of the Condiments and Sauces Sector. Brenda E. Edgerton, VP and Treasurer of Campbell, was named one of the 50 Top Black Executives in Corporate America by *Ebony* magazine in 1992. Minorities also hold such positions as Group Director of Engineering Systems, Senior Director of Nutrition and Toxicology and Director of Ingredient Technology. Claudine B. Malone, President of Financial and Management Consulting, Inc., served on the board of directors for many years, retiring at the end of 1991. Currently there are no minority board members.

Campbell has a long-standing policy of urging buyers to find and buy goods and services from minority-owned suppliers. In 1992, Campbell purchased more than $64 million in goods and services from minority vendors. The company was a charter member of the American Bar Association's Minority Counsel Demonstration Program, through which minority-owned firms are sought out to represent corporate interests in a wide variety of legal matters. Similarly, Campbell is represented on the Corporate Advisory Board of the National Bankers Association, which encourages corporations to use minority banking institutions. Campbell maintains balances in twenty-two such banks across the country.

Campbell's headquarters are in a predominantly minority community (more than 50% of the local population is black, and another 25% Hispanic), and the company has sought to improve the quality of life there, and near its manufacturing sites, by supporting community activities. In Camden, 43% of the people are younger than twenty-one, prompting Campbell to establish a summer program and invest $1.7 million since 1975 in summer jobs, athletics, camping and cultural activities. Grants in the Camden community totaled nearly $2 million in 1991 alone.

Campbell has also committed to a joint venture in the construction of an office tower on thirteen acres of Camden's waterfront. The company will use about half of the building, which will be Camden's tallest.

Among the many Camden organizations the company works with are the Black People's Unity Movement and the Latin-American Economic Development Association. Campbell also works with the school district to promote and support the Management Assistance for Public Schools program, which gives principals and their assistants training in management skills.

The company has for several years supported INROADS, the national program that provides career-related summer jobs for minority students. In 1992, Campbell sponsored eight such interns. The Campbell's Scholar program supports minority scholarships at Rutgers University, Ohio State University and the University of Medicine and Dentistry of New Jersey. Campbell also supports the ASPIRA Process, a New Jersey program aimed primarily at at-risk Hispanic students in Camden's public schools.

The Campbell Soup Foundation's priority is nutrition-related health matters, and the foundation has contributed generously to efforts to improve nutrition in minority communities. In 1992, the foundation gave grants to the Navajo Community College at Shiprock for research on obesity and diabetes prevention among Navajo youth, and to the National Kidney Foundation for work on hypertension and diabetes.

Office locations: The company is headquartered in Camden, New Jersey, and has manufacturing facilities across the United States. Campbell's International Division has operations in fifteen countries, primarily in Europe.

P.O. Box 391
Camden, New Jersey 08103
(609) 342-4800

CHAMPION INTERNATIONAL CORPORATION

Champion International is one of the country's largest manufacturers of paper and wood products. The company's products are used for business communications, commercial printing, magazines and newspapers. Champion manufactures pulp, as well as lumber, plywood, studs and specialty wood products. The company owns or controls 6.4 million acres of timberlands in the United States, making it one of the nation's largest private landowners.

1990 revenues: $5,089,944,000
1991 revenues: $4,786,403,000
1992 revenues: $4,926,471,000

Number of full-time U.S. employees: 20,600

Percentage of these employees who are minorities: 14.4
    Black: 10.8
    Hispanic: 2.4
    Asian/Pacific Islander: .4
    Native American: .8

Number of people in the total management pool: 2,530

Percentage of minorities in the total management pool: 4.4

Percentage of minority managers who comprise each managerial level:
    Vice president: 6.0
    Director: 8.1
    Manager: 9.7

Salary information:

Executive VP/senior VP:	$183,700–$293,000
Vice president–operations:	$88,800–$142,200
Manager—paper manufacturing:	$62,600–$100,200
Systems engineer manager and paper machine manager:	$49,700–$79,500
Senior process control engineer:	$39,400–$63,000
Process engineer:	$32,600–$48,800

Founded in the 1890s as the Champion Coated Paper Company in Hamilton, Ohio, the company eventually merged with St. Regis Corporation, thereby expanding its coated paper and lumber manufacturing business into the area of newsprint and publication paper producing.

Minorities at Champion hold such positions as Director of Project Analysis, Manager of Environmental Health, Manager of Planning and Staffing, Manager of Business Information, Manager of Quality Programs, Facilities Manager, Sales Manager and Materials Analyst, which is a director-level position.

There is one minority person on the board of directors: Sybil Mobley, dean of the School of Business at Florida A&M University.

The company recruits at several universities with large minority enrollment including North Carolina A&T State University, Hampton University, Xavier University, Florida A&M University and the University of Puerto Rico.

According to Thomas O'Brien, Vice President of Equal Opportunity and Work-Family Services, the company has a pilot diversity training program in its offices in Roanoke Rapids, North Carolina. "We're currently using R. Roosevelt Thomas's American Institute for Managing Diversity in Atlanta," says O'Brien, "and we intend to expand the program to our Ohio and Alabama locations. We are beginning with focus groups in order to identify the issues that would be tackled in a training program. Our company's management realizes that we're not going to get where we need to be just because the top executives mandate it. We will get there because all employees will learn to appreciate each other's diverse backgrounds."

According to Lorna Joselson, Manager of Equal Opportunity Affairs, the company is working with an Atlanta-based consultant called Diversity Consultants, Inc., which is helping to develop effective plans for the company's various facilities.

Champion employees take part in a comprehensive education and training program which covers developing skills in facilitating change; team building; implementing management techniques; conflict resolution and negotiating; technical knowledge acquisition; work group training and job redesign.

According to Kenneth Loyd, Sales Administrator at Champion's Hamilton, Ohio, plant, the company formed a Minority Development Task Force in 1988. "We were very successful at recruiting minority employees," says Loyd, a black manager who has worked at Champion since 1986, "but we wanted to find out how we could improve our retention."

Another task force was created by minority members in the accounting division. Before the two task forces eventually merged, both groups conducted studies to see how they could retain more minority professionals. After completing their studies, the two task forces made a presentation to the CEO, president and executive vice presidents. "We recommended that the company develop a Diversity Advisory Council," says Loyd.

The council was made up of the head of Human Resources and cross-functional teams of minorities and nonminorities. One very successful program to come out of the council was the Champion Mentoring Program, which is used to acquaint not just newly hired minorities but also nonminorities with the company. Loyd says mentors are generally senior officers or directors, trained before they are assigned to new recruits. The mentor relationship lasts for a year; mentors give both professional and personal advice to the new recruit on a completely confidential basis. "The Mentor Program has made it easier for people to talk about race and ethnicity," says Loyd.

The company works with the Stamford, Connecticut, schools, a district with a large minority population, on various projects that support the students. The company offers students after-school jobs and summer internships.

Other minority students are hired through the INROADS internship program. Champion also reserves a certain percentage of its summer jobs in mills throughout the country for the college-age sons and daughters of its workers.

The company gives to such minority organizations as the NAACP Special Contribution Fund, the National Urban League, the National Action Council for Minorities in Engineering, the Council on Career Development for Minorities, the United Negro College Fund and the Southeastern Consortium for Minorities in Engineering.

Office locations: Corporate headquarters are in Stamford, Connecticut. Other operations are in a number of states including Minnesota, Texas, New Jersey, Florida, Ohio, North Carolina, Michigan and New York. Champion also has production facilities in Canada and Brazil.

One Champion Plaza
Stamford, Connecticut 06921
(203) 358-7000

CHEVRON CORPORATION

Chevron is the nation's fourth-largest petroleum company and is involved in all aspects of the energy business: exploration, production, manufacturing, transportation, marketing and research. Chevron explores for and produces crude oil and natural gas in the United States and twenty-five other countries. The company has a retail gasoline sales network of more than 12,500 outlets worldwide. Chevron also produces petrochemicals, plastics and consumer products (including the Ortho brand of lawn and garden products), and mines and markets coal for use by electrical utility and industrial customers.

1990 revenues: $42,600,000,000
1991 revenues: $40,945,000,000
1992 revenues: $42,893,000,000

Number of full-time U.S. employees: 40,000

Percentage of these employees who are minorities: 22.8
    Black: 8.5
    Hispanic: 6.5
    Asian/Pacific Islander: 6.3
    Native American: 1.5

Number of people in the total management pool: 5,800

Percentage of minorities in the total management pool: 10.3

Chevron was started in 1879 by wildcatters. From its earliest days the company grew through a balance of smart geography and sharp business judgment. Chevron, known then as the Standard Oil Company of California, developed top-quality fuels during the 1920s, discovered the huge oil fields in Saudi Arabia in the 1930s and pioneered some of the first offshore oil exploration during the 1950s. Chevron's $13-billion acquisition of Gulf Oil Company in 1985 ranked at the time as the largest corporate merger in U.S. history.

The company has begun to distinguish itself as a leader on diversity issues. Jeet Bindra, Group Manager for Projects and Engineering Technology, joined Chevron in 1977, after moving to the United States from India. "When I started, the company was not nearly as progressive as it is today," he notes. "I've seen a steep change in the company's commitment to valuing diversity, particularly under the leadership of CEO Kenneth Derr. He really focuses on valuing diversity, which means appreciating differences and drawing strength from them, rather than just managing diversity, which can turn into a numbers game. I genuinely believe that the company recognizes people for their contributions and rewards them; hard work and strong contributions will definitely be recognized."

Chevron's commitment to creating an environment where those contributions can be recognized begins with the recruiting process. Chevron's Diversity Outreach Program (DOP) is one important way in which the company identifies attractive minority candidates. A group of recruiters is sent to schools with high minority enrollment with the charge of establishing contact with minority student organizations, giving presentations on résumé writing and interviewing skills, and generally creating awareness of the company and the opportunities available. Twenty schools are included in the program, including Howard University, Tuskegee University, the University of Texas at Austin, the University of California and Texas A&M.

In 1991, Chevron established the Hispanic Initiative, increasing its college relations budget to accommodate increased activity with the National Society of Hispanic MBA's; New

Mexico Mathematics, Engineering, and Science Achievement (MESA); the Hispanic Association of Colleges and Universities; the National Hispanic Scholarship Foundation and the Society of Hispanic Professional Engineers. A Chevron manager, Jim Irving, serves on the national board of MESA.

Chevron also works with organizations like the National Action Council for Minorities in Engineering and the National Society of Black Engineers (NSBE) to reach out to the minority community. The NSBE recognized Chevron's new diversity ad campaign, with the theme "we put a lot of energy into developing tomorrow's resources," as an outstanding advertisement, and named the company one of its Top 50 Employers in 1991. Chevron also attended the American Indian Science and Engineering Society National Conference in 1992.

Chevron has several internship programs which expose students to professional life at the company. The cooperative work-study program in engineering and computer sciences and the summer internship program had a total of 307 participants in 1992, of which 90 were minorities. Chevron also participates in INROADS, an internship program designed to interest minority students in careers in business. Chevron is one of the program's leading sponsors: each year the company pays a sponsorship fee of $2,500 to $3,000 for each intern to cover the costs of running the program. Supervisors prepare a career development plan for each student assigned to them. The plan spans four working summers and defines the student's development goals for that period. Students work forty hours a week in professionally oriented paid positions. They also attend weekly workshops to learn communication, personal leadership, technical competence and business skills. INROADS counselors meet regularly with the students. In 1991, the company placed forty-nine INROADS students. Louis Fernandez, a Chevron manager, serves on the national board of INROADS.

The company takes its commitment to developing and retaining minority managers very seriously. "Every year," says Bindra, "we prepare a list of high-potential women and minority candidates at all levels of the company. We then develop a specific development plan for each person, and discuss it with the individual and with the head of each division or subsidiary. The plan is reviewed once during the year to ensure that we're following through on what we committed to."

Besides these efforts, Chevron has a diversity training program that was initiated in 1989 to help sensitize employees to what different people might find acceptable or unacceptable behavior. All top managers have gone through the program, developed by Dr. Roosevelt Thomas of the American Institute for Managing Diversity. Each manager is responsible for ensuring that ultimately all employees are exposed to the program. All professional recruiters receive diversity training. In addition, Chevron holds an annual Managerial Leadership Forum for middle and senior management. The one-week off-site forum includes a half-day session on diversity issues. Says Bindra, "An outside consultant conducts the session, in which we perform role-plays, and then discuss different issues. In one scenario, we were told to pretend that we were planning a picnic, and to consistently ignore the ideas being proposed by two people. At the end, they talked about how they felt, and how to ensure that this doesn't happen in real time with our minority employees." The diversity training seems to be very successful at surfacing issues, and managers seem to appreciate it. "I really think that the value of the sessions is clear to everyone. It's really been institutionalized," says Bindra.

There are no formal minority organizations at Chevron, but the company's Diversity Councils serve as a forum for discussing issues of concern to minorities. In addition, there are strong informal networks among the company's minority employees. Gregory Redmond is a black man who serves as Manager of Tax Planning. He has been with Chevron since 1972 and is a graduate of the University of Michigan and the University of Southern California. "We have a lot of informal meetings, where we get together to discuss issues," he notes. "When we hire a new minority MBA, the person usually goes into Finance, Marketing, or Human Resources. We all know the person is there, and we extend ourselves to help during the transition period. I've been able to find minority mentors within Chevron, and it has made my experience here much more worthwhile."

Chevron has been very successful at promoting minorities into senior positions. Besides Bindra and Redmond, minorities hold such positions at Chevron as Corporate Vice President, Human Resources; General Manager, Audit Staff; Vice President, Finance, Chevron USA; Regional Medical Director; and Principal Consultant. Condoleeza Rice, a black associate professor of political science at Stanford University and former Special Assistant to the President for National Security Affairs, is a member of the board of directors.

The company has instituted strict measures to identify, support and promote minority-owned businesses through its Small, Minority- & Women-Owned Business Program. Headed by Dorothy Lassair, the purchasing program resulted in almost $150 million in purchases from minority vendors in 1992.

Chevron makes generous charitable contributions to the minority community. The company has supported such diverse organizations as Howard University, the Black Engineer of the Year Award, the American Association of Blacks in Energy, the NAACP and the Asian Art Museum of San Francisco. Grants have been made to Family Science, a program designed to encourage minority students to pursue careers in science, the Japanese American Citizens League, SER—Jobs for Progress, the National Council of La Raza, the Mexican American Legal Defense and Education scholarship program, and the League of United Latin American Citizens.

The company provides scholarships through the National Hispanic Scholarship Fund and the League of United Latin American Citizens. It has provided funds for the creation of the

Chevron Top 25 Minority Engineering Scholars Program at the University of California at Davis. Minority scholarships have been endowed at more than fifty universities, including California Polytechnic State, Louisiana State, MIT, Northwestern and Xavier.

Chevron has made significant progress in its attention to diversity issues. "Over the past seven years or so, we've been very successful at hiring and advancing minorities through the company," says Redmond.

"As people retire now," says Bindra, "we constantly ask if there is a qualified minority on the list of candidates to fill the slot, and if there isn't, we ask why not and what we can do to help ensure that next time there will be. Those questions weren't asked fifteen years ago. But they are now." Most importantly, once those slots are filled, Chevron rewards the hard work of the manager, regardless of race. "I'm being fully recognized for my contributions," says Bindra, "and that's the best I can ask for."

Office locations: Headquarters are in San Francisco; Chevron and its affiliates conduct business in most states and in 102 other countries.

575 Market Street
San Francisco, California 94120
(415) 894-7700

CHRYSLER CORPORATION

Chrysler produces a full line of cars, minivans, sport-utility vehicles and light-duty trucks. Its brand name models include Chrysler, Plymouth, Dodge and Jeep. The company's subsidiaries include Acustar, Inc., which produces components for Chrysler vehicles; Chrysler Financial Corporation, which provides financing for dealers and customers; and Chrysler Technologies Corporation, which supports the company's automotive research. The company also owns General Rent-A-Car, Inc.

1990 revenues: $30,600,000,000
1991 revenues: $29,400,000,000
1992 revenues: $36,897,000,000

Number of full-time U.S. employees: 83,620

Percentage of these employees who are minorities: 24.4
    Black: 22.3
    Hispanic: 1.5
    Asian/Pacific Islander: .5
    Native American: .1

Number of people in the total management pool: 7,012

Percentage of minorities in the total management pool: 11

The smallest of the Big Three American auto manufacturers, Chrysler was hailed in the black labor community for its 1991 decision to open a $1-billion dollar manufacturing plant in the center of Detroit. Although the company is based in a suburb outside the mostly minority-populated city, this step was seen as symbolic when so many major companies have left the minority community.

Minorities at Chrysler hold such positions as President of Acustar, Inc.; Vice President and General Counsel; Plant Manager; General Manager of Special Projects; Group Controller; Co-director of UAW–Chrysler National Training Center; Executive Engineer; Manager of Pricing and Component Analysis; Zone Manager in Sales; and Director of Issue Analysis and Policy Development. Earl G. Graves, publisher of *Black Enterprise* magazine and owner of a Pepsi bottling franchise, is a member of the board of directors.

The company has recruited many minority students from such universities as Howard, Florida A&M, the University of Texas at Austin and Hampton. The company also participates in conventions sponsored by the NAACP, the National Urban League, the National Council of La Raza and Operation Push. To aid minority students, the company contributes to scholarship programs directed by the National Action Council for Minorities in Engineering and other groups.

Chrysler's Minority and Women Merit Scholarship Program in Business and Engineering provides summer internships and scholarship support for minority and female students.

One top-ranking minority executive at Chrysler is Forest J. Farmer, president of the company's Acustar subsidiary. A graduate of Purdue University, Farmer had been a supervisor of manufacturing for Volkswagen of America before coming to Chrysler and holding the position of general plant manager at three of Chrysler's assembly plants.

Having held the top position at Acustar since 1988, Farmer feels a strong tie to the Chrysler family. "I would like to be chairman of Chrysler," he explains, pointing out that being black would never hinder one's career at Chrysler. "The auto industry is like a ball game. We're out here to win, and you do that by playing your best players. I don't think that because a person is a female or a minority that Chrysler would turn its back and say the company is not going to play them." Besides manufacturing parts for Chrysler cars, Farmer's division sells 15% of its products to other automakers. He is currently trying to break into the Japanese auto markets.

To increase diversity awareness among its employees, Chrysler established an Equal Opportunity Advisory Committee as a formal management committee. The committee advises senior management on work force diversity initiatives and on other corporate programs that relate to civic activities outside the company. The committee is composed of cross-functional executive-level employees representing a range of key corporate departments.

Jointly with the UAW, Chrysler has implemented a series of training programs that focus on diversity issues. Known as the Equal Application Training Program, the training has involved management and representatives from all Chrysler's plants. The company is the first major American corporation to undertake such a joint diversity initiative. Overseeing the entire diversity program is the Department of Employment Planning, Operations and Training Services, which meets regularly with senior management to provide presentations on new diversity initiatives, affirmative action policies and diversity goals.

According to Patricia Flaherty, Manager of Employment Planning, Operations and Training Services, diversity is an important consideration for both the company and its senior management. "A diverse work force provides a competitive advantage," says Flaherty. "A rich corporate culture naturally provides more voices and more solutions to choose from." Flaherty says that Chrysler's commitment to fairness, diversity and economic opportunity has been continually reaffirmed "by entering into moral covenants and partnerships with the NAACP and the Hispanic Association on Corporate Responsibility (HACR) to further promote diversity issues in our business practices."

She adds, "We became a participant in the NAACP's Operation Fair Share Program on July 11, 1989, when our chairman and NAACP executive director Benjamin Hooks signed a Fair Share Agreement pledging mutual good-faith efforts to assure equality in employment opportunity and business operations." The agreement the company signed represents the commitment of senior management to diversity in such areas as procurement and supply, dealer development, work force diversity, advertising, banking, insurance, professional services, corporate policy development and management structure, and philanthropic contributions.

In 1991, the company entered into a Joint Declaration of a Cooperative Relationship with the Hispanic Association on Corporate Responsibility. It is because of these agreements that Chrysler now leads the auto industry in percentage of minority employee representation.

To advance diversity among its national network of dealers, Chrysler created its Minority Retail Dealer Development Program in 1983. According to Flaherty, "we established an intensive two-year training program for minority dealers. Since 1983, the number of African-American Chrysler dealers increased from nine to eighty-four, and the number of Hispanic dealers increased from fifteen to forty-seven."

Since 1984, Chrysler has had a minority supplier-vendor program which locates and develops qualified minority and women-owned firms to supply products and services to the company. The company's Department of Economic Opportunity and Minority Supplier Relations is headed by black executive Joseph E. Harris, and spends more than $575 million with minority and women-owned suppliers. The company actively supports the National Minority Supplier Development Council.

Office locations: The company is headquartered in the Detroit suburb of Highland Park. Most of Chrysler's manufacturing facilities are in Michigan, Ohio, Indiana, Illinois, Wisconsin and Missouri. Subsidiaries have manufacturing facilities in Canada and Mexico.

12000 Chrysler Drive
Highland Park, Michigan 48288
(313) 956-5741

CLOROX COMPANY

Clorox's principal business is developing, manufacturing and marketing consumer products, such as its well-known line of liquid bleach, Pine Sol cleaner, Kingsford charcoal, Hidden Valley Ranch salad dressing and Control cat litter. The company also manufactures a line of specialty equipment for the fast-food restaurant industry, and markets Deer Park bottled water in several Eastern states.

1990 revenues: $1,484,042,000
1991 revenues: $1,646,489,000
1992 revenues: $1,717,039,000

Number of full-time U.S. employees: 5,406

Percentage of these employees who are minorities: 21.5
    Black: 12.1
    Hispanic: 4.2
    Asian/Pacific Islander: 4.8
    Native American/Alaskan Native: 0.4

Number of people in the total management pool: 888

Percentage of minorities in the total management pool: 10.2

The Clorox Company was founded in Oakland, California, in 1913, and takes its name from Clorox bleach, its first product. Perhaps because of the large minority population in Oakland, the company has long been committed to minority advancement. Clorox recruits at traditionally black schools such as

Morehouse College, Spelman College, Atlanta University, Howard University and Prairie View A&M University. The company also participates in annual career fairs sponsored by the National Black MBA Association, the National Society of Hispanic MBA's, the Society of Professional Hispanic Engineers and the National Society of Black Engineers.

The company's affiliation with INROADS, a national program that places high-potential minority students in business internships, has resulted in a very successful program at Clorox. The company sponsors nine interns at its General Offices and Technical Center. It also hires an average of forty students each summer through its Summer Internship Program; about 50% of these are minorities. Clorox also supports the Oakland Mayor's Youth Summer Jobs Program; 75% of these placements are for low-income minority youth.

Clorox has demonstrated commitment to diversity by creating the position of Manager of Diversity to develop and support diversity programs. Rianne O'Reilly currently holds the position. "We have several initiatives under way to increase sensitivity to diversity issues," she notes. "One is our diversity awareness presentation. Using the Copeland-Griggs videotapes and in-house discussions that we had conducted, I created a training session for senior managers that was delivered throughout the company. Over the next year, we will expand our efforts to reach every manager."

There is also a Diversity Council comprised of senior managers, including the chief financial officer. The council is charged with overseeing all diversity initiatives in the company, based upon the overall strategy approved by senior management. One of those initiatives is the pilot mentor program. "It's a voluntary program," says O'Reilly. "We chose three departments and matched mentors and protegés to discuss career development. The program was not just for minorities, but our diversity strategy calls for a plan to expand the program and ensure minority participation." In addition, the council is overseeing the development of a career development process that will identify high-potential minority employees for development. Finally, equal opportunity and affirmative action were recently made measures of performance for officers and managers.

Vincent E. Alvarez is a member of the company's ten-person Diversity Council. As Director of Technology with Clorox's Technical Center and as a manager who has been with the company since 1976, Alvarez is convinced that the senior executives at Clorox are committed to diversity at every level of management. "Even before we had the council," says Alvarez, "I was impressed with how unimportant office politics were around here. I have always been given the opportunity to cross-train in different disciplines in the company. With a Ph.D. in chemistry, I arrived here as a laboratory scientist. Because my bosses encouraged me to cross-train in other areas as well, and because they promote equitably, I have had the chance to move from scientist to project leader to middle management and to my present management position, where I supervise ninety people."

Alvarez, who has done a lot of minority recruiting—particularly among the Asian and Hispanic student population at the University of California at Berkeley and Santa Barbara, as well as at California State University at Hayward—says finding mentors at Clorox is both easy and beneficial. "During the last seven to ten years of my career, I have sought mentors who were both minorities and nonminorities," he says. "I've also felt that minority issues were always a welcome subject among all groups of employees here."

There are no formal minority employee organizations at Clorox, but there are two focus groups on work force issues, one for African American employees. The group meets regularly to discuss issues of concern, and also serves as an informal support network.

Clorox has been successful at moving minorities into high-ranking management positions. Minorities hold such positions as Group Vice President, Technical; Associate General Counsel; National Sales Manager; Director of Technology; Manager of Process and Production Services; Group Marketing Manager; Area General Manager—International; and Director of Personnel. Daniel Boggan, Jr., a black man who is Vice Chancellor for Business and Administrative Services at the University of California at Berkeley, sits on the board of directors.

The Clorox Foundation provides substantial funding for numerous programs, many of which benefit minorities and youth. In 1992, $2.7 million was provided to organizations like the Berkeley Asian Youth Center, the National Council for Minorities in Engineering, the Spanish Speaking Unity Council, La Clinica De La Raza, the Urban Indian Health Board and the Black Filmmakers Hall of Fame. The company received presidential recognition for its work with the East Oakland Youth Development Foundation, a job training and counseling facility opened in 1978 in a neighborhood where more than 50% of families live at or below the poverty level. The center also has recreational, art and sewing activities.

The company makes annual donations of about $135,000 in scholarships and grants, about half of which goes to minority students and organizations. Examples of these scholarships include $10,000 per year to the Marcus Foster Educational Institute, which benefits the Oakland Public Schools; $7,500 per year to the United Negro College Fund and $1,000 per year each to Hispanic and Native American scholarship funds.

Clorox has made a substantial commitment to Oakland's downtown area at a time when most corporations are moving to the suburbs. Along with Kaiser Aluminum, Clorox invested more than $1 million in the construction of a new hotel and convention center that constituted an integral part of plans to revitalize the downtown area. It also became a limited partner in the rehabilitation of a historic Oakland area known as Victorian Row.

In 1992, Clorox purchased more than $8.5 million in goods and services from minority- and women-owned businesses. The

Minority Economic Development Program Forum, comprised of area representatives from major divisions and staff groups, provides guidance and direction to the Minority Economic Development Program. Clorox is active in the National Minority Supplier Development Council and was the founding member of the Northern California Purchasing Council.

Alvarez has a piece of advice for minority applicants who want to build a career at Clorox: "As minorities, many of us don't want to take risks. We somehow believe that we already have one strike against us because of our ethnicity. Minorities who come to Clorox should realize that the company encourages you to take risks—particularly if you are coming here as a scientist. The company wants you to take cross-training assignments so that you can go beyond your academic training. And this is what will create more minority managers. By their training, scientists are taught never to make judgments unless they have all of the necessary data. Unfortunately, managers sometimes have to take a chance and make a judgment with just a small amount of data. As minorities, we have to have the confidence to take on assignments and responsibilities that we may not have been trained for. This is a company that will reward you for your willingness to be challenged by the unexpected."

Office locations: Clorox is headquartered in Oakland, California, and sells its products in seventy countries. There are more than forty manufacturing facilities in the United States, Puerto Rico and abroad.

1221 Broadway
Oakland, California 94612
(510) 271-7000

COCA-COLA COMPANY

Coca-Cola is the world's largest marketer of soft drinks, with sales in more than 185 countries. Besides its leading product, Coca-Cola, the company's brands include Sprite, Minute Maid juices and Fanta. Coca-Cola is currently the sixth-largest public company in the United States.

1990 revenues: $10,236,400,000
1991 revenues: $11,571,600,000
1992 revenues: $13,073,900,000

Total number of U.S. employees: 10,250

Percentage of these employees who are minorities: 34.7
    Black: 19.9
    Hispanic: 13.0
    Asian/Pacific Islander: 1.5
    Native American: 0.4

Number of people in the total management pool: 1,548

Percentage of minorities in the total management pool: 12.8

Under the leadership of Roberto Goizueta, one of the most prominent Hispanic business leaders in America, Coca-Cola has redoubled its efforts to recruit and develop minority candidates. While the company hires relatively few employees directly from universities, it does have strong relationships with such black schools as Morehouse, Spelman and Morris Brown colleges, Clark-Atlanta University and Grambling State University. Its recruiting activities include advertising in publications aimed at minorities and sending representatives to minority-oriented job fairs like the annual career fair at the National Black MBA Association Conference.

Besides Goizueta, Coca-Cola's chairman and CEO, the company has many other high-ranking minorities, in such positions as President of the Coca-Cola Financial Corporation, Assistant Vice President and Manager of Media and Investor Relations, Assistant Vice President and Manager of Pension Investment and Vice President and Manager of Corporate External Affairs. Carl Ware, Deputy Group President, Northeast Europe/Africa Group, was recently named one of the 50 Top Black Executives in Corporate America by *Ebony* magazine. In August 1991, *Black Enterprise* named Carolyn Baldwin, President of Coca-Cola Financial Corporation, one of the 21 Top Women Executives. Donald F. McHenry, former U.S. Ambassador to the United Nations and Professor of Diplomacy and International Affairs at Georgetown University, and company Chairman Goizueta serve on the board of directors.

The company provides summer internships for minority youths. Since 1985, the company has hired INROADS interns in such departments as trade accounting, financial planning, accounts payable and desktop technology. According to Shirley Dilsworth, Manager of Corporate Equal Opportunity, the company has a goal of adding one intern per year for each functional area.

The company makes efforts to ensure that all employees have the opportunity to advance. Extensive skills training courses are available. The company provides diversity training to all employees, including officers. According to Dilsworth, the diversity training program was created in 1991 and includes a two-day session, with a half-day follow-up. "The training," Dilsworth explains, "focuses on inclusion in groups, change as a process, ways to identify and overcome unconscious bias, and employee development as a management responsibility." The sessions use role-playing and lectures.

Participants in the diversity training program are generally the executive committee members as well as functional vice presidents, directors and others on the senior manager level. Once a functional area's managers have been trained, the program is offered to the next level of employees. Dilsworth says, "We have also worked a Diversity Module into our introductory management development training program. We want our people to be aware of how their biases can affect the selection process in both hiring and promoting."

Dilsworth heads the company's Diversity Task Force, whose mission is to develop the company's strategic diversity vision. Recently the Task Force invited black entrepreneur and Coca-Cola bottling franchise owner Bruce Llewellyn to give a presentation on marketing to the minority community. The Task Force has also sponsored employee-focused events during Asian Heritage Month and Black History Month.

"I feel that the company is extremely sensitive to minority issues," says Verona Smith, Marketing Manager of Grocery Products at the Coca-Cola Foods Division in Houston. An MBA graduate of Northwestern University, Smith is responsible for marketing Hi-C fruit drinks. She has been with the company since 1988 and remembers that when she first interviewed, she was immediately aware that the environment was welcoming to minority professionals. She had already worked in marketing and advertising positions. "The recruiters knew that I would want to talk to other minority managers," says Smith. "So they scheduled a lunch for me so that I could meet with a minority manager and ask the questions that a nonminority might not be able to answer. I was happy to see that there was a black vice president, but since that time, it has been rather easy to develop mentor relationships with other senior managers as well."

Smith, who came into the company as a product manager

for Minute Maid frozen orange juice, became a senior product manager after nine months, and then moved into her present position as marketing manager; she supervises product managers and helps develop new flavors, products and packaging for Hi-C.

The company earmarks special advertising monies for the minority community; these are administered through the African American and Hispanic Consumer Marketing Department.

Last year, the company awarded more than $110 million in purchasing contracts to minority and female suppliers under the Minority and Women-Owned Vendor Development Program. Coca-Cola created the program in 1982 and has committed to a spending goal of $1 billion by 1996.

The primary focus of the Coca-Cola Foundation, headed by Ingrid Saunders Jones, who is also a corporate vice president, is improving education in the United States. In 1992, the foundation aided such organizations as the United Negro College Fund, the National Hispanic Scholarship Fund, the Phelps-Stokes Fund and Pennsylvania State University's minority chemical engineering scholarship program.

Office locations: The company's headquarters are in Atlanta, and offices and plants are in nineteen states and fifty-one countries around the world.

Coca-Cola Plaza
P.O. Drawer 1734
Atlanta, Georgia 30301
(404) 676-2121

COLGATE-PALMOLIVE COMPANY

Although best known for Colgate toothpaste and Palmolive soap, Colgate-Palmolive is a leading global consumer products company which produces such other consumer items as Ajax, Fab detergent, Irish Spring soap, Murphy Oil Soap, Hill's Pet Products, Mennen personal care products, Princess House crystal and Sterno cooking items.

1990 revenues: worldwide $5,691,300,000
1991 revenues: worldwide $6,060,300,000
1992 revenues: worldwide $7,007,200,000

Number of full-time employees: 24,000 worldwide, 7,248 in the United States

Percentage of these (U.S.) employees who are minorities: 17.2

Black:	9.5
Hispanic:	5.4
Asian/Pacific Islander:	2.7
American Indian:	.02

Number of people in the total management pool: 1,096

Percentage of minorities in the total management pool: 13.8

Salary information:

Sales workers:	$30,000–$55,200
Professionals:	$24,500–$134,400
Officers and managers:	$40,800–$300,000+

Founded in 1806, Colgate-Palmolive has become a truly global company, with more than two-thirds of its employees working outside the United States.

Minorities at Colgate-Palmolive hold such positions as Vice President of Finance and Strategic Planning, Vice President of Global Advertising Development, Vice President of Advance Technology in the Oral Care Group, Vice President of Process Development, Associate General Counsel and Assistant Corporate Controller. There is one minority person on the board of directors, Delano E. Lewis, president and CEO of Chesapeake & Potomac Telephone Company.

The company recruits at such black universities as Howard, Morgan State and Florida A&M. There is a recruiting program that reaches many Hispanic graduates of University of Puerto Rico. Many minority interns and minority graduate students are hired from Columbia University and New York University graduate programs.

According to Ronald Martin, Director of Global Employee Relations, the company has several internal minority employee organizations. The Technology Group, based in Piscataway, New Jersey, is the most advanced division in this area. "At that location," says Martin, "there are three very active organizations, including the Asian American Group, which was created in 1987 to give added support to Asian employees and the Asian community outside our company." The AAG has eighty members and offers each new member an employee mentor and role models. Besides sponsoring an Asian American Heritage Week Celebration which includes an India Day and a China Day, the AAG has sponsored science lecture series for high school students, a fund drive for victims of a Bangladesh cyclone and an internship program at Rutgers University.

According to Martin, the Technology Group also formed a Black Action Committee (BAC) in 1987. The committee provides mentors for its newly hired members as a part of its employee retention effort. Internally, the group spearheaded the search for diversity consultants to bring sensitivity training into the division. Outside Colgate-Palmolive, the committee sponsors a summer intern group and a high school mentoring program and has organized fund-raisers for the United Negro College Fund.

Martin, a black manager who held several management positions with CIGNA Corporation, Chevron and Bristol-Myers before coming to Colgate-Palmolive, says he has been involved with the BAC and is impressed with what it brings to the company. "Groups like this can contribute a lot to employee morale," Martin says, "and they are able to thrive in this company because they have the endorsement and the enthusiasm of our top management."

In 1990, the Technology Group also established a Hispanic organization called the Hispanic Action Network. The Network includes Hispanic and non-Hispanic members who are interested in promoting the culture and concerns of Hispanic employees and the Hispanic community outside the company. The group is involved with recruiting at University of Puerto Rico and organizes activities with the Society of Hispanic Professional Engineers. The group has also sponsored a Saturday school for parents and students.

Diversity training at Colgate-Palmolive has been evolving over the past few years and has included work with the Cincinnati-based diversity consultant Merlin Pope & Associates, as well as with the Chicago-based firm Harbridge House. According to Linda Smith, Colgate-Palmolive's Manager of Global Cultural Diversity, the company's newest training program, called "Valuing Differences," will include videotapes and interactive presentations for everyone from chairman Reuben Mark down to first-line supervisors.

Smith explains how the new diversity program was designed. "I had met with our minority employee organizations and interviewed more than three hundred other employees here using one-on-one interviews and focus groups. After performing this needs assessment, we were better able to locate which areas needed greater sensitivity." Smith, who holds a master's degree in speech communications with a focus on intercultural communications from San Francisco State University, brings a unique sociological perspective to the Colgate business world. She has worked extensively with the Ethiopian and Southeast Asian communities in Northern California and has also run job development programs for female immigrants from Southeast Asia.

"We are trying to create an environment where people are individually valued," says Smith, "and we do this by incorporating the various cultural identities of our employees."

Ron Martin adds that because most of the company's employees are outside the United States, the diversity program will focus not only on race, ethnicity and gender, but also on language issues. "As an example," says Martin, "because we have many Asian scientists who were not raised with English as their primary language, we need to sensitize our entire work force to the fact that different accents and word usage are a normal characteristic in a global company."

Although Colgate-Palmolive has no company-wide mentoring program tailored for minority employees, there is a mentoring program for all entry-level supervisors. For one year, each new supervisor is given a mentor who is approximately three grades ahead and who works in the same physical location.

After working with the company since 1988, Gregory Andrews says he has always been able to find mentors to advise him. A black MBA graduate of the University of Wisconsin, Andrews had held various marketing positions with the Clairol division of Bristol-Myers before becoming General Manager of Market Development at Colgate's New York headquarters. "I have never had difficulty developing mentor relationships with white managers at the company," Andrews says. "Colgate-Palmolive is committed to infusing the company with more minorities, and there is a high comfort level here." Andrews, who has participated in recruiting minority students from Florida A&M University, has also introduced minority inner-city elementary school students to the offices during the company's Shadow Day events.

Recently the National Dental Association and Colgate established a group of scholarships for African American students enrolled in dental schools and other course programs leading to dental health-related degrees. The NDA–Colgate Select Scholars program awards five $2,000 scholarships to undergraduates.

The company contributes to such minority organizations as the National Urban League, the National Hispanic College Fund, the New York Chinatown Senior Citizen Coalition Center, the Hispanic Children's Foundation, the United Negro College Fund and the Organization of Chinese Americans.

While the company sponsors many valuable programs in the minority community, it continues to operate in South Africa.

There is a minority supplier-vendor program at the company, the Colgate-Palmolive Minority Procurement Task Force, which spent in excess of $25 million with minority suppliers in 1992.

Office locations: U.S. and global headquarters are in New York City. The company's Technology Headquarters are in New Jersey, Hoyt Labs and Mennen divisions in Massachusetts, Hill's Pet Products in Kansas, Softsoap in Minnesota and Murphy Headquarters in Ohio. The company also has operations in Colombia, Argentina, France, Ghana, Haiti, Saudi Arabia, Thailand, Zimbabwe, Mexico, Japan and the United Kingdom.

300 Park Avenue
New York, New York 10022
(212) 310-2000

ADOLPH COORS COMPANY

Adolph Coors is one of the country's major beer breweries and one of the largest public industrial corporations. This diversified company operates businesses in brewing, aluminum rigid container sheet, ceramics, and folding carton and flexible packaging. Its Coors Light is the third-largest-selling beer in the United States.

1990 revenues: $1,838,000,000
1991 revenues: $1,917,000,000
1992 revenues: $1,911,775,000

Number of full-time U.S. employees: 11,800

Percentage of these employees who are minorities: 14.2
    Black: 4
    Hispanic: 10
    Asian/Pacific Islander: .1
    Native American: .1

Number of people in the total management pool: 700

Percentage of minorities in the total management pool: 10

Percentage of minority managers who comprise each managerial level:
    Executive vice president: 0
    Vice president: 0
    Director: 7.5
    Manager: 9.9

Founded in 1873 by Adolph Coors, this company is still run by members of the Coors family. Bill Coors is chairman and president. Nephews Peter, Jeff and Joe Jr. serve as executive vice presidents, and Grover Coors is a vice president. Joseph Sr. is vice chairman of the board.

Minorities at Coors hold such positions as Director of Risk Management, Director of Finance, Plant Manager and National Accounts Manager. There are two minority directors on the company's board. J. Bruce Llewelyn, CEO of the Philadelphia Coca-Cola Bottling Company and WKBW-TV, has been on the board since 1989. Luis G. Nogales is a member of Nogales Partners, a media acquisition firm, and was previously CEO of United Press International; he has been on the board since 1989.

The company recruits many Hispanic students from such schools as Pan American University in Texas and Florida International University. Coors also recruits many black graduates from such schools as North Carolina State University, the University of Alabama and Florida A&M University, through which the company also has an active summer internship program.

There is a Diversity Task Force with ten members from different racial and ethnic backgrounds. The task force is currently developing a training program which the company will use to train managers and nonmanagement employees.

There are minority employee organizations for both Hispanic and black employees at Coors. The Coors Hispanic Employee Network (CHEN) was formed in 1990 and has approximately 300 members. According to Carlos Soto, National Manager of Community Relations, the network helps Hispanics build their professional skills so that they become more promotable. "A network like this," says Soto, "gives employees the opportunity to exchange information on the corporate culture, internal job openings or programs that can aid their professional development." Soto says the network's board meets each month and plans social events, educational programs and management training workshops. CHEN publishes a quarterly newsletter and frequently offers training programs for members in which college professors are brought to the network's meetings.

Black employees have formed an employee network called the Coors African American Association. According to Felice Barrett, Senior Programmer Analyst and president of the association, the organization was created as a small advisory council to upper-level management. "We reorganized ourselves into an employee organization," says Barrett, "so that now we include all African American employees. We have several committees which are responsible for publishing a newsletter, setting up a mentoring program, monitoring divisions of the company and creating Black Awareness Activities for Black History Month."

According to Joe Fuentes, Media Program Manager, Coors was one of the first companies to formalize agreements with coalitions of black and Hispanic organizations, specifically the National Black Economic Development Coalition and the Hispanic Association on Corporate Responsibility, two organizations that encourage companies to support minority vendors and minority employees. The agreements promise that Coors will spend a certain amount of money with minority contractors in such areas as banking, insurance, public relations and advertising.

Coors contributes to many minority organizations including the Asian Pacific American League, the National Puerto Rican Coalition, the National Urban League, the NAACP, the National Council of La Raza, the American Indian Graduate Center, the American Indian College Fund and the Coalition of Hispanic American Women. The company also funds scholarships through SER—Jobs for Progress.

In 1988, Coors began recruiting minority students from Denver public schools for its High School College Internship

Program. The program has a summer job component. According to Carlos Soto, each student was assigned to an employee who became a mentor for the summer and for the following year of high school. "Each of the students," says Soto, "is given the opportunity to work with the company during his or her college summers, and we give them each a two-thousand-dollar scholarship to use toward their tuition. Our mentors keep up with them and we encourage the students to consider full-time employment with Coors after their graduation."

In his position as Program Director of Supplier Diversification and Development, Patrick Ortiz heads up the company's minority supplier-vendor program, established in 1984. "We spend forty million dollars each year with minority contractors," says Ortiz, "and we have managed to build a network of up to fourteen hundred minority suppliers that offer supplies and services for the company's needs." Ortiz says the company belongs to, and has been honored by, the National Minority Supplier Development Council.

For the minority manager who is worried about the minority presence in Golden, Colorado, several Coors employees point out that the area around Golden and Denver is home to a very active minority population. "I realize that minority people from the East and West Coasts might be intimidated by this area of the country," Soto says. "But they should realize that Denver has had a Hispanic mayor before and at least ten percent of the population here is Hispanic." Soto and his fellow employees are as excited about the diversity of the community as they are about Coors's diverse programs and work force.

Office locations: Coors's headquarters are in Golden, Colorado. The operations there constitute the country's largest single brewery and aluminum can manufacturing plant. There are also operations in Tennessee, Virginia, California, Ohio, Pennsyl-

vania, Texas and Illinois. The company has foreign operations
in Brazil, Scotland and Switzerland.

Golden, Colorado 80401
(303) 279-6565

CORNING INCORPORATED

Corning is organized into four business segments: Specialty Materials, Communications, Laboratory Services and Consumer Products. The consumer products division is best known through its marketing of such products as Corning, Pyrex and Revere Ware cookware, Corelle dinnerware and Steuben crystal.

1990 revenues: $2,900,000,000
1991 revenues: $3,200,000,000
1992 revenues: $3,700,000,000

Number of full-time U.S. employees: 11,427

Percentage of these employees who are minorities: 9.1
    Black: 7.0
    Hispanic: 0.2
    Asian/Pacific Islander: 1.8
    Native American: 0.1

Number of people in the total management pool: 1,103

Percentage of minorities in the total management pool: 6.9

Percentage of minority managers who comprise each managerial level:
    Senior vice president: 8
    Vice president: 5
    Directors: 12
    Managers: 9

Salary information:

Administrative and technical	$14,600–$40,600
Production and maintenance	$21,247–$30,607
Managers and professionals	$27,100–$72,200
Executives	$76,700+

In 1976, long before many other major corporations had addressed the issue, Corning CEO Jamie Houghton decided to expand the company's EEO efforts to include valuing and managing diversity. Corning had always been in compliance with the government's EEO directives, but Houghton decided that although that was necessary, it was not sufficient.

Corning conducts intensive on-campus recruiting at a variety of colleges and universities, including such traditionally black schools as Howard, Florida A&M, North Carolina A&T and Georgia Tech. Michelle Cox, Manager of Recruiting, believes that a new program will make minority recruiting efforts even more successful. "We just started a summer internship for Spelman and Morehouse students," she says. "It's another way to improve our outreach to minority candidates."

CEO Houghton established two teams led by Management Committee members to focus on women and minority employees. These Quality Improvement Teams were given broad charters, including identifying gender and race issues, conceiving remedial actions, recommending funding, guiding program development, monitoring implementation and measuring results. Each team's membership consists of a diagonal slice of the organization to ensure representation by race, gender and salary level. The minority team's efforts have resulted in the reestablishment of the Corning Black Engineering Scholarship and Training Program; the development of career plans for minority employees; an increase in the number of black summer interns; division manager preview of black employee performance reviews; and mandatory awareness training for all employees.

Corning has six training courses designed to help managers

value and manage diversity. The racial diversity courses, designed by Elsie Y. Cross & Associates, range from one- to three-day sessions for all management levels. Trade Marketing Manager Debra Turner was recently interviewed by *Glamour* magazine about the programs, and said, "They definitely had an impact. Now people have a framework and a language to talk about racial issues in the workplace. A lot of white managers thought they should be color-blind. We've taught them that a black person's ethnicity defines who he or she is in America. What you need to do is learn to understand it and value what it can bring to your work environment."

The Black Employees Workshop is for all black salaried employees, and is designed to give them an opportunity to discuss the climate, structure, reward system and developmental opportunities in their units and how they relate to their expectations of Corning. The workshop has been an important tool for helping black employees deal with race-related stress and manage difficult situations.

The Society of Black Professionals (SBP) was established in 1980 by a group of managers concerned about the needs of black professionals at Corning. The SBP was chartered as a non-profit corporation to encourage communication among members and bring members' expertise to bear on the problems and issues confronting black professionals. The society, which has more than sixty-five members, sponsors talks and cultural events, organizes youth and community programs and assists black-owned businesses. It conducts a Community Welcome program for new blacks in the Corning, New York, area, and helped establish a managing diversity curriculum at the Cornell School of Engineering.

In 1992, Corning awarded $3.1 million in contracts to minority suppliers through its minority vendor program. Bob Pavlick, Manager of Purchasing Administration, heads the program. "We help each organization within Corning assess itself based on the goals it has set for minority purchasing," says

Pavlick. "Minority purchasing is one of the key results indicators that we use to measure our performance in the purchasing department. Our goal is to increase our spending five percent each year." Minority suppliers provide Corning with storeroom items, computer equipment and raw materials; minority vendors also include leasing companies, law firms and an advertising agency.

Several minorities have progressed to senior management positions, holding such titles as Vice President, Business Manager, Director of Diversity Programs and Director of Education. Vernon E. Jordan, Jr., former head of the National Urban League, serves on the board of directors.

The Corning Foundation contributes generously to minority civic and charitable organizations, including the National Urban League, the African-American Institute, the United Negro College Fund, the National Black MBA Association, the Southeastern Consortium for Minorities in Engineering and the NAACP.

Corning's response to a changing population was praised in a 1991 *New York Times* front-page article which said, "The company is engaged in one of corporate America's most ambitious experiments in cultural engineering." The article pointed to such steps as mandatory courses and workshops designed to break through racist and sexist attitudes, the assignment of coaches to help new black and women employees, active programs for training and promotion of these employees, and consistently clear messages of commitment from management. The *Times* commented, "All big companies have a long way to go," but went on to note that Corning is "well above the levels of most companies" in the percentage of women and black employees, and that the company has shown a dramatic improvement in its retention of such employees since 1987.

A 1992 *Glamour* profile highlighted the company's efforts and quoted Romaine Crawford-Mulley, who has been running Corning's Glass Center since March 1990. "At my last job, people didn't talk about racial issues. I remember having a conversation with a supervisor and trying to explain that because I'm a black female, sometimes people take 'no' differently from me than they would from someone else. When I tried to explain that to my supervisor, he was aghast. He couldn't believe that I wasn't treated like everyone else. I think people here at Corning are much more aware that it's not proper to make certain remarks and certain jokes. I just don't hear the kind of stuff I used to hear." Crawford-Mulley also described a change which she believes is small but symbolically important. Richard Rahill, president of Corning Enterprises, the division that works to improve the quality of life for black employees, "worked to have BET [Black Entertainment Television] brought up here. Some people say that's not such a big deal, but I think it is. You may not watch it every day, but it's nice to know it's here."

Office locations: Corning has offices and plants across the United States and in Europe, Asia and South America.

Corning, New York 14831
(607) 974-9000

DAYTON HUDSON CORPORATION

Dayton Hudson is one of the nation's largest retailers, operating 708 stores in thirty-three states. Besides its upscale Dayton's, Marshall Field, and Hudson's department stores, the corporation operates Target, a discount store chain, and Mervyn's, a moderate-priced department store chain.

1990 revenues: $14,739,000,000
1991 revenues: $16,115,000,000
1992 revenues: $17,927,000,000

Number of full-time employees: 175,000

Percentage of these employees who are minorities: N/A*

Under the leadership of chairman and CEO Kenneth A. Macke, Dayton Hudson has established itself as an industry leader in recruiting and developing minority managers. The company has set minority employment and job-level goals for every major unit within each operating division. These goals affect the incentive pay of managers and are very specific with regard to minority representation by job level and function. As a result, the percentage of minority managers doubled between 1982 and 1992.

Each operating company pursues campus recruiting specifically to attract minority candidates. The corporation tends to focus on identifying strong minority candidates at Midwestern

*While Dayton Hudson has declined to make public its statistics about minority hiring, the author has reviewed the data and believes that the company is an industry leader in hiring and promoting minority managers.

universities like Michigan State and Minnesota State, and at Harvard, Stanford and the University of Chicago business schools. Dayton Hudson takes this strategy because the company has a well-known presence in the Midwest and has been successful at filling slots from these sources. The company also maintains a presence on the campus of Florida State University to help increase the pool of minority candidates. Besides campus efforts, Dayton Hudson supports the National Black MBA Association with contributions, speakers and recruiting at the annual conference. In areas where the company has had difficulty recruiting minorities, it has placed support money in personnel budgets to fund minority recruiting at the professional level.

These efforts have paid off. In 1991, more than 20% of all college recruits for merchandise management training were minorities. The merchandise management trainee group tends to produce the company's highest-ranking management.

Each operating division takes care to foster an environment that will ensure the development of minority managers. Ed Wingate, Senior Vice President of Personnel, believes the mentoring program is crucial in getting new employees off to a good start. "We have 'buddy systems' in certain companies, where we assign a mentor to each incoming minority employee," says Wingate. "Because the industry was historically not very diverse, many of the new minority management trainees don't have a deep history with the retailing business. The buddy system is one way for them to get up to speed quickly on what the business is like." Dayton Hudson has also encouraged and supported minority employee networks, and has formed diversity councils to serve as sounding boards to upper management on diversity issues. Mary Kwan, an Asian American who is a Division Merchandising Manager for Mervyn's, sits on one of the task forces. "The group has people from middle and senior management, and from a variety of functions, including Merchandising, MIS and Human Resources," she says. "We meet once a month to discuss a lot of different issues: how to recruit more minority candidates, how to retain them, how to increase awareness of diversity. There are task forces in fifteen states just within Mervyn's now." Other operating units also have diversity task forces charged with increasing the number of successful minority employees at all levels of their organizations.

The company also has diversity and cultural awareness training for employees, especially managers and supervisors. An outside firm provides the diversity training, and there is a library of diversity training films.

As a result of these efforts, Dayton Hudson has successfully moved minorities into several top management positions. The top officer in Target's West Coast operations, which accounts for 30% of Target's $9-billion sales, is a black senior vice president. His highest-ranking subordinate, a vice president, is black. Two of the four merchandising officers (both senior vice presidents) in the Department Store Division are minorities: one black and the other a Pacific Islander. The head of merchandising control in Mervyn's is Asian. The officer in charge of MIS at Mervyn's is Hispanic. Michele J. Hooper, a black woman who is president of the Baxter Corporation, sits on the board of directors.

Michael Hyter, Director of Human Resources of Hudson's department stores, summarizes the feeling that many minority managers have about Dayton Hudson's impressive record: "When I came here fourteen years ago, I accepted less money than I was being offered from another company. But I knew it was the right choice. I was an activist in school, and I was looking for a certain environment. Hudson's offered me less money—but they gave me more emotional satisfaction."

Dayton Hudson's has participated in and initiated a wide range of community support programs. For example, in 1990 Mervyn's launched Expressions '90, allocating $650,000 over two years. Fifteen California arts organizations received grants to develop and expand programs for children and families, build audiences for arts in communities of color, and preserve the cultural heritage of these communities. Also in 1990, Marshall Field made a three-year $100,000 leadership grant to operate and expand the Learning Center of Jobs for Youth/Chicago. This group informs dropouts about GED preparation services, provides volunteer mentoring and develops part-time jobs for those who need financial support while they learn. Michael Hyter was involved in the High School Employability Training Program. "We worked with the Detroit public schools, which are almost one hundred percent black, to teach the students how to interview for jobs, write résumés, and survive the job-hunting process," Hyter says. "We brought them to our stores to practice interviewing, and talked to them about the business. The program was so successful that we plan to roll it out to other cities. Even if they decide not to work in retailing, the training helps them attain jobs in other fields." The company also funded Christians United in Business Endeavors, a group of fifteen black churches in Detroit that provides tutoring services and hosts a career fair.

Dayton Hudson has also made generous donations to other minority charitable and civic organizations, including the Asian American Theater Company, Chicanos Latinos Unidos En Servicio, the Indian Health Board of Minneapolis and the NAACP Legal Defense Fund. Total donations to organizations serving people of color totaled $2,700,462 in 1991. In addition, the Target division has a minority vendor program to support purchases of goods and services from minority-owned businesses.

Some of Dayton Hudson's geographic locations might, at first blush, appear inhospitable to minority families. "People don't automatically think of Minneapolis as being a diverse community," laughs Nancy Kimura Fuller, an Asian American senior buyer for Dayton's department store. "But it's much more integrated than most people realize. There are a lot of Japanese and people from Southeast Asia, and we felt totally at home here." It is in Dayton Hudson's best interests to make sure that its minority employees feel comfortable, at work and in their communities. As Mary Kwan notes, "Because we're in so many states now, we have a really diverse customer base. We need to spend time understanding our own diversity so that we can understand theirs."

Office locations: Dayton Hudson is headquartered in Minneapolis; the company has operations in thirty-three states.

777 Nicollet Mall
Minneapolis, Minnesota 55402
(612) 370-6948

THE DETROIT FREE PRESS

The *Free Press*, which is owned by the Knight-Ridder newspaper chain, is one of Detroit's two daily newspapers, with a daily circulation of 631,000.

Number of full-time employees: 267

Percentage of these employees who are minorities: 21.7
    Black: 17.6
    Hispanic: 1.1
    Asian/Pacific Islander: 2.6
    Native American: 0.4

Number of people in the total management pool: 31

Percentage of minorities in the total management pool: 19.4

Salary information:
    Reporter/photographer/copy editor: $27,500–$49,000
    Assistant/deputy editor: $49,500–$57,500
    Assistant/deputy managing editor: $60,000–$89,000
    Managing editor/vice president: $90,000–$105,000
    Editor/senior vice president: $130,000–$160,000
    Executive editor/vice president: $150,000–$180,000

Under the leadership of chairman and publisher Neal Shine, the *Free Press* has built a national reputation as an industry leader in hiring and developing minority managers. The Detroit metropolitan area has a large minority population, and the paper has committed to a work force that reflects this diversity.

The *Free Press* recruits on campus to identify talented minorities, including at black colleges and graduate schools with high minority enrollment. Louise Reid Ritchie, a black Harvard graduate who is Executive Assistant to the Publisher, says, "Most of our hiring is for the newsroom, and we look for minority candidates at schools in Michigan, like the University of Michigan, at black colleges, such as Howard, and at journalists' association meetings, like the Association of Black Journalists. We also sponsor our own job fair." In 1991, the paper hosted a three-day job fair for minorities interested in finding employment in the newspaper industry. The *Free Press* advertises in publications aimed at minorities and actively encourages employee referrals. That's how Larry Olmsted, City Editor and the highest-ranking black manager at the paper, started at the *Free Press.* "One of my colleagues at a paper in Baltimore came to the *Free Press,"* Olmsted says. "Neal Shine was always asking minority employees if they could recommend other people he should pursue, and that person gave him my name."

The paper has several internship programs for minority students. The high school summer intern program provides students with work in the newsroom for twenty hours per week for five weeks at a rate of $6 per hour. The students are recruited from twenty Detroit public schools and through direct applications. Minority freshmen in college can participate in the Project FOCUS internship, which is administered in conjunction with the Society of Newspaper Editors. The *Free Press* also has a general minority summer scholarship program which accepts ten college students each year. The Dow Jones Editing Internship Program is open to all college students.

The paper pursues many philanthropic efforts that may ultimately lead students to employment in the newsroom. The *Free Press* operates a collaborative program with twenty Detroit public high school journalism classes at no charge to the schools or students. A *Free Press* staff member works with the classes, and the students work in the newsroom during business hours to produce their newspapers. *Free Press* staffers also serve as mentors to the classes, and top students are offered part-time summer jobs. The students receive mentors and training over the summer. Of twelve students hired in 1991, nine were black.

The paper offers three scholarships annually (two of $1,000 and one of $750) to minority high school seniors planning journalism careers. Staff members also volunteer as teachers at several summer journalism workshops for high school students. The *Free Press* has also funded, and has staff photographers volunteering in, a photography course for middle school students at a community program in a predominantly black area of Detroit.

The newspaper provides career planning and management training to help employees bolster their skills. All managers undergo sensitivity training, and there are mentoring programs for minority employees. "One of the best things about the *Free Press* is that the paper offers a lot of opportunities—not just for minorities, but for everyone," says Olmsted. "There is a lot of movement between jobs, a lot of cross-training, chances to work on major stories, and the opportunity to travel. There are a lot of different kinds of work you can do, and as a result, many opportunities for advancement."

Perhaps as a result of this mobility, the *Free Press* has done an excellent job of moving blacks into senior management. Besides city editor Olmsted, one of the two managing editors and five of the twenty-three department heads are black. Minorities also hold the positions of Associate Editor and Executive Assistant to the Publisher.

There is no formal minority employee network, but Olmsted believes strong ties exist among the minority employees. "There are so many of us here that I guess we don't feel the need to have an official organization. We have close relationships, and if there is a problem, we mobilize to get it resolved. For example, in 1984, there were no black supervisors in the newsroom, and supervisor is a crucial position for developing younger reporters. So we set up a task force and got senior management to address the issue." Mentoring is critical for advancement in this business, and the *Free Press* has created an environment where everyone understands that part of his or her job is to coach others. "Almost everyone in the newsroom is the type to take people under his or her wing," Olmsted says. "A new person coming in would receive a lot of attention, whether minority or not. But it is nice to see that every newsroom department has minority staff people who can perform this role. At the city desk, ten of the fifty reporters are minorities, as is one of our most prominent columnists."

The company participates in a wide variety of philanthropic efforts in the minority community, donating money to organizations such as the NAACP, encouraging employee volunteerism in minority neighborhoods and providing internships for minority youths. The paper sponsors and supplies teachers for an art workshop for children served by a black organization, sponsors a drive that has supplied more than 300,000 new books to young children (primarily disadvantaged Detroit residents), sponsors a summer reading club based on African American literature for a Detroit elementary school and hosts a Saturday reading club for youngsters in Highland Park, a predominantly black city that borders Detroit. The Free Press Charities organization contributed $40,000 in 1991 to organizations helping children in the Detroit area, many of whom are minorities.

In 1991, the Morris Memo on Minorities and the Media graded 114 daily newspapers with 100,000 or more circulation on their treatment of minority professionals. Only four papers—*The Dallas Morning News*, *The Miami Herald*, *The Seattle Times* and *The Detroit Free Press*—received "A's." Grades were based on minority newsroom percentages reported to the American Society of Newspaper Editors, with emphasis on the number of senior newsroom managers. While the *Free Press*'s numbers are outstanding, the paper's commitment is not only to achieving good statistics. "This is not just a numbers game," says Olmsted.

"We still have a ways to go, and this industry is traditionally pretty bad at integrating its work force. But we have a leadership group that's committed to integrating diversity goals into training, development, assignments and other aspects of professional life. We're trying to do a more sophisticated job at getting these issues addressed."

Office locations: The newspaper is headquartered in downtown Detroit and has operations across Michigan.

321 West Lafayette
Detroit, Michigan 48226
(313) 222-6400

DOW CHEMICAL COMPANY

Dow is the nation's second-largest chemical manufacturer, with markets and products beyond those of a traditional chemical company. Included in its product line are plastics that are replacing steel in the auto industry, pharmaceuticals and consumer products. Dow's most familiar brand names include Saran Wrap plastic film, Ziploc bags and Styrofoam plastic foam. In all, the company manufactures and markets more than 2,000 products in countries throughout the world. The company is the sixth-largest chemical company in the world, and ranks among the twenty-five largest U.S. industrial corporations.

1990 revenues: $19,773,000,000
1991 revenues: $18,807,000,000
1992 revenues: $18,970,000,000

Number of full-time U.S. employees: 24,603

Percentage of these employees who are minorities: 14.3
    Black: 7.0
    Hispanic: 5.1
    Asian/Pacific Islander: 1.9
    Native American: 0.3

Number of people in the total management pool: 4,112

Percentage of minorities in the total management pool: 8.0

Percentage of minority managers who comprise each managerial level:

Vice president: 3.1
Director/manager: 7.4
Foreman: 11.0

The cover of a recent Dow annual report speaks to the company's commitment to a diverse work force. Over a picture of fifteen smiling employees—black, white, Hispanic, Asian—one of whom holds a globe, are the words "Diverse People. Common Goals." The company was founded in 1897 by Herbert H. Dow, and has made great strides in recent years in increasing the number of minorities it employs. Under the leadership of Keith McKennon, former president of Dow U.S.A., and now under William Stavropoulos, the company has taken several steps to ensure that it continues to attract and develop a diverse group of managers.

The company recruits at many campuses for high-potential minority candidates, including traditionally black universities such as Howard, Prairie View A&M, Southern, North Carolina A&T, North Carolina Central and Florida A&M. Dow also recruits at universities with high Hispanic enrollment like the University of Miami and the University of Texas. The company advertises in publications aimed at minorities and sends representatives to minority-oriented job fairs and conferences like the Society of Hispanic Professional Engineers conference, the League of United Latin American Citizens conference and the National Black MBA Association conference. Summer and other internships are provided for minority students, including the Premier Scholarship Program, which provides a $3,000 scholarship and employment for two summers to an undergraduate engineering or chemistry major. The Summer Internship at Dow program, which is open to all students, had a 37.1% minority makeup in 1992.

The company provides employees with ample opportunities to build skills, in keeping with its policy of promoting from within. Dow employees work with the company an average of fourteen years, and the average tenure of the corporate management committee is twenty-seven years. Stan Land, a black manager who serves as Zone Vice President for the South/Central Zone, has worked with Dow since 1979. "I came to Dow," he says, "because the recruiter told me that Dow paid for performance and was committed to promoting from within. I believed that the company would follow through on both of those promises, and it has. It's a family-oriented company, committed to the Dow family values, and when you start, you're being hired for a career, not just an entry-level position."

Those Dow values carry over into the company's treatment of diversity. Diversity issues have been incorporated into employee development courses. In addition, since 1989, Dow managers and supervisors have attended J. Howard & Associates' "Managing Development and Diversity" program, a mandatory two-day training session. For employees with tenure of ten years or less, there is also a six-day course called "Efficacy for Minorities," which focuses on helping minorities develop skills and a career path. Dow places a premium on training generally. On average, each employee spends more than a week each year in formal training, and these efforts are complemented by company-paid courses at colleges and universities.

A mentorship program for all employees, which Stan Land helped develop, is in the pilot stage. The program is based on group mentoring: three to four middle managers meet every other week with three to four new hires. "It's a nonthreatening situation," says Land, "that allows new hires to ask questions, and that allows mentor relationships to build more naturally than the traditional, forced one-on-one programs."

The Diversity Steering Committee was formed to help Dow draw upon the opinions and perspectives of its diverse work force. The current steering committee chair is Don Calvin, Vice President of Research and Development for Chemicals and Performance Products. Rita Schellenberger, Dow's Manager of Diversity, is also a member. "The steering committee has three operating board members: myself, the Director of Personnel Resources, and a VP from one of the business units, on a rotating basis," she says. "We have three subcommittees, one of which is the Management Advisory Committee on Minority Issues. This subcommittee has twelve members, with representatives from each function in the company." The subcommittee is headed by Fred Martinez, Manager of Research and Development Training for Dow U.S.A. The group meets quarterly to discuss diversity issues, and then reports to the steering committee at its semiannual meetings. Schellenberger believes the committee is crucial to Dow's success. "The only way that we ensure quality is through our people. And to keep people enthusiastic, we have to work to build an environment that fosters and values the diverse views of all employees."

Besides the Management Advisory Committee, Dow has two other minority employee organizations, the Michigan R&D Minority Task Force and the Ethnic Minorities Task Force. These groups supplement the informal networking that goes on among minority employees at Dow. "When I joined the company in 1979," Stan Land recalls, "some of the blacks at Dow used to avoid each other; I think some felt we were competing with each other. But over time, we've come to realize that unless we help each other, we reduce our chances for success. Now we make sure that we know each other, and that we're lending support whenever it's needed."

The National Organization of Black Chemists and Engineers is a professional organization that helps blacks at Dow Chemical and Dow Corning build a support network. Land is an active member. "We have a variety of activities. We've sponsored an Efficacy for Minority Professionals program, started a mentoring program to help new minority hires get started on the right track, and adopted a school in Saginaw to help teach math and science."

Dow makes other efforts to foster appreciation of diversity. Martin Luther King Day celebrations are held at headquarters in

Midland, Michigan, and at other locations. Some locations also sponsor days that celebrate other ethnic groups.

Besides Land, minorities hold such titles as Environmental Manager, Vice President of Operations and Executive Vice President of Corporate Planning. There are two minority board members: Willie D. Davis, president and CEO of All Pro Broadcasting, Inc., and Enrique Falla, Dow's Executive Vice President and Chief Financial Officer.

Dow U.S.A. purchased more than $35 million worth of goods and services from minority-owned businesses in 1992, thanks to its Minority Focal Point Team, which was established in 1989 to identify, develop and promote minority-owned suppliers.

The company donates generously to minority organizations. Because much of Dow's work relies on science and technology, Dow has a special interest in education. In 1992, education programs received more than half of all corporate contributions—$10 million of almost $18 million. The Louisiana Division makes a yearly grant to a local high school to develop new approaches to education; the Texas Operations group formed a partnership with local schools to create interest in educational skills and provide information on career opportunities, reaching more than 6,000 students. Since Dow began its Take Initiative Program on Transplantation in 1986, the number of black organ donors in the United States has doubled. Blacks have a higher incidence of kidney failure than other groups, and this education program has saved numerous lives.

The company contributes to Hispanic organizations such as Amigos de SER, the League of United Latin American Citizens and the Society of Hispanic Professional Engineers. Other charitable contributions have gone to the National Urban League, the National Action Council for Minorities in Engineering, the American Indian Science and Engineering Society and the National Society of Black Engineers. In 1985, the company created an award program to recognize the efforts of employees who volunteer in their communities. Since then, more than 1,000 employees have been recognized for outstanding community service.

The National Society of Black Engineers named Dow one of the best places to work in 1992, and in 1990 *Fortune* magazine ranked the company the fourteenth most-admired corporation in the United States. Dow has received awards from the Society of Hispanic Professional Engineers, and was named in 1992 one of the top 100 employers by *Hispanic* magazine. The Engineering & Construction Services Division won the President's Award from the Gulf Coast Alliance of Minority Engineers in 1990 for its employees' involvement in the alliance.

Life in Midland, Michigan, may be the one minor drawback to a career at Dow. The city's population is 4 to 5% minority, and the closest areas with higher minority populations are at least an hour away: Midland is 120 miles north of Detroit and 55 miles west of Flint. Stan Land believes the minority families in Midland are much closer as a result. "We leaned pretty hard on the other black families when we first moved here," he remembers. "We have children, and I wanted them to know other black kids, so we quickly joined the Jack and Jill group in Saginaw, and identified a circle of nine or ten families with the same concerns. Now that we're used to it, I think Midland is actually a good place to raise a family. Dow really makes an effort to provide cultural and social opportunities, so there are plenty of things to do. If anything, it's like a fairy-tale world sometimes, and I wonder how my kids would deal with a big city."

Overall, Dow presents an excellent opportunity to build a successful career. "Dow believes in giving employees immediate responsibility," says Land. "You can go as far here as your abilities will take you."

Office locations: Dow's global operations span the United States, Canada, Latin America, Europe and the Far East; Dow and its subsidiaries operate plants at 181 locations in thirty-three countries. Within each area are manufacturing plants, sales offices and research facilities. Corporate headquarters are in Midland, Michigan.

2030 Dow Center
Midland, Michigan 48674
(517) 636-1000

DU PONT [E. I. DU PONT DE NEMOURS AND COMPANY]

Du Pont is an international company in the business of manufacturing and marketing chemicals, specialty fibers, polymers, finishes, petroleum and coal. It also manufactures insecticides, electronic components, films and medical instruments. Many of Du Pont's trademarked fibers, like Dacron and Lycra, are used in sportswear, carpeting and other home products.

1990 revenues: $40,000,000,000
1991 revenues: $38,695,000,000
1992 revenues: $37,800,000,000

Number of full-time U.S. employees: 95,000

Percentage of these employees who are minorities: 13.9
    Black: 9.8
    Hispanic: 1.9
    Asian/Pacific Islander: 1.5
    Native American: .7

Number of people in the total management pool: 37,000

Percentage of minorities in the total management pool: 10

Percentage of minority managers who comprise each managerial level:
    Vice president: 6.0
    Director: 8.0
    Section plant manager: 3.0
    Midmanagement: 4.0
    Lower-level management: 7.0

Salary information:

Vice president:	$150,000–$250,000+
Director:	$100,000–$150,000
Manager:	$75,000–$100,000
Professional:	$55,000–$75,000
Entry (college):	$30,000–$55,000
Secretary:	$20,000–$35,000

Founded in 1802, the company still has a Du Pont family member on its board. Du Pont is currently led by Ed Woolard, a chairman who has been honored by the White House and by many organizations who have recognized his aggressive steps toward bringing diversity into the corporate workplace. One of Woolard's first moves as chairman in 1991 was to schedule a Du Pont leadership conference which focused on issues of diversity and bringing more minorities into management positions.

Minorities hold many important positions at Du Pont including Vice President of Marketing Sales in Electronics; Vice President of Materials, Logistics and Services; Vice President of Federal Affairs; Vice President of Technology and Professional Development and U.S. Director of Medical/Marketing Services. There is one minority member of Du Pont's board of directors: Andrew F. Brimmer, the well-known economic and financial consultant who also serves on the board of governors of the Federal Reserve Bank.

The company recruits many minority students from such universities as North Carolina A&T State, Howard, Prairie View A&M and Southern.

Du Pont has an Affirmative Action Committee which consists of top executives. The committee was created in 1977 and has been responsible for setting minority recruitment and retention goals, as well as creating a speakers' bureau which has invited Gloria Steinem and columnist William Raspberry, among others, to discuss minority business issues. In 1991, the committee's role was broadened to include teaching employees how to manage Du Pont's diverse work force.

The Committee to Achieve Cultural Diversity has presented proposals to senior management on ways to enhance diversity at the company. The group has helped set up mentoring and career development systems for minorities.

A number of cultural diversity initiatives are taking place at Du Pont. The company offers a five-day Multicultural Awareness Workshop which deals with issues of race and gender in the workplace. A six-day course, "Efficacy for Minority Professionals," designed by the training firm J. Howard & Associates, helps minority employees examine environmental and psychological obstacles to professional development.

Du Pont has several corporate-wide minority employee networks. There are Asian, Hispanic and black women's networks on the corporate level. Most of the other business divisions have their own black networks and/or minority networks. In April 1991, the company sponsored its first Black Leadership and Development Conference, at which 100 black employees came together for three days to discuss the developmental needs of black professionals at the company.

While some of the business divisions have core teams assigned to work on issues of race and gender which are either bicultural or multicultural, each division has developed its own form of diversity training. As an example, Du Pont Engineering developed cultural study groups open to all employees, and the Finance division has embarked on an educational program engaging outside consultants and internal facilitators. Each employee goes through a three-, six- or nine-day process in which issues of race and gender are addressed.

The Agricultural Products group uses a team approach; issues of diversity are discussed in an atmosphere of team building. The Information Systems and Polymers divisions have a full-time manager who heads up all diversity activities. The Materials, Logistics and Services division has fully integrated diversity issues into its training programs, while the Imaging Systems and Medical Products divisions have a Black Issues Core Team which focuses on issues relating to successful career development for black employees. The issues included are networking, recruiting, mentoring and awareness training.

Most of Du Pont's new hires come from such disciplines as chemical engineering, biochemistry, chemistry, physics and finance.

The company contributes to such minority organizations as the National Council of La Raza, the National Urban League, the NAACP, SER—Jobs for Progress and the Interracial Council for Business. It is extremely active in its sponsorship of minority scholarships through such organizations as the American Indian Science and Engineering Society, the National Black MBA Association, the Society for Hispanic Professional Engineers and the National Action Committee of Minority Engineers. Du Pont contributes to the University of Tennessee Minority Engineering Scholarship Program, which provides internships as well as scholarships.

The Du Pont Minority Vendor Program typically spends more than $220 million each year with minority-owned suppliers. It is overseen by a corporate program called TEMPO (To Encourage Minority Purchasing Opportunities).

Of the company's total purchases from contractors, 2½% are made with minority firms. During 1991 and 1992, the company sponsored six development seminars for minority suppliers to help them bid effectively for its business. Such topics as timing of bids, how to construct a bid proposal and proper contacts were also discussed.

Du Pont participates in twelve minority supplier development councils at the national, regional and local levels. The company has sponsored a dozen trade fairs in Wilmington and at plant sites for minority suppliers in recent years. The suppliers are invited to visit the sites and meet with site managers and purchasers. Du Pont is a member of the National Minority Supplier Development Council.

Office locations: Du Pont is headquartered in Wilmington, Delaware. There are other offices and manufacturing facilities across the United States and in cities in Europe, Asia, the Middle East and Africa.

1007 Market Street
Wilmington, Delaware 19898
(302) 774-1000

EASTMAN KODAK COMPANY

Kodak is best known as the world's largest manufacturer of photographic products. Its Imaging business includes the production of color film, black-and-white film, 35mm cameras, Fun Saver cameras, alkaline batteries and motion picture films and processing chemicals. Its Health business includes the Sterling Drug Division, which produces such products as Bayer aspirin, Phillips' Milk of Magnesia and Stridex skin care products. The Health business also includes L&F Products, producer of Lysol disinfectants, Ogilvie hair products and Diaperene baby care products. Kodak's Chemical division produces a large number of resins, waxes and plastics. Kodak's Information Systems business manufactures duplicating machines and duplicating systems that are used by various types of printers.

1990 revenues: $18,908,000,000
1991 revenues: $19,419,000,000
1992 revenues: $20,183,000,000

Number of full-time employees: 80,350 in the U.S., 134,450 worldwide

Percentage of these (U.S.) employees who are minorities: 12.2

Black:	7.3
Hispanic:	3.1
Asian/Pacific Islander:	1.6
Native American:	.2

Percentage of minorities in the total management pool: 6.9

Kodak's commitment to minority causes and the amount of money it gives to innovative minority programs and scholarships are almost unparalleled.

Because Kodak's products are so diverse, there is a wide range of employment opportunities both at the entry level and in upper management. Kodak hires at all levels in sales, marketing, chemical engineering, optical engineering, mechanical engineering, computer science, electrical engineering, physics, biochemistry, chemistry and mathematics. There is a heavy emphasis on research, design and development.

Kodak focuses its campus recruiting at fifty-four universities. Of these schools, eight are predominantly black or Hispanic: Atlanta, Florida A&M, Howard, North Carolina A&T, Prairie View A&M, the University of Puerto Rico, Tuskegee and Xavier. The company does, of course, recruit minorities from majority schools, and it makes use of minority-owned search firms to identify minority candidates. As a part of its recruiting strategy, Kodak advertises for job applicants in such publications as *Hispanic Engineer* and *U.S. Black Engineer*.

Kodak sponsors and attends numerous job fairs and conferences each year. The company has served as primary sponsor of the American Indian Science and Engineering Society's National Conference. It has also been an exhibitor at or a sponsor of conferences for the National Association of Black Accountants (NABA), the National Black MBA Association, the National Urban League, the National Hispanic Engineering Awards, the National Council of La Raza, the NAACP (with strong support given to the renowned ACT-SO program) and the National Action Council for Minorities in Engineering.

To encourage the development of minority professionals, the company provides scholarships and summer internships in cooperation with the National Society of Black Engineers, the Urban League Scholars Program, INROADS and the American Indian Science and Engineering Society. On the graduate level, Kodak sponsors the Graduate Fellowship Award for doctoral candidates in chemistry and chemical engineering through the National Organization of Black Chemists and Chemical Engineers, as well as tuition and stipend scholarships for MBA students through the Consortium for Graduate Study in Management. There is also a co-op program for students who want to work a school term or a summer term at Kodak. Minorities make up about 30% of the co-op program participants.

Experienced minority professionals are recruited by Kodak's Professional Minority Recruitment program. During a young manager's tenure, it is not unusual for Kodak to pay for the individual's advanced part-time education. Edna Soltero, a Kodak manufacturing engineer and chemical engineering graduate from the University of Puerto Rico, was sponsored by Kodak in her MBA studies after she had worked several years at the company. Career Services Centers at various Kodak locations offer individual career counseling, instructional videotapes and self-assessment.

Mee Wing, Director of Corporate Staff Human Resources, has been active in minority recruiting efforts. She has been with Kodak since 1973 and has been a member of Kodak's Corporate Diversity Task Force, which is made up of fifteen managers from different ethnic backgrounds. "In my position and in my experiences on various diversity and minority task forces at Kodak," says Wing, "I have seen that nonminority people have learned to be more sensitive to minority issues. Race and ethnicity are not taboo topics here."

Wing holds an MBA and worked in such other Kodak offices as Atlanta and Washington, D.C., before coming to the Rochester headquarters. She says she has never felt that her ethnicity was an issue on the job or in the community. "Rochester has a large Asian population and a social organization, the Rochester Asian Association, which sponsors family picnics and other social events," she says. "Organizations like this are important for new hires and their families."

Although some might assume that Kodak is a company of socially reticent engineers, many employees are out in the community disproving the stereotype. One black husband-and-wife team at Kodak enjoy almost celebrity status at the Rochester headquarters. Patricia and Mutiu Fagbayi, both chemical engineers, serve on the board of the Rochester chapter of the National Organization of Black Chemists and Chemical Engineers, edit its national newsmagazine and spearheaded a popular Adopt-a-School program which invites volunteers from corporations to share their experiences and knowledge with children in local public schools.

Leonard Redon, General Manager and Vice President of Market Development for the United States and Canada, says Kodak's Network North Star, formed by black employees in 1987, has done a great deal to develop minority (particularly black) managers. Redon, who is black and has a degree in chemical engineering, has been with the company since 1973. "I have found Kodak to be extremely supportive of minority programs and completely dedicated to developing the skills of minority professionals," he says. Network North Star, he says, "provides mentoring and networking opportunities for employees, and we invite outside speakers to talk to us about career planning skills, experiences of other minority managers and important community issues." Network North Star meets once a month, and recently adopted an elementary school in Rochester, with black employees acting as mentors and role models for the students.

"Groups like this," says Redon, "are good for the minority employees and they are good for the company. We can serve as a good sounding board for Kodak when important minority issues arise, and we can keep them aware of concerns that are facing the minority staff."

Company chairman Kay R. Whitmore has been honored by many minority organizations and others for his commitment to developing minority employees and aiding minority causes.

Under his direction, the company supports approximately 120 minority college students yearly with full tuition and internship opportunities as a part of the Kodak Scholars Program.

Two minority members currently sit on Kodak's board of directors: Roberto C. Goizueta, chairman of Coca-Cola Company, and Charles T. Duncan, senior counsel to the law firm of Reid & Priest.

Kodak has received the NAACP's Corporate Image Award in recognition of its national efforts to improve opportunities for African Americans and other minorities through its business practices and its support of education, culture, housing and economic development. The company was also recognized for its support of the American Indian Program at Clarkson University. Recently Kodak has donated $1 million to the United Negro College Fund and $500,000 to Harlem's Schomburg Center for Research in Black Culture, and it has consistently given the largest corporate gift to any single United Way chapter. The company donated the exhibit "Odyssey of a Black American: The Legacy of Ralph Bunche" to the City University of New York to celebrate the black Nobel Peace Prize winner and United Nations official. Kodak's community relations director serves as chair of a new African American Leadership Development Program, created to develop leadership skills among blacks in the communities around Rochester.

Kodak also contributes to scholarships through such organizations as the Society of Hispanic Professional Engineers, the U.S. Hispanic Chamber of Commerce, the Congressional Hispanic Caucus Foundation, the National Hispanic Scholarship Fund and the Society of Mexican-American Engineers. The company sponsored "The Latino Olympians," a traveling exhibit that focused on the history of Latin American participation in the Olympic Games. The company also has a Minority Business Development Program which seeks to develop and use minority suppliers and vendors.

Office locations: Kodak has offices in all states and most countries of the world. Plants are located in most major geographical areas in the world. Corporate headquarters are in Rochester, New York. Major offices and plants are in New York, Tennessee, Colorado, Arkansas, Florida, New Jersey, Pennsylvania, California, Georgia, Illinois, the United Kingdom, France, Germany, Australia, Japan, Mexico, Brazil and Canada.

343 State Street
Rochester, New York 14650
(716) 724-6888

THE EQUITABLE COMPANIES INCORPORATED

The Equitable conglomerate includes the third-largest life insurance company in the United States. It is a leading pension and mutual fund manager and is a major provider of financial services to consumers and businesses. One of its investment subsidiaries is the brokerage firm of Donaldson, Lufkin & Jenrette.

1991 revenues: $6,623,100,000
1992 revenues: $6,298,100,000

Number of full-time U.S. employees: 14,276

Percentage of these employees who are minorities: 22.3
    Black: 10.8
    Hispanic: 5.8
    Asian/Pacific Islander: 5.6
    Native American: .1

Number of people in the total management pool: 3,590

Percentage of minorities in the total management pool: 10.1

Founded in 1859, The Equitable has become much more than a domestic insurance company. It is also a major participant in the investment world, as it manages assets exceeding $140 billion. Its insurance business has six operating divisions, and its investment business includes Alliance Capital Management Corporation, Equitable Capital Management Corporation, Equitable Real Estate Investment Management, Inc., and Donaldson, Lufkin & Jenrette, Inc.

    Minorities at The Equitable hold such positions as Vice

Chairman of Equitable Capital Management Corporation, Managing Director of Equitable Capital Management Corporation, Senior Vice President of External Relations and Chairman and Vice President of Equico Capital Corporation. Dr. Norman C. Francis, president of Xavier University, is a member of the board of directors.

The company recruits many minority employees from such schools as Morehouse College, Xavier University, North Carolina A&T State University and Howard University. Since several senior executives are on the boards of schools with large minority enrollments, the company has had a strong Minority College Liaison Program, which operates an active summer job program at the New York offices.

There are several minority employee organizations at The Equitable: the Hispanic Officers Cabinet, the Hispanic Agency Council, the Hispanic Business Resource Group, the Black Agency Council, the Black Employee Council and the Black Officers Council.

Founded in 1968, the Black Officers Council is a company employee organization created by black employees among The Equitable's sales force. Its purpose was to encourage the hiring, training and advancement of blacks at the company. "I was one of the earliest beneficiaries of the Black Officers Council," says Darwin Davis, Senior Vice President at The Equitable. "During my twenty-six years at the company, I have seen the organization mentor new minority managers, strengthen career networking and improve the hiring policies with respect to the hiring and promotion of minority vice presidents."

Davis, who was the first black line officer at the company, holds a master's degree in mathematics and sits on the boards of Carnegie-Mellon University and Drew Medical School in Los Angeles. He joined the company as an agent in Detroit, then held such positions as district manager, Detroit agency manager, Vice President of Field Development, Vice President for the Eastern United States Region, Head of the Marketing Sector of

Agency Operations and Director of the Office of External Affairs. "What makes The Equitable a good place for minority managers is that our employee councils give us access to the executives who run the company," Davis says. "We have the access to meet with the CEO and discuss minority hiring and other issues that concern minority employees." As an example, Davis explains that the Black Officers Council worked with the company's CEO several years ago to create a 100 Hire Program. The purpose was to get all business heads to focus on the importance of hiring talented black managers. "Because of the program," says Davis, "we went from six black vice presidents in 1980 to twenty-nine black vice presidents in 1990."

Since 1973, the company has sponsored an Annual Black Achievement Recognition Dinner at which it honors outstanding black leaders for their contributions to business and the community. The winners, nominated by members of The Equitable's Black Officers Council, have included Arthur Ashe, Dr. Dorothy I. Height, Oprah Winfrey, Bryant Gumbel and John Johnson, publisher of *Ebony* magazine.

The Equitable's subsidiary, Equico Capital Corporation, is a small business investment company formed in 1971 to bridge the equity gap for minority entrepreneurs. It has helped finance several minority-owned businesses including Essence Communications, Unity Broadcasting Network, Inc., and TLC Group.

The Equitable has had a one-day diversity training program for all management trainees since 1988. The program uses discussion, videos and role-playing. Having worked at the company since 1967, Davis says he has seen the effects of this training. "It's not always enough to introduce minority employees into the work force," he says. "You have to also train coworkers about how to interact in a diverse office environment. I think the training has changed many employees' attitudes about the importance of diversity."

One of the first companies to contribute to the United Negro College Fund, The Equitable was a founding member of the Black Leadership Commission on AIDS. It also provides scholarships for minority students including an actuarial studies scholarship at Florida A&M University and M.D./Ph.D. scholarships at Drew University School of Medicine and Science.

Through its foundation, the company contributes to such minority organizations as the Asian Legal Defense and Education Fund, the National Urban League, the National Puerto Rican Forum, the NAACP, the American Indian College Education Fund and the National Council of La Raza.

With the New York City Board of Education, The Equitable helped found the Join-A-School Program, which pairs public high schools with corporate sponsors. The company was recently the lead corporate sponsor of the New York City Partnership's annual Summer Jobs Program, whereby The Equitable helped place more than 52,000 young people in summer jobs. Each year the company also honors fifteen of its employees who volunteer with community groups. The Equitable Community Leadership Awards provide $1,000 grants to organizations helped by The Equitable's employees. In 1991, grants were given to Hispanic Unity of Florida, which helps new immigrants adapt; the INROADS minority internship program; and the Athlete Mentor Program, in which college football players work with elementary school children to stress the importance of academics.

In 1992, the company worked with the Foundation for Ethnic Understanding to sponsor an art exhibition by public school children in New York called "My Culture, Our City." The company has also supported many projects that encourage improved relationships between blacks and Jews.

Office locations: The Equitable has its headquarters in the new Equitable Tower in midtown Manhattan. There are offices across the United States as well as around the world, in such countries as France, Germany and Japan.

787 Seventh Avenue
New York, New York 10019
(212) 554-1234

ERNST & YOUNG

Ernst & Young, one of the "Big Six" accounting firms, was created during a major reorganization in the fall of 1989 when the accounting firms of Arthur Young and Ernst & Whinney were merged. The firm employs more personnel in the United States than any of its competitors and provides companies and individuals with such services as auditing, tax planning, management consulting and actuarial, benefits and compensation consulting.

1990 revenues: $5,000,000,000 (worldwide),
$2,200,000,000 (U.S.)
1991 revenues: $5,500,000,000 (worldwide),
$2,300,000,000 (U.S.)

Number of full-time U.S. employees: 22,000

Percentage of these employees who are minorities: 12.2
Black: 5.1
Hispanic: 2.9
Asian/Pacific Islander: 4.1
Native American: .1

Number of people in the total management pool: 7,375

Percentage of minorities in the total management pool: 4.4

Percentage of minority managers who comprise each managerial level:
Partner: 2.6
Principal: 1.5

Senior manager: 4.3
Manager: 5.9
Director: 4.2
Associate director: 4.4
Assistant director: 5.3

Salary information:
Entry level, audit and tax: $25,000–$30,000
Partner: $200,000

While the number of minority accountants has grown considerably over the past decade, the profession still compares poorly
with other industries in minority representation. On the high
end is the percentage of Asian accountants, which stands at 7%.
Although many black colleges now offer accounting programs,
the profession is still only 4% black. These numbers explain why
so few minority accountants reach the partnership level in any
of the Big Six accounting firms. At this point, it seems that
Ernst & Young is doing the most to increase the number of minority accountants.

The firm has black partners in its offices in Chicago, New
York, Baltimore, San Jose, Dallas and Cleveland. There are
Asian partners in Atlanta, Chicago, New York, Los Angeles,
Honolulu, Stamford, Salt Lake City and Detroit. Hispanic part-
ners work in offices in Cleveland, Indianapolis, New York, Chi-
cago, Dallas, Phoenix, Honolulu, Miami, Los Angeles, San
Francisco, Houston, Orlando, San Juan and Orange County,
California.

According to Chuck Eldridge, Ernst & Young's National
Director of Recruiting, the firm created the Minority Recruiting
Advisory Committee in 1989 to advise senior staff on specific
issues regarding minority recruiting and retention. The committee, which meets twice a year, consists of nine partners and four
additional managers.

Besides recruiting from about 400 universities across the

country, Ernst & Young recruits at such black universities as Howard, North Carolina A&T State, Hampton, Morgan State and Jackson State. Many Asian students are recruited from the University of California at Berkeley. There is a major recruiting effort for Hispanic graduates at the University of Texas at San Antonio, Baruch College in New York City, New Mexico State University and Florida International University.

"We have designated eleven universities where we focus our minority recruiting effort," says Eldridge, "and we assign a partner to the school in the same way that we would assign a partner to the client. We make sure he or she visits the school at least four or five times a year so that a real relationship is developed."

John Warren, a black accountant in the New York office, says the firm has been successful at recruiting full-time professionals through the INROADS program. "I know of five full-time minority accountants who had previously come to Ernst & Young through our INROADS summer internship program," explains Warren, who acts as Assistant Director of Recruiting. "Of course we sometimes hire experienced hires from other firms, but most of our efforts are aimed at the university campuses or by recruiting recent graduates whom we meet at conferences sponsored by organizations like the National Association of Black Accountants or the American Association of Hispanic CPA's."

Warren, who joined the company in 1978, has a bachelor's degree in mathematics and a master's degree in accounting. After spending five years in professional basketball with the New York Knicks and Cleveland Cavaliers, he decided to make use of his math background and joined the company's audit staff. After four years, he was staffing other auditors on audit teams for various clients. As he advanced in the company, he says, his technical knowledge and assertive personality were important assets. "Young minority professionals," he says, "need to find informal mentors whenever they enter the business world, but first they need to gain as much technical knowledge as possible and become assertive so that others around them notice their abilities."

Cecil Flamer, a partner in the Atlanta office, also helps in the hiring effort as a Director of Human Resources.

Although several of Ernst & Young's offices are aggressive in minority recruiting and diversity efforts, the Chicago office has been particularly successful. One black partner in that office is Anthony Anderson, who joined the firm in 1977, right after earning a bachelor's degree in accounting. A specialist in the firm's insurance practice, Anderson remembers being concerned about finding a place that was hospitable to minority professionals. "When I first visited the Chicago office," he says, "there were practically no minorities. That can be overwhelming when you know that you're facing an eleven-year partnership track."

Anderson, who recalls that he originally looked at the interviewing process as a means to learn whether he would feel comfortable as a black in an overwhelmingly white setting, says he found it easy to develop mentor relationships with his white coworkers.

Today Anderson and another black partner in Chicago have get-togethers at home to bring the young minority accountants at the office into an informal network. "This office makes it a priority to recruit more minorities," says Anderson, who is also a member of the Minority Recruiting Advisory Committee. "We network with college professors, I give lectures to black and other minority students at the University of Illinois. And I keep in touch with these students. When they finally join the firm, we look out for them and give them advice on job decisions and try to make sure they are getting challenging assignments. More companies and firms need to realize that retention is just as important as recruiting."

There are no formal minority employee groups and no minority mentoring program, but most of the firm's offices assign a counselor or "buddy" to each new staff member. The counselor is responsible for helping the new employee with training opportunities, client assignments and getting acclimated to a new city. Most of the larger offices are divided into practice groups so that different accountants specialize in servicing specific industries like pharmaceuticals, media, insurance and financial services.

The firm is currently creating a mission statement on minority recruiting and retention to be adopted by the Management Committee.

According to Paul Ostling, vice chairman of the company and president of the Ernst & Young Foundation, the company provides support to such minority organizations as INROADS, the National Association of Black Accountants, the National Black MBA Association, the American Association of Hispanic CPA's and the United Negro College Fund. Ostling says the firm's minority student internship program plays an important role in increasing the number of full-time minority accountants both at Ernst & Young and in the profession as a whole. "When we can identify and build a relationship with a minority student during a summer or winter-term internship," says Ostling, "we are able to increase the job acceptance rate for our offers. But even more important, we have found that the retention rate for full-time minority employees is three times greater if the employee has previously participated in a formal office internship experience."

According to Cynthia Woltemath, senior associate in the New York office, the firm sponsors a $12,000 Junior Leadership Award at North Carolina A&T, as well as college internships through the Sponsors for Educational Opportunity program, and scholarships that are awarded at the National Association of Black Accountants convention.

There is no formal minority supplier-vendor program at Ernst & Young, but the firm did recently hire the minority accounting firm Mitchell, Titus & Co. to perform the audit of the Ernst & Young Foundation.

Office locations: The firm is based in New York City and has offices across the United States in such cities as Atlanta, Dallas, Miami, Chicago, San Jose, Baltimore and Los Angeles. There are also operations in Mexico, Canada, Africa, South America, the Far East and Russia, and more than 200 offices in Europe.

787 Seventh Avenue
New York, New York 10019
(212) 773-3000

EXXON CORPORATION

Exxon is an international company engaged in the exploration for, transportation of and production of crude oil, natural gas and petroleum products. The company has various divisions that operate under the names Esso, Standard Oil and Imperial Oil. In the United States, Exxon markets its gasoline and motor oil through approximately 17,000 retail outlets. The company also has an interest in electric power generation in Hong Kong.

1990 revenues: $117,000,000,000
1991 revenues: $116,500,000,000
1992 revenues: $117,100,000,000

Number of full-time U.S. employees: 42,000

Percentage of these employees who are minorities: 23.5
    Black: 14
    Hispanic: 6.3
    Asian/Pacific Islander: 2.8
    Native American: .4

Number of people in the total management pool: 6,400

Percentage of minorities in the total management pool: 11.6

Percentage of minority managers who comprise each managerial level:
    Officials and managers: 11.6

Founded in 1882 as Standard Oil Company by John D. Rockefeller, Exxon Corporation is made up of several divisions which operate around the world. Its largest divisions are Exxon Company U.S.A. and Exxon Company International, which is responsible for oil and gas operations outside North America.

There have never been large numbers of minority professionals in the petroleum business. Although the titles do not sound very glamorous or powerful, Exxon has one of the best records in the industry for promoting minorities into management positions, including Production Manager, Human Resources Finance Director, Marketing Manager and Engineering Manager. There is one minority person on the board of directors: Randolph W. Bromery, a black professor at the University of Massachusetts at Amherst as well as the president of Geo Science Engineering Corporation.

The company recruits at such black universities as Prairie View A&M, Howard, Southern and Clark Atlanta. A major recruiting effort is aimed at Hispanic students who attend Texas Agricultural and Industrial College and other minority students who attend Texas A&M University, the University of Oklahoma and the University of Florida. A large number of these recruits are students with graduate degrees in engineering.

Besides its recruitment effort, Exxon supports minority colleges through its financial contributions. Recently the company gave $137,000 to the Hispanic Association of Colleges and Universities, $42,000 to the American Indian College Fund and $230,000 to historically black colleges and the United Negro College Fund.

In 1990, the company created a Minority Scholarship Program for students pursuing degrees in math, science and engineering which distributes approximately $100,000 annually to fifteen minority students at ten universities. Exxon also offers summer internships to the scholarship students.

According to Robert W. Gentry, Senior Policy Advisor, the company has worked with diversity consultants since 1987. "We have offered on-site presentations and workshops for our employees," says Gentry. "At the corporate headquarters, we have worked with Roosevelt Thomas, head of the American Institute for Managing Diversity, as well as with the program 'Diversity Awareness for the Nineties,' which was created by diversity professionals at Harbridge House."

There are several minority employee organizations at Exxon, mostly informal. A few exist for Hispanic employees, but most were created by the many black employees in different parts of the United States: the Dallas Black Employee Network, the North East Black Employee Network, the Polymer division's African American Network and the Black Employee Council, which is based at the corporate headquarters. The council acts as an advocate for black employees, advises management and provides networking and mentoring for new black employees. Most of the employee groups also contribute to neighborhood youth organizations and participate in community development programs.

Gerald McElvy, Assistant General Auditor of Exxon Company International, says that though the company does not have many formal minority employee organizations, he has always been able to meet senior managers and develop mentoring relationships with both black and white executives. "I joined the company in 1976 and I've seen the development and evaluation process create a level playing field so that minorities can not only create mentor relationships with whites, but so that we can compete for the same top jobs as our nonminority coworkers." McElvy, who is black and holds graduate and undergraduate degrees in business, has held such positions as Manager of Finance, Executive Assistant to the President, Financial Services Manager and Production Accounting Manager, all within the Exxon USA division.

McElvy, who recently relocated from Houston to Florham Park, New Jersey, says minority employee organizations were small and informal in the Houston Controller's Department and Informations Systems Department. The Northeast locations appear to have more active minority employee groups.

William Wigglesworth, Division Human Resources Manager, has been with Exxon USA since 1978. As an Asian person, he acknowledges that when he first considered Exxon as an employer, he was concerned about whether he would feel comfortable. "Different minority groups face different barriers," he says. "Among Asian employees, language is often the barrier. No matter how well educated he or she might be, there are Asian professionals who worry that because English is their second language, they may not be as fluent as they should be. I've had the opportunity to talk about these kinds of issues with my coworkers at Exxon."

Wigglesworth holds a master's degree in organizational behavior from Purdue University and became the corporation's first minority recruiting coordinator in 1988. He says that virtually every division has formal or informal minority networking or support groups that make young minority professionals feel comfortable at Exxon.

Exxon hires such employees with backgrounds in engineering, earth science, accounting, law, computer science and business. Graduates with MBAs or computer or human resource backgrounds have the greatest number of choices among the company's different businesses. Engineers are likely to work for a refinery or in some other area of production.

Through Exxon's Early Minority Identification Program, the INROADS program and the company's high school partnership program, the company provides mentoring and summer employment opportunities for minority high school and college students.

Exxon has given generously to such minority organizations as the American Indian Science and Engineering Society, the National Black MBA Association, the Society of Hispanic Professional Engineers, the National Society of Black Engineers, the NAACP, the National Puerto Rican Forum and the National Council of La Raza. A great deal of funding is also provided to minority groups through the Exxon Education

Foundation, which includes an Elementary and Secondary School Improvement Program.

Besides being a member of the National Minority Supplier Development Council and working with regional minority purchasing councils, Exxon spends more than $150 million each year with more than 1,800 minority-owned businesses. It also contributes to the Interracial Council for Business Opportunity and the Urban Business Assistance Corporation.

Office locations: The company is headquartered in Irving, Texas, a town outside Dallas. It also has offices and locations in seventy-nine other countries including Mexico, Saudi Arabia, Germany, Kenya, Senegal, Uganda, China, Bermuda, Chile, Australia, Colombia, France, the Netherlands, Malaysia, the United Kingdom, Japan, Belgium and Canada.

225 East John W. Carpenter Freeway
Irving, Texas 75062
(214) 444-1000

FEDERAL EXPRESS CORPORATION

Federal Express is an international delivery company that handles letters, packages and larger cargo across the United States and in more than 130 other countries. It transports packages more than 1.8 million miles each day with more than 400 airplanes and 30,000 trucks.

1990 revenues: $7,015,069,000
1991 revenues: $7,688,296,000

Number of full-time U.S. employees: 72,048

Percentage of these employees who are minorities: 32.8
    Black: 24.7
    Hispanic: 5.7
    Asian/Pacific Islander: 2.0
    Native American: .3
    Other: .1

Number of people in the total management pool: 4,928

Percentage of minorities in the total management pool: 18

Percentage of minority managers who comprise each managerial level:
    Senior vice president: 9.1
    Vice president: 6.3
    Managing director: 12.7
    Senior manager: 12.9
    Manager: 19.6

An extremely young company, Federal Express was conceived and founded by its chairman, Frederick Smith, in 1973 with just eight planes. An entrepreneurial atmosphere pervades almost every aspect of the company.

Minorities at Federal Express hold such positions as Senior Vice President of Personnel, Managing Director of Human Resource Compliance and Managing Director of Corporate Employment. There are also vice presidents in several departments. On the fourteen-member board of directors, there is one minority board member, Joshua I. Smith, chairman and CEO of Maxima Corporation.

Federal Express developed a program which has helped many minorities enter management positions. The Leadership Effectiveness and Awareness Program (LEAP) is designed to help nonmanagement employees work through a leadership qualification process with their current manager acting as coach. A LEAP endorsement, which includes an employee profile, a manager's focused recommendation, a peer assessment and a panel interview, is required for first-line management positions.

According to Suey Coleman, Manager of Equal Employment Opportunity and Affirmative Action, the company offers employees diversity training through the Managing Diversity Program. "We have several cultural diversity training programs," says Coleman. "Some are aimed at management and some are available to all employees through our Leadership Institute." The institute is Federal Express's "in-house college," offering courses on a wide range of issues at the Memphis headquarters. These courses can also be viewed by employees in offices across the country on the Federal Express cable TV station.

For a long time, Coleman says, the company had a race relations class and a course that dealt with issues surrounding female employees. The two courses have been merged into a course called "Cultural Diversity."

Albert Alexander, Senior Manager of Employee Relations, is enthusiastic about Federal Express's diversity courses. A black manager who has worked with the company since 1982, Alexander had previously held jobs at Honeywell and Ford Motor Company. "Employees are able to face and manage ethnic diversity at Federal Express for several reasons," he says. "Not only are diversity issues discussed in our race relations and cultural diversity program, but they are also important components in the management courses that are taught in the company's Leadership Institute." Alexander says discussion groups, videotapes and role-playing encourage employees to get more involved with the subject matter than simple lectures would allow. "Since our course training is taught by senior managers from the company, employees recognize that the company takes these issues seriously," he adds.

There are no minority employee organizations at Federal Express, but Alexander insists that new minority hires should have no problem feeling comfortable around their coworkers. "There are many senior-level minority executives here who look forward to mentoring other young minority employees," he explains. "Even in my position, I can still call and get advice from some of the minority executives who are managing directors with the company."

Federal Express recruits at colleges with large minority enrollments like Le Moyne-Owen College and Shelby State University in Memphis. The company also works with the Tennessee Employment Services and West Memphis Employment Services to identify and recruit minority job applicants. The company hires accountants, auditors, programmers, account executives and sales representatives, as well as financial analysts with bachelor's and master's degrees.

The company has also established a partnership at three historically black colleges by providing money to fund campus-based chapters of the International Association of Students in Economics and Business Management. Through the partnerships, the company has also hired fifteen student interns. Federal Express also hires minority interns through the INROADS program.

The company supports many minority organizations including the Urban League, the NAACP, the U.S. Pan Asian American Chamber of Commerce, the National Hispanic MBA Association, the National Black MBA Association, the Black Airline Pilots Association, the National Civil Rights Museum and the United Negro College Fund, and has helped fund such events as the National Urban Coalition "Salute to Cities" Dinner, the Memphis NAACP Freedom Fund Gala and the U.S. Hispanic Chamber of Commerce annual conference.

Federal Express sponsors an Adopt-a-School scholarship at the mostly minority Booker T. Washington High School in Memphis. In adopting the 500-student inner-city school, the company funds annual scholarships and student activities, provides technical equipment, purchases computers, sponsors annual career fairs and individual tutoring and counseling, and offers educational tours of the company offices.

By working with the Memphis City Schools, Federal Express employees have created Development Clubs that help students who want to investigate certain careers while still in high school. The clubs focus on careers in engineering, finance, law, marketing, math/computer science and media art. Federal Express employees with these occupational backgrounds serve as consultants to the students. Currently more than 100 employees are working with the program. Volunteer employees also serve as role models and classroom speakers.

Federal Express contributes significantly to the minority community through its Corporate Neighbor Team (CNT) Program, which encourages employees to volunteer with community organizations. Although there are teams in other cities, Memphis currently has ten teams with a total of 1,500 volunteers. The teams choose specific areas of need, like the arts, youth, senior citizens and health.

One of the company's black pilots, Drew Brown, an economics graduate of Southern University, is responsible for founding the American Dream Program, which arranges motivational lectures to minority students who are considering dropping out of school. In 1991 the company received the prestigious Malcolm Baldridge National Quality Award.

Since the 1980s, the company has had a Minority/Women Business Development Program, which spends approximately $30 million annually with minority contractors.

Office locations: Corporate headquarters are in Memphis, Tennessee. The company has offices across the United States in such cities as Indianapolis, Newark, Oakland, Los Angeles and Anchorage. There are also facilities in 135 other countries including France, Italy, the United Kingdom and Germany.

P.O. Box 727
Memphis, Tennessee 38194
(901) 369-3600

GANNETT CO., INC.

Gannett is a diversified news and information company that publishes newspapers, operates broadcasting stations and outdoor advertising businesses and is engaged in research, marketing, commercial printing, a news wire service and news programming. The company publishes eighty-one daily newspapers, fifty nondaily publications and the national paper *USA Today*.

1990 revenues: $3,441,621,000
1991 revenues: $3,382,035,000
1992 revenues: $3,468,957,000

Number of full-time employees: 37,000

Percentage of these employees who are minorities: 21.4
    Black: 13.1
    Hispanic: 4.6
    Asian/Pacific Islander: 3.2
    Native American: .5

Number of people in the total management pool: 5,798

Percentage of minorities in the total management pool: 11.7

Percentage of minority managers who comprise each managerial level:
    Management committee: 6.0
    Publishers/general managers: 9.0

Vice presidents: 7.0
Department heads: 9.0

Founded in 1906 by Frank Gannett, the company was privately held until 1967. The total average paid daily circulation of Gannett's papers exceeds 6 million. The company owns and operates ten TV stations and fifteen radio stations in major markets. Gannett also encompasses the country's largest outdoor advertising operation.

Gannett stands well above many other companies when it comes to putting minorities into positions of power. According to José A. Berrios, Director of Personnel and EEO Programs, minorities at Gannett hold such positions as President of the Gannett Television division, President of the Detroit Newspaper Agency, Publisher of the Honolulu *Star-Bulletin*, Assistant Treasurer of Gannett Co., Inc., Controller for Gannett Outdoor, Publisher and Regional President of Gannett Newspapers, President and General Manager of WGCI Radio and Vice President and General Sales Manager of KUSA-TV.

Gannett's board is also impressive in its large representation of women and minorities. Its four minority members include Carl T. Rowan, the Washington columnist; Andrew F. Brimmer, the economist; Stuart T. K. Ho, chairman of Capital Investment of Hawaii, Inc.; and Dolores D. Wharton, president of the Fund for Corporate Initiatives. Former First Lady Rosalynn Carter is also a member of Gannett's board.

The newspaper division recruits at such black universities as Howard and Florida A&M and at universities with large Hispanic enrollments such as San Jose State, the University of Texas at Austin and San Diego State. The division recruits for journalism as well as business (primarily advertising) students. Gannett's broadcast division also recruits at Howard and the University of Texas at Austin, in addition to Spelman College, Clark University and North Carolina A&T State University.

An overall diversity program at Gannett, the Partners in Progress program, was launched in 1979. According to José Berrios, this program uses several committees including the EEO Advisory Committee and the Public Responsibility Committee. The purpose of the program is to establish a partnership between communities and the company; the company believes it will be able to recruit, develop and promote minorities only if it can develop a relationship with the communities in which these people live.

Gannett identifies promotable minorities and places them in the Gannett Management Development Program or the Gannett Executive Development Program. In order to train its managers to work with people from different cultures, Gannett puts them through a program called "EEO: The Competitive Edge."

Gannett is not only concerned with bringing diversity into its work force; it is also aggressive in showing diversity in its newspapers' articles and photos. It is commonplace, for instance, to pick up a copy of USA Today and see a front-page photo of a minority person portrayed in a positive light. Berrios says that there are programs to ensure that newsroom staff use sources that reflect diversity within the community.

The company's newsletter often shares advice on how to more fairly portray minority subjects in articles. A recent newsletter story pointed out the importance of including minority people in group photos that accompany feature stories. It noted that while the white reader may not notice the continual absence of people of color, minority readers will find it offensive.

According to Berrios, the company has established an EEO Advisory Committee (EEOAC) in each of its divisions. "Each committee," he says, "which consists of key managers, is designed to meet regularly and report to the corporate EEOAC on the hiring of minority employees, and on how more minorities can be brought into higher levels of management at the company." The Broadcast Division has recently expanded the focus of its advisory committee to include initiatives to actively recruit individuals with disabilities.

Gannett's different operating units use a diversity training syllabus titled "It Takes All Kinds" which offers managers a collection of case studies and other ideas to be presented to employees. "We provide them with an explanation of changing demographics and compelling business reasons for addressing diversity issues," says Berrios, "and we offer tips for interpersonal skills training sessions, a comprehensive group of video-based programs and case studies covering interviewing, performance improvement and coaching."

The company supports the black, Hispanic, Asian American and Native American journalist organizations and the National Black Media Coalition. In addition, the broadcast division supports the California Chicano News Media Association. The Gannett Communities Fund makes contributions to such minority organizations as the Puerto Rican Youth Development and Resource Center, the Minority Arts and Education Foundation, Concerned Black Men of Massachusetts, the Rockford Area Indochinese Service Center, the INROADS Program and the Martin Luther King, Jr., Memorial Society. The fund contributes more than $4 million to nonprofit groups each year.

According to Berrios, Gannett's Partners in Progress program includes an overall attempt to hire minority suppliers and vendors. While the Gannett Supply subsidiary has been responsible for identifying minority vendors since 1984, there has been no unified program to assess the amount of minority business conducted with the company. While there are no formal company-wide minority employee organizations, certain local Gannett businesses like *The Des Moines Register* have such groups.

Office locations: The corporate headquarters are in Arlington, Virginia, which is also where *USA Today*, Gannett News Service and Gannett Telemarketing, Inc., operate. The company has facilities in forty-one states in addition to the District of Co-

lumbia, Canada, Guam, the U.S. Virgin Islands, the United
Kingdom, France, Switzerland, Hong Kong and Singapore.

1100 Wilson Blvd.
Arlington, Virginia 22234
(703) 284-6000

GENERAL ELECTRIC COMPANY

General Electric is an international company with thirteen key business areas including aerospace; aircraft engines; household appliances under such brand names as GE, RCA and Hotpoint; financial services through GE Capital and Kidder, Peabody; industrial and power systems; lighting; medical systems; plastics; communications; electrical distribution; electric motors; transportation systems; and television broadcasting through its ownership and operation of NBC.

1990 revenues: $58,414,000,000
1991 revenues: $60,236,000,000
1992 revenues: $62,202,000,000

Number of full-time U.S. employees: 198,000

Percentage of these employees who are minorities: 11.6
    Black: 7.7
    Hispanic: 2.1
    Asian/Pacific Islander: 1.6
    Native American: .2

Number of people in the total management pool: 19,600

Percentage of minorities in the total management pool: 6.1

Founded in 1892 through the merger of the Edison General Electric Company and the Thomson-Houston Electric Company, General Electric was merged with RCA in 1986. While many consumers associate General Electric only with household appliances and light bulbs, that is but one-tenth of the company's business. Besides manufacturing heavy equipment and power systems, GE owns Employers Reinsurance Corporation and other insurance operations; Kidder, Peabody, the brokerage firm; and the NBC television network. With a total of thirteen industry segments, GE offers opportunities in engineering, finance, broadcasting, chemistry, medicine, law, accounting and many other areas.

Minorities hold many positions at General Electric including President of Genstar, a division of GE Financial Services; Vice President of Manufacturing; General Manager of Corporate Sourcing; Senior Systems Engineer in the GE Aerospace division; and General Manager in the GE Transportation Systems division. The board of directors has one minority member, Barbara Scott Preiskel, an attorney and the former senior vice president of the Motion Picture Association of America.

The company recruits at such black universities as Tuskegee, North Carolina A&T, Howard and Prairie View A&M, as well as at schools with substantial Hispanic enrollments like the University of Texas at El Paso. According to Gene Skogg, Manager of Recruiting and University Development at GE, the company has created strong recruiting relationships with minority student organizations at targeted colleges by asking GE employees to act as campus liaisons or "university executives."

Skogg says, "We have created a GE Speaker Series so that minority and nonminority managers from the company can visit the schools and discuss the newest issues relating to our research, technology and other advances in the areas of science and engineering. For several years, the company has also sponsored Student Leadership Conferences where we bring all the student leaders from these schools to our offices for daylong conferences on business topics and other issues."

According to Skogg, General Electric believes it can attract more minorities into its work force if it can create more personal contacts with student leaders at schools with large minority enrollments, reducing students' fears about entering and competing in a large corporation.

Because of GE's size and decentralization, diversity training programs are run differently in each of the separate businesses. The overall diversity initiative is informed by Dr. Eugene Andrews, who has the title of Manager of Workforce Diversity and is based at the corporate headquarters. "My job," says Andrews, "is to work with the diversity managers at each of our thirteen businesses. Since diversity is one of the company's major issues, we want to be sure that all of our businesses are given direction and understand the strategies that are being used at different locations."

Because there are different diversity managers and different needs at each of the thirteen businesses, programs differ. The GE Appliances division has a well-developed program which uses diversity awareness training workshops as well as a mentoring program to match minority employees with more senior managers. This division also has formed relationships with minority fraternities and sororities, as well as creating a summer internship program for visiting minority professors.

At another division, GE Capital, a cultural diversity office uses role models and mentoring to improve minority retention. At GE Medical Systems in Milwaukee, Karen Nelson is Manager of Diversity. A black manager who has been with the company since 1990, Nelson oversees an equal opportunity program that serves 8,000 employees. Andrews says the aerospace business is using an interactive video in its diversity workshops. "The video technology is so sophisticated," she says, "that it allows the workshop trainee to watch different scenarios and to change the race, ethnicity and gender of the actors in the scenario and to test the trainee's own biases. This type of training tool gives the trainee complete privacy and encourages him to be even more honest about his biases than he would in a group workshop. Here he is honest, but he is also challenged."

Andrews says that he and the thirteen diversity managers

come together quarterly to discuss any new successes or failures in the various programs. Since many of them are using different training consultants, they share their advice on those professionals as well.

One GE minority employee organization, the African American Forum, was established by black employees and is open to all business divisions. It encourages networking and mentor relationships, sponsors self-help programs that aid in employee development and meets three to four times a year. Asian and Hispanic employees have talked about forming a similar employee organization, but Andrews says the groups have not yet been created.

General Electric gives to such organizations as the NAACP, SER—Jobs for Progress, the National Urban League, the National Hispanic Scholarship Fund and the United Negro College Fund. Not only is GE's vice chairman, Edward Hood, on the board of the National Action Council for Minority Engineers, but the company has consistently been the largest donor to this organization, which provides scholarships for minority students entering the engineering professions. The company has focused large sums of money to aid public inner-city schools across the United States in such cities as Camden, New Jersey, Albuquerque, New Mexico, and Cleveland, Ohio.

The GE Foundation Scholars Program helps academically motivated minority students pursue engineering and business degrees. Besides providing a scholarship for all four college years, the Scholars Program also provides summer internships with GE businesses.

The company also aids students with a ten-year initiative called "Faculty of the Future," created to increase the number of minority researchers and professors in academia. The program gives money to colleges and graduate schools, which, in turn, award scholarships to minority individuals who are planning teaching careers and attempting to earn master's and doctoral degrees.

Each of GE's separate business divisions operates its own minority supplier vendor program.

Office locations: Corporate headquarters are in Fairfield, Connecticut. There are also facilities in all fifty states and Washington, D.C., as well as in more than fifty other countries, including the United Kingdom, Japan, Germany, Canada, China, India and Mexico.

3135 Easton Turnpike
Fairfield, Connecticut 06431
(203) 373-2211

GENERAL FOODS USA

As recently as 1983, General Foods was an independent consumer packaged foods company with its own board of directors and hundreds of famous-name products. Today the company is a division of Kraft General Foods, Inc., an entity that was created by the conglomerate Philip Morris when it bought General Foods and Kraft and then merged the two. Some products marketed by General Foods USA are Jell-O Gelatin and Puddings, Kool-Aid drinks, Minute Rice, Post Cereal, Maxwell House Coffee and Entenmann's bakery products.

Number of full-time employees: 5,561

Percentage of these employees who are minorities: 15.2
    Black: 9.7
    Hispanic: 3.0
    Asian/Pacific Islander: 2.3
    Native American: .2

Number of people in the total management pool: 4,128

Percentage of minorities in the total management pool: 15

Percentage of minority managers who comprise each managerial level:
    Executive vice president and president: 13
    Vice president: 7

Director:	11
Senior manager:	10

Salary information:

Product manager/district sales manager/financial manager/reasearch scientist:	$70,000–$112,000
Associate product manager/key account executive/supervisor/superintendent:	$50,000–$77,000
Assistant product manager/financial associate/senior scientist/department head/territory sales manager:	$40,000–$62,000
Sales representative/analyst/assistant engineer:	$33,000–$51,000
Accounting assistant/associate engineer:	$27,000–$42,000

While General Foods is seen only as an operating unit of Kraft General Foods, there is no question that General Foods deserves to be highlighted separately because of its history of retaining and promoting minority executives. The company has been particularly successful in training minority women.

High-ranking minority members at General Foods USA include Ann Fudge, Executive Vice President and General Manager of the Dinners and Enhancers Division (a $530-million business); Paula Sneed, President of the Foodservice Division (a $350-million business); Manmohan Mehra, a Director of Strategic Planning; Nancy Wong, Marketing Director in the Dinners and Enhancers Division; Raymond Garcia, District Sales Manager for Maxwell House Coffee Company, and John Parnell, Research Director with the Beverage Division.

There are two minority members on the board of directors

of General Foods' parent, Philip Morris: Richard D. Parsons, chairman of the Dime Savings Bank of New York and Dr. José Antonio Cordido-Freytes, president of C. A. Tabacalera Nacional.

The company uses its Minority Recruiting Task Force to develop strategies for recruiting at minority and other colleges and universities. At nonminority schools, General Foods' recruiting staff always assigns at least one recruiting contact for minority students. The company has also worked closely with the National Black MBA Association.

On the high school level, General Foods' minority internship program, Project Opportunity, has more than 1,500 alumni who have received summer jobs in General Foods' offices since 1967.

While the Diversity Management office is run day to day by Jean Spence, the company has a Diversity Management Steering Committee, chaired by General Foods' president. Ten senior executives also serve on the committee, which directs the strategy that is carried out by Spence's office. According to Spence, the majority of the company's employees have already been trained in the diversity program. It has become a part of what the company calls its Total Quality Management initiative.

In the area of minority employee organizations, General Foods has an Ethnic Diversity Council, established in 1989, through which employees advise senior management on how to improve such areas as recruiting and minority employee development. Thus far, the council has recommended ten projects to improve minority recruiting methods. According to Spence, management not only approved and implemented all ten recommendations, but also incorporated some of the same strategies in the overall recruiting program. The organization meets monthly and presents quarterly reports to the Diversity Management Steering Committee.

There is also a Black Sales Council, which has been active

since 1990 and is currently focusing on the retention of black salespeople. The Hispanic Sales Council is concentrating its efforts on recruiting more Hispanic sales employees.

Sheryl Adkins-Green is an enthusiastic supporter of and participant in the company's Ethnic Diversity Council. Since 1990, she has acted as the council's chairperson. As a black woman, she has seen firsthand that the company is willing to promote talented employees from every ethnic and racial background. A graduate of Harvard Business School, Adkins-Green has held a number of positions since coming to General Foods in 1983. "I am currently Category Manager in the Desserts division, where I am responsible for refrigerated desserts like Jell-O brand puddings and gelatins," she says, "but I've had some wonderful product manager positions that have introduced me to the wide range of products in our business."

Adkins-Green's experiences are a marketer's dream. Starting from the beginning of her career at General Foods, her positions have included Assistant Product Manager for Gains Pet Foods, Assistant Product Manager for Stove Top Stuffing, Associate Product Manager and Product Manager for Good Seasons Salad Dressing, Product Manager for Post Bran Flakes Cereal, Senior Product Manager for Pebbles Cereal, Group Product Manager for Adult Cereals, Category Manager for Cereal Development and Director of Productivity.

"When minority students are interviewing with employers," says Adkins-Green, "they need to look at the type of experience they'll be getting, but they also need to look at the diversity of the workplace. To begin with, they need to look at the diversity of the interviewers who come to the campuses. When I recruit with General Foods, I always make sure to attend the minority conferences that are sponsored at the various business schools like Columbia, Wharton, Harvard, Duke, the University of Michigan and Northwestern."

General Foods believes its mentoring program, available to all employees since 1990, is particularly beneficial to young minority professionals. It is entirely up to the mentee to say what type of assistance he or she would like from a mentor. According to Spence, "Typically, the mentee states his or her particular focus (e.g., career development, understanding corporate culture, utilizing company resources), and then we match him or her with a mentor who is two levels above the mentee and who is outside of the mentee's chain of command. We want the mentoring process to help with the informal information that a junior person sometimes misses." All mentors go through a training program.

Adkins-Green says new hires have been aided by activities sponsored by the Ethnic Diversity Council. She says that since the organization sponsors panel discussions and guest lectures, it makes minorities feel more welcome while also sensitizing nonminority employees to issues that are important to minority coworkers. "We sponsor networking events, roundtable discussions and other programs that contribute to the diversity efforts at the company," she adds.

General Foods has a long history of contributing to minority communities and causes. The company gives to such organizations as the National Urban League and National Council of La Raza.

Since 1987, the company has awarded two fellowships each year for minority employees to obtain a graduate degree (usually an MBA). The program provides up to $50,000 for university charges and gives each recipient a summer job at a General Foods office. Upon completion of the degree, the company places the graduate in a full-time management position in the recipient's sponsoring division.

Recently the National Organization of Chinese Americans selected General Foods' director of strategic planning, Flora Lee, to receive its Annual Asian American Corporate Achievement Award. Lee was recognized for her help in the launch of ECHO, a company employee volunteer group, as well as her fund-raising work with United Way.

The company's Manager of Minority Vending oversees the use of minority-owned suppliers and vendors. Each division has a specific goal, and progress toward these goals is reported quarterly to the Diversity Management Steering Committee.

Office locations: Kraft General Foods is in the Chicago area; the General Foods unit is in White Plains, New York, a suburb of New York City.

250 North Street
White Plains, New York 10625
(914) 335-2500

GENERAL MILLS, INC.

General Mills is a consumer packaged foods company which also owns and operates restaurant chains. The company is best known for its "Big G" ready-to-eat cereal division, which manufactures Cheerios, Wheaties, Total, Trix and Lucky Charms. General Mills also produces the Betty Crocker product lines, which consist of Hamburger Helper, Pop Secret microwave popcorn, Fruit Roll-Ups, Nature Valley Granola Bars and the many Betty Crocker cake mixes and icings. Gold Medal Flour, Bisquick, Yoplait Yogurt and Gorton Frozen Seafoods are other examples of the wide variety of foods marketed by General Mills. The company also owns and operates the Red Lobster Restaurants and a relatively new Italian dinner restaurant chain called the Olive Garden.

1990 revenues: $6,400,000,000
1991 revenues: $7,200,000,000
1992 revenues: $7,777,800,000

Number of full-time employees: 96,488

Percentage of these employees who are minorities: 25.7
    Black: 14.2
    Hispanic: 8.0
    Asian/Pacific Islander: 2.2
    American Indian: 1.3

Number of people in the total management pool: 5,658

Percentage of minorities in the total management pool: 10.9

Many minority professionals will tell you that they have crossed some corporations off of their job-hunting list because of the communities in which these companies are based—communities that might be "too white" or too insensitive to a minority population. This should not be a concern for those who are thinking about Minneapolis.

In addition, General Mills has an impressive record of promoting minorities and working with the minority community in Minneapolis. Luis E. Rubi, a Marketing Research Manager in the company's Big G Cereal division, says, "I am a Hispanic person who grew up in the Little Havana section of Miami and I had no problem fitting into the Minneapolis community." Rubi, who has been with the company since 1985, says people are wrong to assume that Minneapolis is a city without a minority population.

Dr. Reatha Clark King, President and Executive Director of the General Mills Foundation, says minority business and civic groups are very much alive in the city. "We give grants to the Minneapolis Economic Development Association so that they can continue to foster black entrepreneurship in the city, and we have supported the Minneapolis YMCA's Black Achievers Program for several years. We also help to sponsor an annual Martin Luther King Breakfast, where such people as Alex Haley and Cicely Tyson acted as guest speakers."

King, who is black, is one of many General Mills employees who praise the company for its activism. In 1992, she approached American Indian community groups to ask them to send her grant proposals for their activities or research. James Moody, director of the company's Equal Employment Opportunity office, is particularly proud of the fact that in 1992 31% of all marketing hires and 42% of all sales hires were minorities. He says that because the company employs many scientists and engineers, it sponsors the Associate Food Scientist Program, which "provides us an avenue to identify top black chemistry, food science and biology majors at the undergraduate level. We hire them at full salary while they work flexible hours and attend daytime and evening classes in the graduate program in food science at the University of Minnesota."

Moody says General Mills has an aggressive recruiting program which identifies minority candidates through active participation, including board memberships and other personal involvement with such schools and organizations as North Carolina A&T State University, Hampton and Lincoln universities, the National Association of Black Accountants, the National Society of Black Engineers, the National Black MBA Association, Lifeworks, Inc., and INROADS. The company not only attends the minority career fairs at universities like Ohio State, the University of Texas and Purdue, but it also provides financial support for the Minority Scholarship Fund at Washington University, the Minority Apprenticeship Program at Michigan State University, the American Indian Science and Engineering Scholarship Fund, the Consortium for Graduate Studies in Management, the Minority Engineering Program at Purdue and many others.

The company is also concerned with educating its entire employee pool on issues that arise in a diverse workplace. In 1989, General Mills initiated a company-wide training program, "Managing a Diverse Workforce," which teaches managers how to promote, appraise and work with employees in a diverse environment. In 1990, General Mills initiated yet another diversity training program called "Understanding and Managing Diversity," which teaches managers how to both work in and service a culturally diverse marketplace.

Sherri Hall, Manager of Customer Relations with the Olive Garden Restaurant division in Orlando, Florida, believes she has benefited from the company's willingness to work with and promote minority employees. "As a black person, I was initially concerned about where I would fit in when I started here in 1980. I came into the company as a secretary without a college degree. But because our senior management has made a commitment to reward talented and hardworking people, I now hold a management position."

In her capacity as head of the General Mills Foundation and as a vice president of the company, Reatha Clark King says she has been able to see that younger minorities at the company have access to all the company resources. "When I came to the company in 1988, I was looking for a place where a minority woman would feel comfortable. I wanted an environment where people are not looking over their shoulder to see what you are doing. And most of all, I wanted a place where I could be creative and productive—a place where I was trusted and respected." King says that young minority women frequently drop by her office for job and career advice. "I like the kind of informality that encourages this kind of mentoring. I don't want to be in an office where my secretary asks for an employee's life history before he or she can come in and talk to me about a special concern."

Chuck Chakrabarti is Director of Research and Development in the Sperry division, which manufactures flour and baking products. "When I came to General Mills in 1980, I looked at the company's market share and what the company stood for." Chakrabarti was born in India and holds a doctorate in food engineering. He is actively involved in minority recruiting and often gives special presentations at North Carolina A&T. He says job applicants are surprised to find that Minneapolis has a thriving minority community. "There are at least five thousand Indian people in the city, and it is easy to either assimilate or to stay within your own ethnic community. That's totally up to you."

The company has a black board member, Gwendolyn A. Newkirk, a professor and chairman of the Department of Consumer Science and Education at the University of Nebraska.

General Mills places emphasis on identifying and hiring minority vendors. The company holds periodic luncheons at the Minneapolis headquarters at which prospective minority suppliers sit with the appropriate General Mills buyers. General Mills also maintains financial or advisory participation with the Minority Purchasing Council, the American Indian Chamber of Commerce, the Urban League, the Minnesota Hispanic Chamber of Commerce, the Organization of Chinese Americans, the Twin Cities Opportunities Industrialization Center, Inc., and other groups that facilitate the development of minority businesses.

Office locations: Headquarters are in Minneapolis, with offices and plants across the United States. Offices are also located in Canada, Japan, England, Switzerland, Holland and France.

One General Mills Boulevard
P.O. Box 1113
Minneapolis, Minnesota 55440
(612) 540-2311

GENERAL MOTORS CORPORATION

General Motors is a manufacturer of cars, trucks and buses, as well as aviation equipment. Besides operating its Chevrolet, Pontiac, Buick, Oldsmobile, Cadillac and Saturn car divisions and the GMC Truck Division in the United States, it operates General Motors Europe, which includes a 50% ownership of Saab Automobile and various ownership shares of other auto manufacturers. The company owns Electronic Data Systems Corporation, which provides information technology to more than 7,200 corporate customers in twenty-seven countries; Hughes Aircraft Company, which produces air defense systems, missiles and satellites; Delco Electronics Corporation, which manufactures auto sound systems and semiconductor devices; and GMAC Mortgage Corporation, which provides mortgage services for home buyers, builders and developers.

1990 revenues: $124,700,000,000
1991 revenues: $123,056,000,000
1992 revenues: $132,400,000,000

Number of full-time U.S. employees: 403,000

Percentage of these employees who are minorities: 20.6
    Black: 16.8
    Hispanic: 2.8
    Asian/Pacific Islander: .7
    Native American: .3

Number of people in the total management pool: 34,703

Percentage of minorities in the total management pool: 12.5

Founded in 1908, General Motors is the only Big Three auto manufacturer that has kept its corporate headquarters in Detroit. The company's commitment to this city, with its large black population, is just one example of its desire to maintain ties to the minority community.

Minorities at General Motors hold such positions as Vice President of Consumer Market Development, Division General Manager, Manufacturing General Manager, Executive in Charge of Corporate Strategic Planning and General Director of Marketing and Product Planning.

There is one minority member on the board of directors: the Reverend Leon Sullivan, former pastor of Zion Baptist Church of Philadelphia, who was made famous by his Sullivan Principles, which established guidelines for companies that conducted business in South Africa.

Part of GM's commitment to minorities can be seen in the way the company has dealt with its continuing need to downsize its work force at management as well as nonmanagement levels. In spite of this downsizing, minority representation has not been reduced. In fact, the percentage of women and minorities has increased.

Jerry D. Florence, General Director of Marketing and Product Planning for the Cadillac Motor Division, says minorities are not only very visible at the company, but have also gained executive positions and have acted as mentors for younger minority managers. Florence, who has been with the company since 1983, is the head marketing person for Cadillac. He says, "Even before I got to Cadillac, when I was in the AC Rochester division, I was given the opportunity to lead the negotiations of a contract between GM and what was then the Soviet Union's largest automotive company, Volga Automotive Associated Works. I led a senior team in negotiating a plan for upgrading the Soviet cars' emission systems and standards."

Recognizing that there are minorities at GM who hold positions from which they direct as many as 15,000 employees, Florence says minority managers who learn the culture of the company have no problem advancing. He points out that two of the top ten managers in his division are black. "What I like about the company," he says, "is that I don't have to assimilate myself out of my ethnicity and my black culture in order to succeed here. I have found mentors who are both black and white—and I have never had to give up who I was in order to move ahead."

An important aspect of GM's business is its car and truck dealerships. Of its approximately 9,400 dealerships, almost 200 are minority-owned. The company has announced that it will increase the total number of black, Hispanic, Asian and Native American dealers by 40% by 1995. To improve opportunities and to address the concerns of minority dealers, GM created a Minority Dealer Steering Committee in 1990. The committee has helped create the Corporate Minority Dealer Development Department, which helps recruit and train new minority dealers.

The company recruits at such black universities as North Carolina A&T, Florida A&M, Howard, Southern, Tennessee State, Prairie View A&M, Tuskegee and Atlanta. GM assigns certain key executives to focus on specific schools. Balancing his schedule at Cadillac with his responsibilities as a key executive with Prairie View A&M University, Jerry Florence is able to coordinate scholarships, job offers and contributions that are awarded by GM to the university and its students. "I'm their contact person," Florence explains, "so if the school ever needs special financial support or would like the company to provide speakers for a special program, I will help coordinate the project. It helps to maintain good relations with a school that produces bright future employees."

The company established the General Motors Engineering Excellence Awards Program, which provides scholarships to eight historically black colleges. In 1991, twenty-seven students received awards of $15,000 for their sophomore, junior and senior years. Based on the guidelines of an agreement that GM established with the Equal Employment Opportunity Commission, the company has provided more than 2,000 educational scholarships for minority and women GM employees, including spouses and children.

To assist the development of minority lawyers, GM has established a $600,000 fund at six major law schools: Georgetown University, Howard University, the University of Michigan, Northwestern University, the University of Texas and Vanderbilt University. Each school receives $100,000, payable over five years.

Since 1987, the company has also sponsored an Annual Black Collegian Conference in Detroit at which more than 500 black college summer interns hear about full-time opportunities in the company and the auto industry.

Although diversity training has been conducted for the top leadership of the company, GM does not have a specialized diversity office or diversity training program. Diversity and affirmative action issues are handled locally.

Among the minority employee organizations at GM are the Black Executives Forum and the Hispanics Initiatives Group, which both aid in recruiting and serve as networking support groups.

In 1989, GM signed a Statement of Fair Share Principles with the NAACP, reaffirming the company's commitment to equal economic opportunities for blacks and other minorities. The principles stress equal treatment of minority employees and contractors in purchasing, banking, insurance, construction, advertising, dealerships, public relations, professional services, philanthropic contributions and employment.

Today it is difficult to attend a minority conference or convention that GM has not contributed to or sponsored. Among the many minority organizations that have benefited from GM's generosity are the Urban League, the National Council of La Raza, the NAACP and the Organization of Chinese Americans.

The company also supports the Leadership Education and Development (LEAD) Program, a summer program at the University of Michigan designed to introduce outstanding minority high school seniors from across the country to business, economics and management.

There is a minority vendor program at the company called the General Motors Minority Supplier Development Program. Since GM is currently purchasing more than $1 billion worth of products and services from minority suppliers, it easily has the largest minority vendor program. Besides being the first company to receive a leadership award from the National Minority Supplier Development Council, GM was recently named Corporation of the Year by the council for its support of minority contractors.

GM has also been aggressive in pursuing minority suppliers in the area of professional services. Since 1988, it has doubled the number of minority-owned law firms which represent it. GM asks majority-owned firms to allow their minority partners and associates to represent the company.

GM also has programs that encourage the participation of minorities in insurance and banking. In 1991, GM contracted to have $14.7 billion worth of property serviced by five minority insurance brokers. The company also maintains deposits in more than ninety minority-owned banks, which represents nearly every U.S. minority-owned commercial bank.

Office locations: Corporate headquarters are in Detroit; the company has offices in many other towns in Michigan and operations in thirty-two other states. There are plants in Canada and Mexico and assembly, manufacturing, distribution and warehousing operations in thirty-two other countries including Australia, Brazil, Chile, Colombia, France, Germany, Hungary, Ireland, Japan, Spain, Taiwan, the United Kingdom and Venezuela.

General Motors Building
3044 West Grand Boulevard
Detroit, Michigan 48202
(313) 556-5000

HALLMARK CARDS, INC.

Founded in 1910 by Joyce C. Hall, Hallmark manufactures greeting cards, calendars, candles, baby products, gift wrap, crayons, puzzles, party goods, mugs, wedding products, plush toys, pens and writing papers under such brand names as Hallmark, Ambassador, Crayola, Springbok and Magic Marker. Except for approximately 175 company-owned stores, all retail stores carrying the Hallmark name are independently owned, not franchised. Hallmark is a privately held company.

1990 revenues: $2,700,000,000
1991 revenues: $2,800,000,000
1992 revenues: $3,100,000,000

Number of full-time employees: 24,100

Percentage of these employees who are minorities: 11.6
    Black: 7.0
    Hispanic: 3.4
    Asian/Pacific Islander: 1.0
    Native American: .2

Number of people in the total management pool: 5,000

Percentage of minorities in the total management pool: 8.6

Percentage of minority managers who comprise each managerial level:
    Senior management: 2.3
    Middle management: 3.0
    Beginning management: 9.0

Hallmark is much more than a greeting card company. Besides owning retail outlets, it manufactures and markets toys, gift items, paper products and Crayola products. Because it is a privately held company and does not release the kind of information about itself that publicly held companies of its size do, few realize that Hallmark would rank in the top half of the *Fortune* 500 list of corporations. It is among the top fifty on *Forbes* magazine's list of the largest private companies. Hallmark is responsible for almost 50% of all greeting cards sold in the United States. Through the employee profit-sharing and ownership plan, employees own about one-third of the company. Hallmark remains very much a family-type company; chairman Donald J. Hall is the son of founder Joyce Hall.

The company has an Equal Opportunity Affairs department, created to develop company programs that address issues of interest to minority employees, suppliers and retailers. As Director of Corporate Diversity, Tom Wright is responsible for managing that department. Wright says his office provides employees with diversity awareness training through a day-and-a-half workshop. "In 1986, we began working with Dr. Price Cobbs, the consultant from Pacific Management Systems," says Wright, "in order to develop awareness training. We started by training our top executives and then moving on to all managers. We also use the Copeland-Griggs diversity training videotapes. Our workshops are run in groups of fifteen to twenty-five people, and our strategy is to get managers to discuss these issues with their team. Training is not the end-all; ongoing discussion is what must be promoted."

Minorities at Hallmark hold such positions as Managing Director for Continental Europe, Director of Internal Audit, General Manager of the Christmas Celebration Unit, Director of Corporate Diversity and Production Center Manager. There are no minorities on the board of directors.

The company recruits at such black universities as Prairie View A&M, Florida A&M and Clark-Atlanta. It recruits many

Hispanic students from such schools as the University of Arizona, the University of Texas at Austin and Arizona State University. To strengthen relations with these schools, Hallmark has a Visiting Educators Program, through which the company gives presentations on the company's operations, finance and marketing departments to college administrators. Tom Wright explains, "We build a better relationship with colleges when we can give professors tours of the company and Kansas City and introduce them to new business issues. As an example, we might have the director of minority engineering at Michigan State University or a director of placement from a college visit the company and meet with senior management for a three-day period." In 1992, Hallmark welcomed eight university faculty members.

The company also supports the Consortium for Graduate Study in Management, the nine-university alliance which helps prepare minorities for management-level positions in corporate America.

Hallmark makes a special effort to reach the minority job hunter through its monthly job opportunity bulletins, sent to such minority organizations as the Urban League, Blacks in Management, the National Black MBA Association and the League of United Latin American Citizens.

Since 1979, the company has hired minority interns through the national program INROADS. In 1985, Hallmark created its Minority Scholarship Internship Program, which offers ten-week paid internships and scholarship assistance for college students who major in communications and visual arts. It has awarded these internships and scholarships to minority students at such universities as San Jose State, Stanford and Northwestern.

Paul Quick, Internal Audit Director, is an enthusiastic supporter of Hallmark's minority internships and recruiting efforts. An MBA graduate of Pepperdine University, Quick has been with the company since 1983, beginning his career in sales a short time after he spent three summers at Hallmark as an IN-ROADS intern. "Having gained some great experience here as an intern for three summers," Quick says, "I had the opportunity to go to several other top companies like Procter & Gamble or IBM. I decided to come here because it was obvious to me that minority employees were given the same challenging responsibilities that everyone else was given."

Like other new hires, Quick went through the career development program, which required that he rotate through sales, administration, purchasing, inventory control and product management. Each assignment lasts three or four months. After the rotations, Quick worked in the sales division in Southern California for three years, and then returned to the Kansas City headquarters, where he worked for the Shoebox Greeting division for two years as a marketing strategist. "I then spent two years on the seasonal cards line as marketing manager," he says. In that position he was responsible for all cards and other merchandise that relate to all holidays other than Christmas. Now that he is in a finance position, he has gotten a broad view of the company's operations. "I've learned that as a black person, or as a member of any minority group," he says, "we have to demonstrate an ability to complete any job we are given."

Hallmark hires in sales, advertising, finance and many artistic disciplines that aid in product design. The company advertises many of these positions in such magazines as *Hispanic*, *Hispanic Business* and *Black Enterprise*.

According to Wright, Hallmark's CEO in 1989 created a Minority Advisory Council which consists of twelve employees and advises the CEO on the issues that the Hallmark minority community is concerned with. The group meets regularly and reports to the CEO periodically.

A minority employee organization called the Hallmark Minority Exchange was established in 1990. Since it is run by employees, it serves as a networking and social group, sponsoring picnics, holiday parties and other events.

Additional networking opportunities are available to minority employees at Hallmark through the company's Minority Forum, begun in 1989 by Wright's office. "Any minority professional from Hallmark can participate in the Minority Forum," says Wright. "We have quarterly meetings and talk about business and career development issues." In the past, such people as training consultant Dr. Price Cobbs and Dr. Gene Chavez of the Center for Intercultural Communication have made presentations at meetings of the Forum. "The Minority Forum exposes me to business issues that can be very helpful to the minority professional," says Quick.

Hallmark contributes to many minority organizations including the National Urban League, the National Council of La Raza, the NAACP, the United Negro College Fund and the Hispanic Chamber of Commerce. Through a partnership with a Kansas City inner-city performing arts magnet school, Hallmark has given a great deal of computer equipment and other supplies.

The Hallmark Minority Supplier Development Program was created in 1985 and currently spends in excess of $25 million each year with minority contractors. The company also attends conventions sponsored by the National Minority Supplier Development Council and regional purchasing councils.

Office locations: Hallmark's corporate headquarters are in Kansas City, Missouri. Most of its divisions are based there as well. There are offices and production centers in Kansas, Georgia, New York, Illinois, Texas and California.

P.O. Box 419580
Kansas City, Missouri 64141
(816) 274-5111

HEWLETT-PACKARD COMPANY

Hewlett-Packard makes computing and electronic measuring equipment for people in business, industry, science, engineering, health care and education. Among the company's 12,000 products are computers and peripheral products; testing and measuring instruments and computerized test systems; networking products; handheld calculators; medical electronic equipment; and instruments and systems for chemical analysis.

1990 revenues: $13,200,000,000
1991 revenues: $14,500,000,000
1992 revenues: $16,400,000,000

Number of full-time U.S. employees: 53,400

Percentage of these employees who are minorities: 19.5
    Black: 4
    Hispanic: 6
    Asian/Pacific Islander: 9
    Native American: .5

Number of people in the total management pool: 8,300

Percentage of minorities in the total management pool: 11

Percentage of minority managers who comprise each managerial level:
    Senior management: 7.0
    Middle management: 10
    First-line management: 16

Hewlett-Packard was founded in 1939 as a partnership of William Hewlett and David Packard, and the company's roster of officers and board members still carries the names of both founders and their offspring. The company's first product was an electronic test instrument known as an audio oscillator. The company's first major customer was Walt Disney Studios, which used the oscillators to develop a sound system for the movie *Fantasia*.

Minorities at Hewlett-Packard hold such positions as Group Controller, North American Field Operations Manager, Research Development Manager, General Manager and Division Marketing Manager.

The following areas at the company have strong minority representation: Entry-level engineers in Research and Development and Marketing is 26% minority. Information Technology is 21% minority. Product/process engineers in Research and Development and Marketing is 18% minority. There is a minority member on the company's board of directors: Condoleeza Rice, a black professor at Stanford University and a former adviser to President Ronald Reagan.

With 70 national recruitment teams and 106 local university recruitment teams, the company hires approximately 1,000 college and university students each year, and recruits at such black colleges and business schools as Howard University, Tuskegee University, Florida A&M University and North Carolina A&T State University, and at several universities with large Hispanic enrollments including the University of Texas at El Paso and the University of Texas at Austin. As a part of its minority recruiting effort, the company participates in career conferences sponsored by the National Black MBA Association, the National Hispanic MBA Association, the National Society of Black Engineers, the American Indian Science and Engineering Society and the National Urban League. Of new hires at Hewlett-Packard, 70% have technical degrees.

Hewlett-Packard hires employees with backgrounds in

many areas including computer science, engineering, business, chemistry and physics.

The company promotes diversity in the workplace through its Managing Diversity/Affirmative Action Program, introduced in 1988 as part of the management development curriculum. The three-day program consists of nine modules, each containing awareness exercises, definitions, business rationale, legal framework and practical application—all structured in a way that lets local Hewlett-Packard entities tailor the program to their specific needs. The program uses lectures, case studies, discussions, role-plays and videotapes. Besides cosponsoring the production of the seven videotapes in the "Valuing Diversity" program series from Copeland-Griggs Productions, Hewlett-Packard also produced five in-house videotapes. One tape, "Managing Diversity at Hewlett-Packard," highlights the experiences of company managers and employees who comment on working in diverse groups.

Certain offices and sites have developed their own Affirmative Action Advisory Boards. These Advisory Boards are all company-sanctioned. At the San Jose Components Group site in San Jose, California, the advisory board reports directly to the group's general manager. At the Avondale, Massachusetts, location, the Affirmative Action Advisory Board has created minority mentoring programs and community outreach programs, and has also hired diversity training consultants. At the Colorado Springs facility, the Advisory Board examines minority career development issues and meets quarterly.

To help further develop minority professionals at the company, Hewlett-Packard offers a specifically tailored seminar that helps high-performing minority professionals. According to Corporate Diversity Representative Nettie Calamia, the seminar is a six-day course for twelve to twenty participants at a time. It is conducted off-site in two three-day sessions scheduled one month apart and covers such topics as competitive behavior, goal setting, psychological barriers to performance, risk taking and personal motive assessment.

Leading a popular trend that is occurring at other diverse and progressive companies, Hewlett-Packard implements the "executive-on-loan" concept carried out through the Consortium for Graduate Study in Management in St. Louis, Missouri. Harry Portwood, a black corporate manager at the company, was recently a visiting faculty member at the consortium, which is on the Washington University campus. Portwood is also a member of a network of black managers who mentor rising black managers at the company.

Calamia says there are different minority employee organizations at various Hewlett-Packard facilities across the country. "There is a very active black employee network in our Waltham, Massachusetts, facility," she says, "and in 1988, black employees in the San Francisco area organized the Bay Area Black Manager Network. The network has developed mentor programs for new employees and has sponsored outside speakers and local community programs."

The company has sponsored a Hispanic Student Youth Day in the San Francisco Bay Area: Hispanic high school students were given tours of the company and attended workshops on team building and future careers. Another program the company has targeted at minority youth is its MESA (Math Engineering Science Achievement) Day, at which academic competitions and training sessions are set up for minority children in kindergarten through twelfth grade. Hewlett-Packard employees volunteer to teach the students at local MESA centers.

The company is extremely generous in its financial contributions to minority organizations. Its philanthropic program includes an Affirmative Action Grants Advisory Board which makes cash and equipment grants to educational and nonprofit community programs that focus on increasing representation and promote opportunities for minorities. According to Calamia, "In 1991, Hewlett-Packard awarded over $530,000 in cash and equipment to minority educational and community programs throughout the U.S."

The company also supports many student internship programs. It offers an internship opportunity called SEED (Student Employment and Educational Development), which emphasizes the participation of women and minorities. This summer internship program allows students to work in research and development, manufacturing, marketing, finance, personnel and information systems. Each student is assigned a mentor who helps the student make the transition from school to workplace.

The Minority Business Program, a minority supplier-vendor program created in 1968, spends more than $70 million each year with minority contractors.

Office locations: Headquarters are in the Silicon Valley town of Palo Alto, California; the company has offices in several other cities in California, as well as in Colorado, Idaho, Massachusetts, New Hampshire, New Jersey, Pennsylvania, Oregon, Washington State and Puerto Rico. There are also offices and manufacturing sites in approximately 100 countries including Brazil, Canada, China, France, Germany, India, Japan, Italy, Korea, Malaysia, Mexico, Spain, Singapore and the United Kingdom.

3000 Hanover Street
Palo Alto, California 94304
(415) 857-1501

HOECHST CELANESE CORPORATION

Hoechst Celanese is a manufacturer and marketer of chemicals, dyes, fibers, plastics, industrial gases, engineering ceramics, paints, synthetics and pharmaceuticals. The company is a division of the German conglomerate Hoechst AG.

1990 revenues: $5,300,000,000
1991 revenues: $6,800,000,000

Number of full-time U.S. employees: 20,941

Percentage of these employees who are minorities: 18.8
Black: 13.2
Hispanic: 4
Asian/Pacific Islander: 1.4
Native American: .2

Number of people in the total management pool: 1,215

Percentage of minorities in the total management pool: 7

Percentage of minority managers who comprise each managerial level:
Management: 7.4
Senior management: 6.7
Executive management: 8.3

Salary information:
Management: $81,000
Senior management: $110,000
Executive management: $150,000

Hoechst Celanese Corporation was created in 1987 when the German parent company, Hoechst AG, merged the Celanese Corporation, an American company, with Hoechst's American division.

Minorities at Hoechst Celanese hold such positions as Vice President of Finance and Administration, Group President, Vice President and General Counsel and Vice President of Communications. The company is owned and run by its German parent, and there is no American board of directors.

The company recruits from such black universities as North Carolina A&T, Prairie View A&M, South Carolina State, Tuskegee, Howard and Hampton, and at universities with large Hispanic enrollments such as the University of New Mexico. The company sponsors a corporate-wide internship program for students and offers a six-month co-op student work program that runs throughout the year.

In 1988, the company created the Hoechst Celanese Corporation Equality Committee to help define and achieve the company's vision of equality and diversity. The committee was made up of employees with different ethnic backgrounds, business locations and business functions, and was asked to develop strategies that would promote equality and diversity within the company. The committee was also to identify community and educational programs which the company could sponsor in order to continue building a diverse work force. By 1990, the committee submitted a complete proposal of strategies to the operating committee of the corporation.

By June 1990, the company held its annual conference, but this time with a focus on diversity issues. According to Jane McBunch, Director of Equality and Work/Life Initiatives, "One hundred fifty senior managers participated in sessions that explored personal biases and shattered stereotypes. Our CEO, Dr. Ernest Drew, encouraged all of the employee participants to sponsor similar conferences on diversity and respect for individual differences within their own separate business groups."

Some of Hoechst's offices and plants established their own Equality Committees as early as 1981, while others are still developing these groups now. Since these activities are decentralized, management at each location sets diversity objectives. In any case, these objectives must be consistent with the overall company's Equality Policy.

The diversity-related activities that have been sponsored by the different Hoechst offices include equality workshops and training programs for employees, implementation of a "buddy system" to ease new and transferred employees' adjustment to the community culture, a Diversity/Respect Conference, an Equality Awareness Day, development of a video presentation which addresses the changing population, implementation of a mentoring program which addresses developmental needs of minority and female employees, and establishment of a local Toastmasters Club which was motivated by a desire to help interested employees—particularly Hispanic employees—improve their public speaking and presentation skills.

The company's Advanced Materials Group has demonstrated a strong commitment to sensitizing its workers to minority issues. The group recently celebrated a monthlong tribute to Middle Eastern culture. Rick Ramirez, who serves as Director of Environmental Health and Safety Affairs in the Group's Chatham, New Jersey, office, says he was impressed by the creation, several years ago, of a minority council in his division. "The president of my division created and chaired a minority council," Ramirez explains, "which met monthly and discussed barriers in career opportunities for minority employees." Ramirez, who holds a bachelor's degree in forensic chemistry and a master's degree in health and safety management, has been with the company since 1981. Ramirez says he came to the company because of its progressive reputation and because of the opportunities to develop as a manager.

The president of Ramirez's division, the Advanced Materials Group, is Ed Munoz, a Mexican American executive who is also the chair of the division's Diversity Council. "Our Diversity Council," says Ramirez, "is supposed to develop awareness and sensitivity among employees. There are representatives on the council who come from different offices and plants throughout the country. They keep us informed about what is going on in the other offices, and they then report back to their coworkers after each of our quarterly meetings. Since I began serving as a representative, we have begun using the 'Valuing Diversity' videotapes and we have sponsored Diversity Conferences where managers hear presentations made by diversity consultants and other experts." The Diversity Council is also responsible for tracking the minority hiring and retention statistics.

The minority employee organizations that exist at Hoechst Celanese are those that are formed on a local level. No one group exists in all of the plants and offices.

Because of its continued support of SER—Jobs for Progress, Hoechst Celanese was recently given the Amigo of the Year Award by this organization, which addresses the needs of the Hispanic community.

The company supports many other minority organizations including the NAACP, the American Indian College Fund, the National Action Council for Minorities in Engineering, the National Urban League, the National Hispanic Scholarship Fund and the Interracial Council for Business Opportunities.

Besides being a member of the National Minority Supplier Development Council, the company has a Minority Vendor Steering Committee which directs purchases from minority contractors.

Office locations: Although its parent is based in Frankfurt, Germany, Hoechst Celanese has its headquarters in Somerville,

New Jersey. There are offices and plants in other areas of New Jersey and in Alabama, North Carolina, South Carolina, Kentucky, Virginia, Rhode Island and New York.

Route 202–206
P.O. Box 2500
Somerville, New Jersey 08876
(908) 231-2000

HOGAN & HARTSON

Founded in 1904, Hogan & Hartson is the oldest major law firm headquartered in Washington, D.C. The firm offers a broad range of practice areas including antitrust, banking, bankruptcy, communications, corporate, election law, environmental, estate planning, food/drug, health care, international trade, labor, litigation, lobbying, real estate, tax and transportation.

1991 revenues: $103,500,000 (as reported by *The American Lawyer*)

Number of partners: 75

Number of these partners who are:
  Black: 4

Number of associates: 210

Number of these associates who are:
  Black: 9
  Hispanic: 2

Number of summer associates employed in 1992: 40

Hogan & Hartson has a distinguished ninety-year history and employs attorneys who have served in many important government and political positions. Among attorneys currently at the firm are Paul Rogers, the former Florida congressman; William Fulbright, the former senator from Arkansas; Frank Farenkopf, the former head of the Republican National Committee; and

Tony Harrington, general counsel in Bill Clinton's presidential campaign.

Minority job-seekers should not assume that these credentials describe a firm that is a bastion of white male conservatism.

The firm's hiring committee, partnership selection committee and evaluation committee each include a black partner. Each summer a black partner at Hogan or at another major Washington firm throws a networking party to welcome the black law students working as summer associates in the Washington area. According to Vincent Cohen, a black partner who specializes in labor and litigation at Hogan, "These parties are important because they allow these young black professionals to find each other and to build their business and social networks."

Cohen also says that there is informal mentoring for black and Hispanic associates who join the firm. The minority partners meet almost monthly with the minority associates to discuss any systemic problems. "Of course these and other associates can stop in and talk to us at any time," says Cohen, "but over the past few years we have found that these monthly meetings create a greater comfort level for those who might otherwise feel nervous."

The firm assigns two mentors to each new associate. While it is not required, associates typically rotate through three or four departments over a year before settling on one practice area.

Hogan recruits from Howard University Law School. Like most progressive law firms, Hogan sends representatives to conferences sponsored by minority law student associations at various law schools around the United States, and the firm buys tables at or helps to underwrite fund-raisers sponsored by such minority organizations as the National Bar Association, the Washington Bar Association and Howard University's annual Charter Day Dinner. Two years ago, the attorneys at Hogan decided to forgo their spring dinner dance and instead gave $25,000 to five homeless organizations in the Washington area.

They had a much less lavish get-together at the black photo exhibit "Songs of My People" at the Corcoran Gallery of Art.

Several attorneys also volunteer with the firm's summer minority tutoring program, established in 1983. For two months, four days a week, Hogan attorneys meet with minority students who are about to enter law school. The students are given lessons on writing briefs, using the Socratic classroom method and preparing oral arguments.

One unique feature of Hogan is the fact that since 1970, it has had a pro bono department, officially the Community Services Department, staffed by a full-time partner and a full-time associate with the assistance of other associates who volunteer on a rotating basis. Cohen says the firm can have more of an impact on civic and community issues when it approaches them through a full-time department.

Office locations: The firm's main office is in Washington, D.C. There are satellite offices in Baltimore, Bethesda, Maryland, McLean, Virginia, Brussels, London and Warsaw.

555 Thirteenth Street, N.W.
Washington, D.C. 20004
(202) 637-5600

HONEYWELL INC.

Honeywell is an international manufacturer of control components, products, systems and services for homes and buildings, aviation and space. Its products are also used in industrial processes. It supplies the autopilot mechanisms, flight controls and navigation systems for many commercial and military aircraft. The company manufactures security systems as well as controls for heating and air-conditioning equipment.

1990 revenues: $6,309,100,000
1991 revenues: $6,192,900,000
1992 revenues: $6,222,600,000

Number of full-time U.S. employees: 59,000

Percentage of these employees who are minorities: 13.7
    Black: 5.1
    Hispanic: 5.2
    Asian/Pacific Islander: 3.0
    Native American: .56

Number of people in the total management pool: 4,717

Percentage of minorities in the total management pool: 6.40

A company that attracts those who are interested in engineering and manufacturing, Honeywell was originally known for its manufacturing of military defense equipment, control switches and mechanisms. After a recent five-year transformation, the company is now organized into four business groups: Space and

Aviation; Homes and Buildings; Industrial and International. Homes and Buildings represents the largest share—approximately 35%—of Honeywell's business.

Among the minority professionals at Honeywell are several Divisional Directors and Vice Presidents, as well as a Corporate Director and Group Executive. There is one minority member on the board of directors: A. Barry Rand, a high-ranking black executive at Xerox.

The company recruits minorities from many universities and has particularly aggressive recruiting efforts at several black colleges. According to Thomas Lawrence, Manager of University Relations and Minority Recruiting, "We have targeted five historically black schools with which we have formed partnerships. We have formed Industry Clusters with each of these institutions. The schools are Florida A&M University, North Carolina A&T University, Prairie View A&M University, Tuskegee University and Howard University."

Between 1986 and 1992, the company hired twenty-two permanent and thirty-seven summer employees from Florida A&M, twelve permanent and twenty-five summer employees from Howard, twenty-two permanent and sixty-three summer employees from North Carolina A&T, ten permanent and fourteen summer employees from Prairie View A&M, and twenty permanent and forty-six summer employees from Tuskegee.

Honeywell has also been very successful at recruiting Hispanic students from the University of Puerto Rico and the City College of New York. The company occasionally loans top-level researchers to work as instructors at universities with large minority enrollments.

Lawrence points out that Honeywell has also contributed financially to these schools to establish research grants, engineering facilities and professorships. The company also provides financial support for scholarships through the Society of Hispanic Professional Engineers, as well as support for scholarships distributed by the American Indian Science and Engineering Society.

According to Barbara Jerich, Director of Workforce Diversity, Honeywell began a diversity training program for management in 1986. Originally the company used such outside consultants as Merlin Pope & Associates and J. Howard & Associates. Now diversity training is performed by in-house staff for all levels of supervisors.

Since 1990, the corporate office has had a Diversity Council which identifies new issues and suggests new programs. The council, which meets monthly, includes various managers, as well as the heads of the minority employee organizations. Diversity Councils are being formed at individual offices and plants in Arizona, Texas and Florida.

There are several minority employee organizations at the company. According to Reed Welke of Honeywell's Office of Workforce Diversity, these include the Asian-American Council of Honeywell, the Honeywell Black Employees Council, the American Indian Council and Hispanos Honeywell. Welke says the Black Employees Council, formed in the mid-1970s, offers diversity awareness training and career development programs for its participants. Each organization meets monthly during work hours and has access to funding from Honeywell. "Employees need to feel connected to their company and they need to feel that they are being heard," Welke says. "These organizations give the employees greater access to each other while also providing them with a real voice in the company."

According to Tom Lawrence, black employees in Minneapolis are currently forming another group called the Honeywell Black Planning Committee.

Within the minority community, Honeywell is a generous contributor to several engineering organizations, as well as to the NAACP through the Roy Wilkins Scholarship and the Honeywell/NAACP Scholarship Fund, the National Consortium for Graduate Degrees for Minorities in Engineering and Science Inc., the Urban League and the New Mexico Society for Hispanic Professional Engineers.

The Honeywell Foundation contributes a great deal to schools that educate minority students. It awarded $300,000 to Florida A&M University for engineering scholarships and $100,000 to that university's School of Business; $240,000 to Howard University's engineering program; $320,000 to North Carolina A&T State University to establish research grants and endow science and accounting scholarship funds; $250,000 to Prairie View A&M University to establish a professorship in electrical engineering and award research grants; and $300,000 to establish the General Chappie James Physical Education and Engineering Facility at Tuskegee University.

Although Honeywell has a minority supplier-vendor program, it is not administered at a central office. According to Welke of the Workforce Diversity office, thirty separate offices and plants manage and monitor their own relationships with minority contractors.

Office locations: Corporate headquarters are in Minneapolis, with other major offices in Phoenix, Arizona; Clearwater, Florida; Albuquerque, New Mexico; and Freeport, Illinois. Manufacturing facilities are in San Diego, California; Golden Valley, Minnesota; Akron, Ohio; Richardson, Texas; and York, Pennsylvania. There are also offices and plants in more than ninety other countries including India, Germany, Switzerland, Venezuela, Mexico, Belgium, Malaysia, Canada and China.

Honeywell Plaza
P.O. Box 524
Minneapolis, Minnesota 55440
(612) 870-5200

INTERNATIONAL BUSINESS MACHINES CORPORATION

IBM is the world's largest manufacturer and marketer of computer technology, software and business equipment. Founded in 1914 by Thomas Watson, an inventor, the company also offers its customers a wide range of information services.

1990 revenues: $69,018,000,000
1991 revenues: $64,792,000,000
1992 revenues: $64,523,000,000

Number of full-time employees: 205,500 U.S., 373,000 worldwide

Percentage of these employees who are minorities: 17.5
    Black: 9.1
    Hispanic: 3.5
    Asian/Pacific Islander: 4.6
    American Indian: .3

Number of people in the management pool: 26,945

Percentage of minorities in the total management pool: 13

Although IBM has recently undergone a large reorganization and shrunk its employee base by more than 40,000 employees the company has always been a corporate leader in providing opportunities for minority employees. Unlike other major corporations that waited until the Civil Rights Act of 1964, IBM had formulated and published its equal opportunity policy in 1953. It was the first corporation to contribute to the United

Negro College Fund, in 1944—long before many in corporate America recognized the talented students who were graduating from historically black colleges.

Today minority members hold such positions as Vice President of Business Development; Vice President of Information and Telecommunications Systems; Treasurer; Vice President of Technical Plans and Controls, Research; and General Manager of Marketing and Services. In 1991, IBM formed the $2-billion revenue-producing IBM Federal Systems Company and named Arthur Johnson president and chief operating officer. Johnson, a black executive who has spent most of his career working with IBM's federal customers, had served as general manager of company facilities in Houston and Westlake, California.

The company has one minority member on its board of directors: John Slaughter, president of Occidental College.

According to Ted Childs, Director of Workforce Diversity Programs, the company offers a diversity training program for managers which was designed with the help of the Sable Group, a diversity consulting firm in Connecticut. The program, "Realizing the Diversity Advantage," uses lectures and role-playing. "We have been using this four-hour training module since 1991," says Childs, "and we include it in our New Managers School at our Armonk headquarters, as well as at other company locations when training our more senior managers." Childs says the diversity training program is designed to examine a manager's biases and show him or her why such views are incorrect, unfair and unproductive.

Although the company has no minority employee organization like those found at Xerox or Polaroid, and although there is no task force or committee that focuses on minority issues, the company does have the IBM Mentoring Program, which is intended to provide a special mentoring process for minority or female employees hired since 1990.

"We created the Mentoring Program," says Childs, "in

order to help people adjust to the business and to provide them with early career assistance. We wanted these new employees to have a place where they can get penalty-free advice." Mentors, who are not necessarily minorities, are assigned to new employees and are asked to commit to a two- or three-year relationship.

A black employee who has been with the company since 1967, Childs tells a story which describes IBM's approach to making minorities feel comfortable in the work environment. "When we first stepped up our efforts to recruit more blacks to work in one of our large upstate New York office complexes," he recalls, "we realized we had to do more than offer jobs to these people. We knew that we had to make sure that the community would be hospitable as well. We set up a housing office and got local residents and landlords to post their apartment vacancies. To make sure that our new black employees would not be faced with prejudiced landlords, we first sent one black IBM personnel staffer and then a white IBM personnel staffer to each of the apartments. If they didn't feel that the landlord was going to be hospitable to our new black hires, we just took the apartment off of the housing list."

Childs adds, "IBM realizes that employees will stay with us when we create a hospitable environment. And part of that environment is the ethnic tolerance that is demonstrated both inside and outside of our offices."

The company recruits at a number of black universities including Hampton, Tuskegee, Florida A&M, Atlanta, Xavier, Howard and Southern.

Although IBM recruits at many colleges with large minority populations, creates partnerships with such Hispanic groups as SER—Jobs for Progress and attends minority-oriented job fairs, the company has no plans to create formal on-site minority professional groups. Childs says, "We want our managers to be the focal point for all problem issues. As a black executive, I have a responsibility to be a role model for younger minority employees. Since the minority executives here are easily approachable, we do not see the necessity to establish a formal group."

The company has a Minority Campus Executive Program in which IBM executives are assigned to act as liaisons to a minority college or graduate school. The executives visit the campus frequently, meet with professors, deans and the president and identify ways in which IBM can aid the school through providing resources, managers to teach specific courses, etc. Childs says, "When you create this type of a relationship with a school, you can better identify qualified students, and they can better evaluate you as a potential employer."

Maria Magana, a senior engineer and manager based in San Jose, California, says, "I have been here since 1974, and what's kept me at IBM is the encouragement and support I get from the company whenever I want to give back to the community and participate in minority activities. I have traveled to various California high schools with large Hispanic enrollments in order to discuss careers in the science fields. I also work with Project Breakthrough, a program we sponsor, where professionals act as mentors to minority students at six local colleges. Since they are all in the engineering disciplines, we give them workshops on related careers and we hire many of them for summer employment."

A member of the Hispanic Professional Engineers Association, Magana says an important part of every management review assesses the effort a manager has made to recruit and retain minority employees.

The company established a United Negro College Fund IBM Faculty Fellowship Program through which IBM sponsors certain minority college professors so that they can pursue and complete their advanced degrees. In 1992, IBM pledged $10 million to the fund's Campaign 2000. The company has also supported minority students through scholarship programs like those sponsored by the National Action Council for Minorities in Engineering, Chinese for Affirmative Action and the National Hispanic Scholarship Fund.

Since 1971, the company has had a Faculty Loan Program in which fifty-five IBM employees are "loaned" to colleges where most of the students are black, Hispanic, Asian or American Indian. The employees receive full pay and benefits while they spend a year acting as instructors in computer science, engineering, mathematics or business administration. "Students will be able to see minorities who have had successful technical careers," says Hubert Whigham, an IBM employee from Atlanta who participates in the program. "Hopefully, the students will want to emulate them." In 1992, IBM executives were on loan at the Institute of American Indian Arts in Santa Fe, New Mexico; Navajo Community College; Tuskegee University; National Hispanic University; Florida A&M University; Morehouse College; Spelman College; Southern University; Hampton University; the University of Puerto Rico; and the American Indian Science and Engineering Society in Boulder, Colorado.

IBM has had a successful minority vendor program since 1968.

Office locations: Headquarters are in Armonk, New York, outside New York City. Offices are located in many other cities across the United States and in 138 countries.

Old Orchard Road
Armonk, New York 10504
(914) 765-1900

JOHNSON & JOHNSON

Johnson & Johnson is the world's largest and most comprehensive manufacturer of health care products serving the consumer, pharmaceutical and professional markets. It manufactures body powder, cotton swabs, lotions, contact lenses, antibacterial medicines, cold medicines, dental rinses, bandages, orthodontic appliances, tampons, surgical appliances and numerous prescription drugs. J&J's brand names include Tylenol, Imodium A-D, Monostat 7, Acuvue Contact Lenses, Band-Aid Brand Bandages and Shower to Shower.

1990 revenues: $11,232,000,000
1991 revenues: $12,447,000,000
1992 revenues: $13,753,000,000

Number of full-time U.S. employees: 32,650

Percentage of these employees who are minorities: 24.7
    Black: 11.8
    Hispanic: 8.1
    Asian/Pacific Islander: not released
    Native American: not released

Number of people in the total management pool: 5,357

Percentage of minorities in the total management pool: 12.7

Percentage of minority managers who comprise each managerial level:
    Executive (board-level equivalent):   6.6
    Upper management (director level):   11.3

Middle management (department manager): 11.6
Lower management (supervisors)   18.0

Founded more than 100 years ago, Johnson & Johnson has grown into a conglomerate with nearly thirty individual subsidiaries. The company is organized into three primary business segments: Consumer, Professional and Pharmaceutical. Besides recently receiving the U.S. Department of Labor's Opportunity 2000 Award in 1991 for its commitment to attracting and promoting people of color and women, J&J is often credited with the revitalization of its hometown of New Brunswick, New Jersey, a largely minority-populated community that was suffering economically until the early 1980s.

Both the corporate parent and its many divisions have shown that Johnson & Johnson is an enthusiastic employer of minority professionals. According to Marion HochbergSmith, Director of Corporate Equal Opportunity, minorities at Johnson & Johnson hold such positions as president of the subsidiary Chicopee Worldwide, Vice President of Operations, vice president of an internal division and Assistant Treasurer of Investor Relations. There is one minority member on the company's board of directors: Ann Dibble Jordan, a black former assistant professor at the University of Chicago and a director of the Child Welfare League, Primerica and ABC Capital Cities.

The company recruits at such black schools as Hampton University, Howard University, Florida A&M University and Morehouse College, and at universities with large Hispanic enrollments such as the University of Texas at Austin. Johnson & Johnson also subscribes to the service HispanaData, which provides job recruiting data on Hispanic university students throughout the country.

The company supports many black colleges when its black executives volunteer with the National Urban League's Black Executives Exchange Program, which brings black corporate executives to historically black colleges to teach seminars and discuss their experiences as minority managers in the business world.

Clarence Lockett is one black Johnson & Johnson executive who has participated in the Black Executive Exchange Program. An assistant treasurer at the corporate parent, Lockett says, "The program shows upcoming generations that they can go out and accomplish their goals. They can learn the expectations of the business community and learn how to prepare themselves to take advantage of their opportunities."

Johnson & Johnson's many divisions hire a large number of black and Hispanic students for summer internships through the INROADS program. The company's Minority Industrial Engineering Scholarship Program provides summer jobs and scholarship money to top black and Hispanic high school graduates who want to pursue undergraduate engineering degrees. Students are also aided by Johnson & Johnson employees who act as mentors for the Minority Access to the Professions Scholars Program, which teaches students about the work ethic and surviving in a large corporate environment.

Jim Rose, Vice President of Human Resources at Johnson & Johnson's Ortho Pharmaceuticals division, is extremely proud of the company's diversity training program, Managing Diversity, which was begun in 1986. "One of the purposes behind our diversity program," says Rose, "is to aid the upward mobility of our minority employees. At the beginning of our diversity initiative, we used the Philadelphia consulting firm Elsie Y. Cross Associates to develop the educational phase of our program. Now we are in the cultural phase of the program."

Rose comments on what had happened at the company before the diversity program was implemented: "We saw that minority employees were leaving us after they got here. We could recruit them, but we saw that when they realized that promotions were not coming their way, they left quickly. Both women and people of color didn't feel valued or respected."

Rose says that in getting employees to celebrate a changing

culture, they can be better sensitized to people who come from different ethnic and racial backgrounds. He established a Cultural Change Committee made up of employees from different management levels and ethnic groups. The group sent out a survey to all employees to identify attitudes regarding different cultures and then began implementing weeklong and three-day workshops to discuss stereotyping and other sources of conflict in a multicultural workplace.

Having tracked the turnover and promotion rates of minorities before the Managing Diversity program was implemented, Rose says both rates have improved to a point where diversity training has proved itself an important aspect of running a good business.

Several minority employee organizations at Johnson & Johnson help minority managers mentor each other or network within or between divisions. They are endorsed and supported by the company, which often provides the groups with corporate facilities, speakers, advisers and other services. An organization for black employees called HONOR (Helping Our Neighbors with Our Resources) was formed in 1976 as a regional group to improve networking among minority employees. The organization raises money to provide scholarships and holiday gifts to inner-city children.

In 1989, the Association for Minority Women's Issues was begun to help minority women employees network and develop a more comfortable environment. In several of the Pennsylvania and New Jersey plants and offices, other minority employee groups focus on a wide range of minority issues.

HochbergSmith says the minority employee groups are good for the company. "I am also glad to see that we have a great deal of mentoring here," she adds. "I feel that you can never have enough mentors. Hitching yourself to just one person may not be appropriate because people leave the company, and when that happens, the mentor can end up leaving behind an employee who has no other support system. And mentors are not just for new hires. We feel that they can help people who want to channel their careers in new directions."

HochbergSmith adds that many plants and offices at Johnson & Johnson, such as those in Florida, North Carolina, Arkansas and Georgia, offer English as a Second Language courses to facilitate the fuller participation in the work force of non–English-speaking employees. The company hires professors from local community colleges to teach these courses.

The company's Contributions Program donates to many minority organizations and programs that serve the minority community: the National Puerto Rican Coalition, the NAACP, SER—Jobs for Progress, the Urban League and the U.S. Hispanic Chamber of Commerce. Because it manufactures so many health care products that can benefit medically underserved people, Johnson & Johnson often donates products in addition to cash. Overall, the company donates in excess of $40 million annually.

The company funds a community-based program, the Head Start–Johnson & Johnson Management Fellows Program, which U.S. Secretary of Health and Human Services Louis Sullivan praised as a program "designed to provide Head Start Directors with the opportunity to receive the highest-quality management education available in America." Head Start is one of the most successful preschool education programs in the country. J&J's program trains directors who work in the hundreds of Head Start centers around the United States with skills that can better serve the many minority and disadvantaged children who attend Head Start.

The company also sponsors the Johnson & Johnson Bridge to Employment Program, which provides young people who have dropped out of school or are at risk of doing so with counseling and training in clerical and other employment skills. It has selected largely minority communities in Tampa, Florida; Albuquerque, New Mexico; Ponce, Puerto Rico; and central

New Jersey and provided them with $25,000 grants to create employment training programs for their young residents.

J&J has also formed a partnership with the National Council of La Raza through which it gives grants to nonprofit organizations that work with medically underserved communities in the United States and Puerto Rico.

The company's Minority Vendor Program actively seeks out and develops relationships with companies owned by women and minorities. Johnson & Johnson's operating companies spend approximately $80 million each year with minority contractors.

Office locations: Johnson & Johnson is based in New Brunswick, New Jersey, and has a large share of its U.S. operations in the New Jersey area. The company also has offices and plants in California, Massachusetts, Florida, Ohio and Pennsylvania. There are operations in Canada, Argentina, Colombia, Venezuela, England, France, Austria, Germany, Greece, Hungary, Italy, Portugal, Spain, Switzerland, Australia, China, Hong Kong, India, Japan, Kenya, Malaysia, Zambia and Zimbabwe.

1 Johnson & Johnson Plaza
New Brunswick, New Jersey 08933
(908) 524-0400

KELLOGG COMPANY

While Kellogg's is best known as a producer of breakfast cereal, it is a diversified international company that manufactures and markets a number of convenience foods. It manufactures such cereals as Rice Krispies, Corn Flakes and Special K, as well as Pop-Tarts Toaster Pastries and frozen pies and waffles under the Mrs. Smith's and Eggo labels. The company also produces soups and other food products for restaurant and institutional use.

1990 revenues: $5,181,400,000
1991 revenues: $5,786,600,000
1992 revenues: $6,019,000,000

Number of full-time employees: 6,595 in Kellogg corporate and U.S. Food Division

Percentage of these employees who are minorities: 17.4
    Black: 13.1
    Hispanic: 2.5
    Asian/Pacific Islander: 1.5
    American Indian: .3

Number of people in the management pool: 792

Percentage of minorities in the total management pool: 10.7

Salary information:
    Officers: $125,000–$250,000
    Directors: $75,000–$125,000
    Managers: $50,000–$75,000
    Supervisors: $30,000–$50,000

Founded in 1906, Kellogg has long been the world's largest producer of ready-to-eat cereals. Its products are sold in more than 150 countries.

It is apparent that the company is enthusiastic about its commitment to minority hiring and retention. The chairman's office publishes and distributes to Kellogg employees an astounding amount of EEO literature and policy information, constantly reminding managers of the importance of diversity. A clear Equal Employment Opportunity/Affirmative Action policy is implemented through a decentralized method. Each plant location has annual meetings with managers to discuss successes and goals in hiring and placement. Corporate headquarters arranges meetings with all area vice presidents to discuss the same concerns as at the plant locations.

The Kellogg board of directors has two minority board members: Dolores D. Wharton, president of the Fund for Corporate Initiatives, Inc., in New York, and Claudio X. Gonzalez, chief executive officer of Kimberly-Clark de Mexico in Mexico City. Minorities at Kellogg's hold such positions as Senior Vice President of Corporate Affairs, Executive Vice President of Sales and Marketing, Senior Vice President of Nutrition Marketing, Director of Business Information Development and Program Director of Worldwide Technology.

Kellogg's managerial staff can be broken down into four levels: managers, third-level executives, second-level executives and top-level executives. Minorities make up 8% of all managers, 3% of all third-level executives and 7% of all top-level executives. At the time of our survey, there were no minorities among the second-level executive staff.

Of the professional hires filled by outside candidates in 1991, 13% were minorities. The summer employment program, which has been further developed to attract minorities to professional-level positions, had a 15% minority makeup in 1991.

The company recruits at such predominantly black universities as Southern, Clark-Atlanta, Hampton, Alabama A&M and Tuskegee.

Developmental programs to assist and encourage the promotion of qualified minorities to upper management include specially selected external programs such as the American Management Association Management Program, the Fund for Corporate Initiatives—Young Executive Program and on-the-job training assignments.

One of the highest-ranking minority executives at Kellogg is Joseph Stewart, Senior Vice President of Corporate Affairs. Stewart, who has been with the company since 1979, had run a school nutrition program in Washington, D.C., before coming to Kellogg. "There was no question that I was concerned about working in a company that was supportive of minority managers," says Stewart, who has a bachelor's degree in nutrition and came to the company as Director of Child Nutrition Marketing. "Before I accepted the offer here, it was important that I first meet the other senior officers. During my early years here, I was mentored by white men, but they were managers who had no hangups on minority issues."

Since Stewart also had a background in public affairs and a great knowledge of regulatory issues through his experiences in the Washington school system, he moved into the position of Director of Corporate Communications after a year and a half with Kellogg. In 1984, he was made Vice President of Corporate Affairs, and eventually became responsible for a staff of fifty-four employees who dealt with consumer affairs, government relations, public relations, investor relations support and global media and strategy.

"Nobody walks around here expecting to get nailed for asking the wrong questions," says Stewart. "This is a wide-open organization that welcomes mentor relationships. I have mentored many young minority managers who are looking for advice on their careers here. There is a history of minority success here, and that exists because there is a high comfort level when it comes to talking about issues of race and ethnicity." Stewart says all officers are responsible for reporting on EEO progress in hiring and promotions within their departments.

Kellogg has an intensive one-day EEO Training Program directed to all supervisors and managers. Thus far, 900 have participated. The company says one goal of the program is to show how affirmative action benefits all employees.

According to Annette Zalner, Manager of Personnel Adminstration, there was a pilot diversity training program at the San Leandro, California, plant, but no company-wide program has been implemented. "In 1991," says Zalner, "the company established a task force to develop and evaluate plans for diversity training. That task force has been formalized into a fourteen-member Diversity Steering Committee which is made up of senior managers as well as support staff from different ethnic backgrounds. The committee meets periodically at our headquarters and is currently looking at what other companies are implementing in the area of diversity training."

Outside its own work force, Kellogg has demonstrated its commitment to minority issues through its Minority Accounting Scholarship Program and an unusual "Challenge Your Horizons in Flight" Summer Program aimed at introducing minority high school students to careers in aviation.

Besides recruiting at many universities with high minority enrollments, Kellogg representatives attend career expos where they establish networks with minority students. Each year, the company attends such programs as the University of Illinois Minority Career Day, the Howard University Career Day and the Purdue University Black Engineer Career Fair.

Kellogg's philanthropic efforts include financial and manpower contributions to fund-raisers for the United Negro College Fund. Many company employees serve as telephone volunteers during the UNCF's annual "Lou Rawls Parade of Stars Telethon." During the telethon, Kellogg matches every employee dollar with an additional $2 contribution. SER, Inc., the NAACP and the National Urban League are also supported by Kellogg. Community grants are given by the W. L. Kellogg Foundation, a private grantmaking institution created by the company's founder.

In spite of its enthusiastic support of many minority causes, the company continues to conduct business in South Africa.

Kellogg is an active member of the U.S. Government's Minority Bank Time Deposit Program and maintains time deposits and operating accounts with more than thirty-five minority-owned banks. Since 1984, the company has tracked and developed relationships with minority suppliers. Today the company spends approximately $16 million each year with minority-owned businesses.

Office locations: Products are manufactured in seventeen countries, with cereal plants and offices in Battle Creek, Michigan; Omaha, Nebraska; Memphis, Tennessee; San Leandro, California; and Lancaster, Pennsylvania. There are overseas facilities in Spain, Japan, Venezuela, Great Britain, Mexico and France.

One Kellogg Square
Battle Creek, Michigan 49016
(616) 961-2000

LEVI STRAUSS & CO.

Levi Strauss & Co. is the world's largest apparel manufacturer. Besides making Levi's jeans and jeans-related products for men, women and children, the company manufactures and markets Dockers branded products and other casual sportswear for men and women.

1990 revenues: $4,200,000,000
1991 revenues: $4,900,000,000
1992 revenues: $5,600,000,000

Number of full-time employees: 22,894 in the U.S., 31,000 worldwide

Percentage of these U.S. employees who are minorities: 56
    Hispanic: 42
    Black: 9
    Asian/Pacific Islander: 4
    American Indian: 1

Number of people in the management pool: 1,429

Percentage of minorities in the total management pool: 35

Although Levi Strauss is more than 140 years old, with annual revenues approaching $5 billion, the company is still privately owned and run by descendants of the founder, Levi Strauss. Robert D. Haas, the youthful and liberal great-great-grand-nephew of Levi Strauss, is chairman of the board and CEO.

Haas was a Peace Corps volunteer and a White House Fellow in the Lyndon Johnson administration. This Harvard Business School graduate and former consultant with McKinsey & Company is also one of the most prominent business leaders to speak out on AIDS research. Because of the company's strong support of gay rights, it took a vocal stand against the Boy Scouts when that organization announced it would not permit gays to join.

The company offers its minority employees the opportunity to express their concerns about ethnic issues through the Diversity Council, established in 1989, which meets monthly and includes representatives from Levi Strauss's many minority employee organizations. The twelve-member council serves as an advisory and resource group to help senior management on minority issues and the company's diversity program.

According to Michael Giannini, Manager of EEO Programs and Human Resource Policies, minority employees at Levi Strauss belong to such company organizations as the Hispanic Leadership Association, the Black Professional Organization, and the Asian and Pacific Islander Employee Association. The company also has a Gay and Lesbian Employee Association. The company provides some funding to these organizations, and senior management tries to meet with each organization at least two or three times each year. Giannini says that while each organization focuses on networking and mentoring its members, the groups also sponsor guest speakers and schedule activities during celebrations like Asian Awareness Week and Black History Month.

Each group sponsors social and business get-togethers to improve networking and quality of life among minority employees. The Black Professional Organization publishes a quarterly newsletter called *Newsline* which spotlights a different black manager in each issue, as well as providing information on new developments, listing new black employees, highlighting upcoming social events and featuring poetry and book reviews by black writers and journalists. The Hispanic Leadership Association also publishes a quarterly newsletter, *El Noticiero*. A recent article profiled Ed Alvarez, manager of the company's Kastrin Street sewing plant in El Paso, because of his recent appointment to the board of directors of the Levi Strauss Foundation. Alvarez is also an officer of the Hispanic Leadership Association at Levi Strauss.

According to Giannini, minorities at Levi Strauss hold such positions as President of the Britannia Division, Vice President of Tax and Customs, Deputy General Counsel, Vice President of Sales, Director of Risk Management, Assistant General Counsel and Assistant Treasurer of the International Division. Nine of the twelve board members are related to the Haas family. There is one minority board member, Patricia Salas-Pineda, who is also a director with the NUMMI auto company, a joint venture of General Motors and Toyota.

There is a Valuing Diversity Training Program for all employees. It is part of what Levi Strauss calls its CORE Curriculum training. According to Giannini, the diversity program is a four-day off-site course which began in 1989. "Our program is highly experimental and is designed to get people to actively examine their own belief systems," says Giannini, who worked with outside consultants to design the program. "We train sixteen to twenty people at a time and we are training everyone, including our most senior executives and most junior employees." The program explores stereotypes and biases and discusses the frustrations of their targets. Each class is mixed ethnically and usually includes at least one employee from the overseas offices and plants.

Levi Strauss does not actively recruit at any college campuses. The company uses many headhunters and works with certain organizations like the National Black MBA Association to recruit minority employees. As Giannini explains, most people who start new jobs at Levi Strauss have already worked for other companies. New hires are sent through the company's training programs in merchandising and other business areas.

Students are also attracted by the company's internship program. The company currently employs twenty-four summer interns, ten of whom are minority students. Besides hiring minority interns through the INROADS summer program, Levi Strauss hires student interns during school semesters.

The Levi Strauss Foundation has begun an ambitious social program called Project Change, designed to help communities reduce racial prejudice and improve racial and ethnic relations. In 1991, the foundation contributed $3.3 million to begin the program in pilot cities in New Mexico, Texas and Georgia. According to Joyce Bustinduy, Corporate Communications Manager, the company and the foundation also contribute to such other minority organizations as Chinese for Affirmative Action, the NAACP Legal Defense and Educational Fund, the National Urban League, the United States–Mexico Border Health Association, the Mexican American Legal Defense and Educational Fund, the National Coalition of Hispanic Health and Human Services Organizations, the National Minority AIDS Council and the National Council of La Raza.

The company's Minority Purchasing Program has purchased more than $160 million in goods and services from minority business enterprises. More than 20% of the Human Resources budget is used to advertise to minority vendors. Since 1985 the company has advertised and sponsored programming on Spanish-language TV.

Office locations: Levi Strauss has 73 locations worldwide. U.S. regional sales offices are in New York, Chicago, Atlanta, Dallas, Los Angeles and San Francisco. Production, finishing and distribution facilities are in Arkansas, California, Georgia, Kentucky, Mississippi, Nevada, New Mexico, North Carolina, Tennessee, Texas, Virginia and Washington. International production takes place in twenty-one foreign countries including Japan, England, Canada and Mexico.

1155 Battery Street
P.O. Box 7215
San Francisco, California 94120
(415) 544-6000

McDONALD'S CORPORATION

McDonald's is the largest food service company in the world. The company, restaurant managers, franchisees and joint-venture partners operate more than 12,400 McDonald's fast-food restaurants in fifty-nine countries. Most famous for its hamburgers, the chain sells other types of meats, sandwiches, salads, desserts and beverages.

1991 systemwide sales: $19,928,000,000
1992 systemwide sales: $21,885,000,000

Number of full-time employees: 107,000

Percentage of these employees who are minorities: 42
    Black: 23
    Hispanic: 10
    Asian/Pacific Islander: 4
    Native American: 1.6

Number of people in the total management pool: 16,910

Percentage of minorities in the total management pool: 30.6

Percentage of minority managers that comprise each managerial level:
    Executive: 14.7
    Department head: 20.0
    Middle management: 20.5
    Store management: 34.1

Salary information: McDonald's publishes a six-page pamphlet that describes the management career path of an employee who joins as a manager trainee. Some early management-level positions available on this career path are operations consultant, personnel supervisor and training consultant. These lower management positions pay up to $59,000 per year and include use of a company car.

In 1962, Robert Beavers, Jr., began working at McDonald's part-time while he was a college student in Washington, D.C. Today the black executive is a Senior Vice President, a Zone Manager and a member of the board of directors. During his tenure at the company, he has moved from Washington to Chicago to New York and back to Chicago. He has held such positions as Operations Manager, Director of Urban Affairs, Assistant Licensing Director, Manager of the New York District Office, District Manager and Adviser to the Board. "Actions speak louder than words," says Beavers, who opted to join McDonald's full-time before completing college. "This company's commitment to talented minority employees is obvious with regard to myself, other minority managers and the many minority licensees who operate McDonald's stores throughout the country. We have the most expansive network of minority licensees in the world."

Beavers says the company sees special importance in mentoring minority managers. "Not only have I mentored many minority managers and executives myself," he explains, "but so have our white executives acted as mentors to minority employees. Throughout the country, I have seen our mentoring and networking meetings work and help minority managers reach their potential. This is the kind of company where minorities can expect to head major offices and divisions."

Some top jobs held by minorities at McDonald's are Senior Vice President and Zone Manager; Regional Vice President in Bloomfield, Michigan; Zone Manager and Vice President; Regional Vice President in Detroit, Michigan; Regional Vice President in Hartford, Connecticut; and Senior Region Manager. Beavers is the only minority board member.

Since 84% of McDonald's restaurants are owned by franchisees, the company's policies and developments are heavily influenced by individuals outside the corporate office. Approximately 25% of franchisees are minorities and women. At the company-owned restaurants, 70% of the restaurant management employees are minorities and women. Because of this diversity, McDonald's in 1979 began offering career development and management seminars tailored to its diverse work force. Since that time, more than 14,000 employees have participated in more than 900 seminars on such topics as black career development, Hispanic career development and managing cultural differences.

Affirmative action training is given to almost 3,000 employees each year through the Mid-Management Training Classes and Advanced Operations Courses at McDonald's well-known employee management training school, Hamburger University.

To encourage employees to share common perspectives, the company supports organized minority employee networking groups, which have representatives that periodically meet with company management. According to Melvin Hopson, McDonald's Director of Affirmative Action, there are minority employee groups at most of the forty regional offices, as well as at the corporate headquarters. "The McDonald's Black Employee Network was created in 1980," says Hopson, a black manager who has been with the company since 1980. "The group's objectives are to advance our own career development and to act as a bridge between the corporation and the minority community." There is an Asian Network group on the West Coast and a Hispanic Employee Network that has been in existence since 1985.

According to Hopson, the company is a leader in diversity programs. "We have had diversity and sensitivity training since the 1970s," he explains. "Today, we offer nine different diversity training programs. In our program 'Managing Cultural Differences,' we teach our managers to not just tolerate ethnic and racial differences, but to also value them and to see how these differences can contribute to our business environment."

Many students begin their careers at the company by participating in McDonald's Management Intern Program, which is available to college juniors and seniors. The program offers flexible hours to work around college course schedules and introduces interns to such business issues as finance, marketing, operations, personnel management and sales. The internship program leads into the full-time Management Development Program.

According to Hopson, McDonald's does not have a national college recruiting program, but it has maintained close ties to minority colleges and students through its scholarships and contributions. McDonald's has contributed more than $8 million to the United Negro College Fund and more than $2 million to Hispanic educational programs. Begun as a local McDonald's program in 1985, Hispanic American Commitment to Education Resources (HACER) is a scholarship program that was developed in partnership with the National Hispanic Scholarship Fund.

While some companies aggressively pursue minority consumers, yet fail to use minority advertising and marketing companies, McDonald's has a long history of working with minority-owned marketing firms. Burrell Communications Group, a major black-owned ad agency, has represented McDonald's in its black-consumer advertising campaigns since 1972. The largest single-brand advertiser on Hispanic television today, McDonald's hired its first Hispanic-owned advertising agency in 1976.

McDonald's has a program which develops minority entrepreneurs and buys products and services from minority-owned businesses. The company works with food, paper and equipment suppliers, manufacturers, construction companies and service organizations such as banks, law and accounting firms and advertising and employment agencies. In 1992, purchases from businesses owned by minorities and women exceeded $400 million. The many suppliers include Normac Foods, a Hispanic-owned company that supplies beef to McDonald's restaurants in fourteen states, and A&D Distribution Center, a black-owned company that distributes McDonald's supplies to more than 230 McDonald's restaurants in Ohio.

Since the late 1970s, McDonald's has had a minority banking program through which it maintains lines of credit as well as depository and service-based relationships with many minority-owned banks, some of which also provide financing for the company's franchisees.

McDonald's top executives serve on the boards of many minority organizations including SER—Jobs for Progress, the NAACP, the National Urban League, the United States Hispanic Chamber of Commerce and the National Council of La Raza. The company contributes to many groups through the Ronald McDonald Children's Charities, including the Boys' Choir of Harlem, the NAACP ACT-SO youth competition and the Congressional Hispanic Caucus Institute Summer Internship Program. The company also honors outstanding black high school students in its print and TV advertising during Black History Month. In recognition of what McDonald's has done for the minority community, it was named Corporation of the Year in 1991 by the U.S. Hispanic Chamber of Commerce.

Office locations: The company is headquartered outside Chicago, in Oak Brook, Illinois. There are locations in all fifty states and in fifty-eight other countries.

One McDonald's Plaza
Oak Brook, Illinois 60521
(708) 575-3000

MARRIOTT CORPORATION

Marriott Corporation is one of the world's leading hospitality companies. Founded in 1927, the company began as a root beer stand. Today Marriott runs 698 hotels around the world. Through the Marriott Management Services division, the company manages food facilities in office buildings, hospitals and schools. Through its Host/Travel Plazas division, the company sells food and merchandise in airports and on toll roads. Marriott Senior Living Services division develops and operates retirement communities in several states.

1990 revenues: $7,646,000,000
1991 revenues: $8,331,000,000
1992 revenues: $8,722,000,000

Number of full-time employees: 188,562

Percentage of these employees who are minorities: 43.5
    Black: 21.6
    Hispanic: 16.6
    Asian/Pacific Islander: 5.0
    Native American: .3

Number of people in the total management pool: 21,219

Percentage of minorities in the total management pool: 14.3

Percentage of minority managers who comprise each managerial level:

Senior management: 5.2
Midmanagement: 9.3
Entry management: 17.7

When one looks at employer records for hiring and promotion, the hotel industry has a clear leader. No other hotel chain seems as aggressive or as committed to minority recruiting and retention as Marriott.

The company recruits at several colleges with large minority enrollments including Virginia State University, Bethune-Cookman College, Howard University, Morris Brown College, Tuskegee University, Grambling State University and Georgia State University. The company also targets Hispanic recruits at such schools as the University of Houston and New Mexico State University. Marriott managers are represented on advisory boards at seven historically black colleges.

Minorities at Marriott hold such top positions as Regional Vice President in Charge of Operations, Vice President of International Project Finance, Vice President of Development, Regional Vice President for the Distribution Center, and Vice President of Human Resources. The company has one minority board member, Dr. Floretta Dukes McKenzie, formerly superintendent of the District of Columbia Public Schools and Deputy Assistant Secretary of Education.

According to Maruiel Perkins-Chavis, Manager of Affirmative Action Compliance, within many of the company's divisions managers are rated on their affirmative action goal attainment efforts, which, in turn, affects their annual compensation. Perkins-Chavis says the company has implemented several initiatives to promote diversity. "For example," she says, "our Marriott Management Services Division developed a diversity program entitled 'Spectrum,' which is a management training program designed to enhance cross-cultural communication skills. More than two thousand managers including the executive vice president and the general manager have been trained with the four-hour program." The training uses a facilitator, instructional videos and group exercises.

Perkins-Chavis says the Hotels and Resorts Division established a Valuing Diversity Committee in 1989. "The group's purpose is to make recommendations to senior management regarding diversity training programs and other interventions," she explains. "The group consists of general managers, staff vice presidents, the corporate human resource vice president, the corporate EEO/Affirmative Action vice president and management staff." The committee retained a diversity consultant to assist in developing a program to create diversity awareness among managers and supervisors.

Curtis Dean, who has been with the company since 1973, was the first black employee to begin his career at Marriott and rise to the position of general manager. Previously general manager of a Marriott Hotel in Saddle Brook, New Jersey, Dean now runs the Fullerton Marriott in Fullerton, California. "When I first entered this business in the early 1970s," says Dean, who is one of a handful of minorities who run hotels in the United States, "you usually only saw blacks working in human resources or working in housekeeping positions. One of the reasons why blacks did not move into management in the same way we moved up in other industries is because there were no hotel management schools at black universities and there were no hotel management courses offered at black colleges until recently." Today many Hispanic students are preparing for hotel management at schools in the California State system and the University of Nevada at Las Vegas. "Twenty years ago," says Dean, "the industry focused only on the hotel school at Cornell University."

The holder of a B.S. in business from the University of Cincinnati, Dean was trained as a front desk manager in a Washington, D.C., Marriott. When he entered the business, he says, front desk requirements focused on the employee's personality. Today there is more of a focus on the employee's management and computer skills.

A member of the company's Cultural Diversity Committee and the chairman of the Marriott Community Relations Committee to Rebuild Los Angeles, Dean says he has always been able to find mentors of different backgrounds at Marriott. "This company has had minority personnel directors for many years," he says, "and the company has spearheaded sensitivity training for nonminorities so that they can better understand minority concerns." He says the Cultural Diversity Committee has the support of the company's chairman and meets quarterly to discuss such issues as hiring and promotion goals, in addition to diversity training.

The company recently aired the National Urban League's program "Beyond the Glass Ceiling, Career Strategies and Successes" by interactive satellite at the corporate headquarters. The program focused on the importance of minority role models and discussed career strategies for employees.

Perkins-Chavis adds that the company is doing a lot to help minority professionals outside the company. Marriott developed a minority counsel engagement program designed to employ minority lawyers as outside counsel. This venture recently resulted in an award from the American Bar Association in recognition of the support and assistance provided to minority-owned law firms and minority attorneys.

Marriott was recognized as Corporation of the Year in 1991 by the Washington, D.C., chapter of the National Black MBA Association. The company belongs to the National Minority Supplier Development Council and has developed more than 60 alliances with minority and women entrepreneurs at twenty-seven airports across the United States through the company's Host International division. Host's Disadvantaged Business Enterprise Program, created in 1977, has found minorities to operate snack bars, cocktail lounges, cafeterias, gift shops, newsstands and bookstores at airports in Chicago, Dallas/Fort Worth, Los Angeles, Detroit, Tampa, San Francisco, Cleveland, Baltimore and Minneapolis/St. Paul.

The company is a regular financial contributor to the National Association for Equal Opportunity in Education, the National Society of Minority Hoteliers, the NAACP, Project Equality, the Mexican American Legal Defense and Educational Fund, the National Council of La Raza and the National Urban League.

Recently the company provided sponsorship for the White House Initiative on Historically Black Colleges and Universities and for the Cornell Minority Hoteliers Conference. Marriott's national employment marketing department worked with the University of Delaware's Hotel, Restaurant and Institutional Management Department to sponsor a one-hour TV satellite broadcast of a program, "Valuing Diversity," at more than 200 colleges in the United States.

Office locations: The company is based in Washington, D.C., and has locations across the United States and in many other countries around the world.

Marriott Drive
Washington, D.C. 20058
(301) 380-9000

MCI COMMUNICATIONS CORPORATION

MCI provides a full range of basic and advanced telecommunications services domestically and internationally. The company is the second-largest long-distance carrier in the United States and the seventh-largest carrier of international traffic in the world.

1990 revenues: $7,680,000,000
1991 revenues: $8,440,000,000
1992 revenues: $10,560,000,000

Number of full-time employees: 22,700

Percentage of these employees who are minorities: 24
  Black: 15
  Hispanic: 4
  Asian/Pacific Islander: 4
  Native American: 1

Number of people in the total management pool: 3,996

Percentage of minorities in the total management pool: 14

Percentage of minority managers who comprise each managerial level:
  Executives: 6
  Managers: 11
  Supervisors: 26

MCI is a young, entrepreneurial company which took on what was once this country's largest monopoly. MCI is a long-distance telecommunications company founded in 1968. The company has eight business divisions, each with its own human resources office.

The company recruits at such black universities as Hampton, Atlanta, Howard, Prairie View A&M and Morgan State. There is also a targeted effort to recruit Hispanic students from the University of Colorado at Colorado Springs. MCI sends representatives to and recruits at conferences sponsored by the National Urban League, the National Association of Black Accountants, the Society of Hispanic Engineers and several other organizations.

At MCI, minorities hold such top management positions as Senior Vice President for Business Markets Finance, Vice President of Administration, Director of Customer Service Systems Development, Director of Disbursement Accounting, Director of Human Resources and Senior Manager of Training and Development. There is one minority person on the MCI board, former Secretary of the Army Clifford L. Alexander, Jr.

The company sensitizes its employees with a noncentralized diversity training program. According to Walter Sanderson III, Director of Human Resources, most of the diversity training is administered by the different company divisions. "There is a two-hour company-wide diversity briefing," says Sanderson, "which is intended for all supervisors, whether they are white, Asian, Hispanic, black or Native American. We realize that there are cultural undertones that exist and that can be misunderstood by someone from any background."

According to Sanderson, the company also offers Equal Employment Opportunity Roundtables four times each year to keep managers aware of EEO legal issues and various minority internship or scholarship programs. "It was at one of the EEO Roundtables," says Sanderson, "that we were all introduced to the successful INROADS minority internship program." Human Resources directors from each of the divisions meet four times each year as well, to discuss diversity management ideas.

Sanderson says that since the company is so young, the top executives have no hard-and-fast rules or traditions of long-term bias. "We think like young entrepreneurs," he says. "For example, when we opened our Colorado Springs office, we immediately contacted the local Urban League office in order to establish a relationship for leads to qualified minority job hunters. And in Sacramento, we formed a relationship with the Sacramento Black Chamber of Commerce and the local NAACP to establish a job bank."

Every quarter, Sanderson says, a list of the company's minority managers is updated and distributed to individuals who want to get together for social or business reasons. "Of course it's true that minority managers need to find nonminority mentors," he says, "but it's equally important for minority managers to know each other in the company."

Carlton Stockton, Vice President of Employee Relations, says he and other top-ranking black executives have met with senior managers to discuss black employee issues. "Diversity and race relations are not taboo topics at MCI," says Stockton. "I recently met with forty black managers to discuss their experiences and impressions of the company."

MCI created and endowed a minority scholarship program in 1991 at the University of Colorado to attract top minority students who would study computer science or electrical engineering at the school. The company also sponsors LEAD, a program that brings talented minority students to universities in the summer, teaches them business skills and offers them jobs upon graduation. MCI also offers minority internships through the INROADS program.

MCI actively supports a variety of organizations such as the Black Data Processing Association's computer competition and scholarship award and the SER—Jobs for Progress career counseling seminars. The MCI Foundation provides monetary contributions to the United Negro College Fund, the Urban League and many other organizations. MCI sponsored the 1992 Essence

Awards, an annual salute to the achievements of African American women. Many employees are active volunteers at public schools, drug abuse prevention centers, homeless shelters and neighborhood organizations. In 1991, MCI served as the national sponsor for the forty-fourth-annual Toys for Tots program, which aids many minority children.

The company's minority vendor program received the award of Corporation of the Year in 1993 from the Washington, D.C./Maryland Minority Suppliers Development Council.

Office locations: Headquartered in Washington, D.C., MCI has major locations in suburban Washington (Maryland and northern Virginia), Georgia, New York, Texas, Colorado, California and Illinois. The company has smaller offices in all fifty states. There are approximately sixty overseas offices in fifty countries.

1801 Pennsylvania Avenue, N.W.
Washington, D.C. 20006
(202) 872-1600

MERCK & CO., INC.

Merck is a multinational pharmaceuticals company that develops and markets health care products and specialty chemicals. While the Merck name may not be easily recognizable, the company is the provider of many over-the-counter and prescription products. It produces drugs that aid sufferers from high blood pressure, arthritis, glaucoma and many other disorders. Mylanta, the popular antacid, is one of Merck's over-the-counter products.

1990 revenues: $7,671,500,000
1991 revenues: $8,602,700,000
1992 revenues: $9,662,500,000

Number of full-time employees: 18,683

Percentage of these employees who are minorities: 16.8
Black: 10
Hispanic: 3.1
Asian/Pacific Islander: 3.3
Native American: .4

Number of people in the total management pool: 3,685

Percentage of minorities in the total management pool: 10.7

Percentage of minority managers who comprise each managerial level:
Senior management: 7.8
Middle management: 11.8
Lower management: 11.8

Salary information:
Officials/managers:	$65,000–$100,000+
Professionals:	$33,000–$100,000+
Technicians:	$33,000–$70,000
Sales workers:	$35,000–$100,000+

It is difficult to find a company that can beat Merck as an employer. Commitment to minority advancement is embedded deeply in Merck's corporate culture. Founded in 1890, Merck has a long history of progressive initiatives, suggesting that commitment to a diverse work force has become a standard feature of its management practices. John Horan, CEO from 1962 to 1986, told the story that in the early 1960s he pleaded with Merck sales managers in the South to hire black sales representatives. When the managers failed to respond, Horan announced that if blacks weren't hired as sales representatives, year-end bonuses would be withheld, and if no blacks were hired by the end of the second year, the unresponsive sales managers would no longer be working for Merck.

Merck's progressive approach to hiring minorities and contributing to the minority community in recent years has been spearheaded by the company's well-respected chairman, P. Roy Vagelos, M.D., who considers the company to be not only in the pharmaceuticals business, but also in the business of shaping public policy. Vagelos has aggressively developed the company's affirmative action program by implementing incentives to reward managers who achieve specific minority recruiting goals. Every manager must, on his or her list of annual objectives, separately list an affirmative action objective. These goals are then reviewed and evaluated by human resources and upper-level managers. Progress is measured quarterly, and success in achieving these goals is one of the criteria for determining year-end bonuses.

According to B. Lawrence Branch, head of Merck's Equal Employment Affairs office, minorities hold many positions at the vice president level, as well as such jobs as General Counsel of the Astra/Merck division, Assistant General Counsel, Marketing Director, Product Manager for the Human Health Division and Vice President of Research in the Montreal office.

Merck recruits from more than 200 universities, including Howard, Tuskegee, Dillard, Xavier and Hampton universities and Spelman and Morehouse colleges. Because of a strong relationship with Florida A&M University, the company has hired more than seventy-five interns from the school in the past few years. Branch says, "We try to establish a presence among minority students at such universities as MIT, Columbia, Wharton, Rutgers, UVA and Cornell by working with and sponsoring programs that are hosted by the campus minority organizations. Many of our employees also lecture at colleges through their volunteer activities with the Urban League's Black Executive Exchange Program."

"Hiring minorities for executive-level positions is an important part of the recruiting process," says Timothy Proctor, Merck's Associate General Counsel, who recently helped recruit two black attorneys—one a former law firm partner and the other a former associate—for the company's legal department. Proctor, who is also black, holds a law degree and an MBA and has been with Merck since 1981. He says, "I have advanced through four positions during my tenure here and my race has never been an explicit consideration. Our chairman, Dr. Vagelos, has always emphasized that career advancement is a function of performance."

The company has both formal and informal minority employee organizations. The Black Employee Network at the Rahway, New Jersey, and West Point, Pennsylvania, offices has provided networking opportunities for employees since the mid-1980s. Other minority organizations create mentoring programs.

In the early 1980s, the company instituted a mandatory daylong affirmative action training program called Phase III. All employees with at least one year's tenure were required to attend sessions that focused on minority recruitment and reverse discrimination. The program was so successful in addressing the concerns of minority and nonminority employees that it was adopted for use by other companies. All royalties from marketing the program to outside corporations are given to affirmative action groups outside the company; to date, well over $3 million has been raised.

Merck requires all employees to be trained in diversity and affirmative action issues. The company's Equal Employment Affairs office produces information for employees, and works with the David Winfield Foundation to train adult minority leaders who work with such organizations as the Boy Scouts and Boys Clubs of America. The company also recently sponsored a PBS film and workshop program designed to encourage minority students to enter the math and science professions.

Merck offers a ten-week Minority Summer Internship Program to minority college students who have completed their junior year and maintained at least a 2.75 grade point average. The company is also an employer member of the National Consortium for Graduate Degrees for Minorities in Engineering, through which it offers summer internships to minority students. Through its participation in the INROADS program, Merck offers jobs to minority high school graduates and college students.

Another of Merck's initiatives is the Merck Black University Liaison Committee Program whereby high-potential students at fourteen black colleges are identified and encouraged to enter Ph.D. programs. A network is created between the faculty at these schools and the company so that job openings and career paths are made known to students. Dr. Alvin Foster, Associate Director of Animal Science at Merck and chair of the Liaison Committee, knows what kind of talent can be found in historically black colleges. A graduate of Tuskegee University College of Veterinary Medicine, Foster says the program started "as a result of Dr. Vagelos's desire to make young, intellectual blacks more aware of industry and more science-conscious."

Merck places a high premium on employee satisfaction, which bolsters its affirmative action efforts. The company regularly conducts seminars to increase management sensitivity to employee needs. One outcome of these seminars has been the development of an employee benefits package called the Work and Family Life Program, which includes flexible hours, employee sabbaticals and child care vouchers.

Positions are available at Merck in marketing, sales, research and development, operations, finance and human resources.

The company participates in the National Hispanic Conference and is affiliated with ASPIRA, Inc., to help train and guide Hispanic youths toward careers in science. Merck is a significant contributor of funding to minority causes, including the United Negro College Fund, the Puerto Rican National Coalition, the NAACP and the Puerto Rican Family Institute. The Merck Company Foundation contributed more than $18 million in cash to charitable causes in 1992.

The company's minority purchasing program spends approximately $45 million with minority and women-owned businesses annually.

Merck has been honored for its achievements in equal opportunity by the National Urban League, the NAACP, the Interracial Council for Business Opportunity and the United Negro College Fund. It was also recently selected by *Fortune* magazine as America's Most Admired Company.

Office locations: Corporate headquarters are in Rahway, New Jersey; there are offices and plants in other parts of New Jersey, California, Pennsylvania, Missouri, Georgia, Texas, Virginia, North Carolina, New Hampshire, West Virginia and Oklahoma. There are offices, plants and laboratories in Japan, Mexico, Australia, Canada, Costa Rica, Ecuador, England, France, Germany, Holland, Pakistan and Spain.

P.O. Box 2000
Rahway, New Jersey 07065
(908) 574-4000

MERRILL LYNCH & CO., INC.

Merrill Lynch & Co., Inc. is a holding company with subsidiaries and affiliates that provide investment, financing, insurance and related services. Its principal subsidiary, Merrill Lynch, Pierce, Fenner & Smith Incorporated, is a major securities firm which acts as a broker in securities, a dealer in options and in corporate and municipal securities and an investment banking firm.

1990 revenues: $11,100,000,000
1991 revenues: $12,400,000,000
1992 revenues: $13,400,000,000

Number of full-time employees: 34,750

Percentage of these employees who are minorities: 17.3
    Black: 8.2
    Hispanic: 5.4
    Asian/Pacific Islander: 3.6
    Native American: .1

Number of people in the total management pool: 8,253

Percentage of minorities in the total management pool: 6.4

Percentage of minority managers who comprise each managerial level:
    Senior vice president: 0
    First vice president: 5.0

Vice president: 4.6
Assistant vice president: 9.0
Managing director: 4.8
Director: 3.1

Founded in New York in 1885, Merrill Lynch & Co., Inc., consists of several subsidiaries including Merrill Lynch, Pierce, Fenner & Smith, the securities firm which acts as a broker dealer and an investment bank; Merrill Lynch Asset Management, which manages mutual funds and provides investment advisory services; Merrill Lynch Government Securities Inc.; Merrill Lynch Insurance Group; and Merrill Lynch Life Agency, which sells life insurance and annuities.

Although there are no minority directors on the board, minorities at Merrill hold such positions as Vice President of Municipal Markets and Director of Strategic Planning. There are also minority executives in the positions of Managing Director for such divisions as Debt Markets, Equity Markets and Corporate Finance.

Valerie Johnson, a director in Merrill's Municipal Markets division, looked to one of these minority executives for mentoring when she arrived at the company in 1985. As a black executive with a graduate degree from the Yale University School of Management and a few years' experience at a Big Six accounting firm, Johnson was savvy enough to seek advice not only from someone whom she admired, but also from someone who knew what it was like to be a minority investment banker. "I was extremely happy," says Johnson, "when I saw that Merrill already had a black managing director in my department. Although I have since been able to network and meet minority brokers and others at the company, my transition was easier because I knew there was someone here I could go straight to for advice."

Johnson, who volunteers a great deal of her time as a "big sister" mentor with the Harlem YMCA/YWCA and the I Have a Dream Foundation, is extremely enthusiastic about Merrill's support of minority youth in Harlem as well as of the minority students who come to the company through its various internships and analyst programs.

The company recruits at many black colleges such as Florida A&M University, Spelman College and Howard University. When Merrill's Operations Division relocated to New Jersey, the company contacted all colleges and universities in the area and established relations with the adviser for each of the minority student organizations.

The company produced and distributed an EEO Source Directory for 850 of its managers and recruiters. The directory identifies minority recruitment sources such as employment agencies, executive headhunter firms, minority newspapers and community organizations.

According to Margaret Ingate, an officer in Merrill's Equal Employment Department, different divisions have different forms of diversity training. "In 1991," Ingate says, "our corporate staff area began a program called 'Bridging the Gap,' which is a diversity workshop that uses videotapes and role-playing. The program uses actual situations that have taken place at the company. In our Private Client division, we have a two-day program which uses videotapes and discussion in lieu of role-playing. By the end of 1993, all of these managers will have undergone diversity training."

Although the company is ahead of many other Wall Street financial firms, this industry as a whole lags far behind many others when it comes to developing minority employee organizations and creating aggressive diversity training programs for its entire staff. It is therefore refreshing to know that Merrill has had the wisdom to invite CEOs from other racially and ethnically progressive companies like Merck to visit and speak to senior executives about diversity issues.

Merrill's efforts in minority recruitment are most evident in its many internship programs. Besides offering ten to twelve summer college internships to minority students through the INROADS program, it worked with public schools in New Jersey to create a program called Financial Industry Readiness Skills Training for inner-city high school students interested in business. The courses, which are administered by employees of Merrill, focus on managing a securities portfolio, brokerage mathematics and interpersonal skills. The program runs for an entire school year and offers student participants the opportunity to work in a summer position once the classes are completed.

The company also participates in Sponsors for Educational Opportunities (SEO), through which it hires minority college-age students for summer internships. During the year, Merrill attends or contributes to various minority conferences sponsored by such organizations as the National Hispanic Scholarship Fund, the National Urban League, the NAACP and the National Black MBA Association. The company sends representatives to the annual Black Expo in New York.

According to Ingate, the company conducts annual management review meetings during which senior managers identify high-potential women and minorities who hold midlevel or lower-level positions.

While Merrill has no formal minority-supplier vendor program, it is a member of the National Minority Development Council and the New York/New Jersey Minority Purchasing Council.

Besides aiding minority organizations like the National Urban League and SER—Jobs for Progress through its funding, in 1988 Merrill created its own impressive educational incentive program, which aids students from Boston, Chicago, Detroit, Houston, Los Angeles, Miami, New York, Philadelphia and Washington, D.C. Through its Scholarship Builder Program, Merrill created a scholarship fund to pay for the college education of 250 students who will graduate from participating high schools in the year 2000. The National Urban League is helping to administer the program, and employees at Merrill serve as big brothers and sisters to the students.

Office locations: The corporate headquarters for Merrill Lynch are in the Wall Street area of New York City. Merrill Lynch has offices in all fifty states, as well as in twenty-seven foreign countries.

World Financial Center
North Tower
New York, New York 10281
(212) 236-1000

METROPOLITAN LIFE INSURANCE COMPANY

MetLife and its affiliates provide a broad range of insurance, pension, investment and financing, real estate and related products and services. Founded in 1868, the company and its affiliates insure or administer coverage for more than 45 million people in the United States, Canada, Europe and Asia. Included among MetLife's affiliates are Century 21 Real Estate Corporation, the world's largest real estate franchise sales organization; MetLife Capital Corporation, a division that provides commercial finance and equipment financing; and MetLife HealthCare Management Corporation, a holding company for MetLife's HMOs.

1990 revenues: $38,200,000,000
1991 revenues: $39,500,000,000
1992 revenues: $37,800,000,000

Number of full-time employees: 41,860

Percentage of these employees who are minorities: 20.4
    Black: 10.2
    Hispanic: 4.4
    Asian/Pacific Islander: 5.3
    Native American: .5

MetLife became the first North American insurer to achieve $1 trillion of life insurance in-force. There are two minority members on MetLife's board of directors: A. Luis Ferre, president and publisher of *El Nuevo Día*, and Roscoe Robinson, a retired four-star general in the U.S. Army.

Although the company has not maintained a recruiting program at predominantly minority colleges since 1991, it is working with several black fraternities and sororities like Alpha Kappa Alpha, Omega Psi Phi and Alpha Phi Alpha to bring more minority students into its Management Associate Program. "This is our fast-track management training program," says Myra Pilson, Managing Consultant in the EEO Unit at MetLife's Corporate Human Resources. "For two years, each of the Management Associates is given rotational assignments in the different business areas. Each of the participants is assigned to a mentor, who will assist the new employee during his or her advancement toward a management position."

MetLife hires graduates to work in each of its major lines of business including pensions, personal insurance, group insurance and investments, as well as corporate staff departments. Assignments include marketing, product development, financial analysis and research.

The company recruits at many minority-targeted events such as China Expo in California, the Asian Festival in Texas and programs sponsored by the Urban League, the National Black MBA Association, the Koreatown Association of Los Angeles and other organizations across the country.

Since MetLife enjoys a special relationship with the INROADS minority internship program, it attracts many INROADS alumni into its management training program and other full-time positions. Catherine Rein, one of MetLife's executive vice presidents, sits on the INROADS New York City board of directors, and the company also employs at least twenty INROADS interns in line and staff operations. The company incorporates a mentoring program as a part of its training of INROADS interns.

MetLife has implemented an affirmative action training program for its human resources professionals that includes lectures, videotapes and discussion groups. After these professionals are trained, they are responsible for returning to their divisions and planning one-on-one presentations with key managers and executives.

"Every eighteen months we have a corporate-wide equal opportunity conference," says Pilson. "This is a four-day program where we utilize outside consultants and bring them to MetLife to present lectures and workshops. We discuss employment discrimination, attitudinal barriers and other issues that relate to diversity. During the four days, we train our senior line executives as well as our human resources managers."

According to Pilson, the company's Program for New Managers and the Transition to Supervision program both offer an equal employment opportunity component which uses case studies to address ways of dealing with diversity issues.

MetLife and its foundation have a particularly impressive record for supporting the Asian community. According to Gus Gomez, consultant in MetLife's Equal Employment Opportunity Office, aid has been given to the Chinese Health Service Center of Houston, the Wichita Asian Association, the Asian American Arts Center in New York, the Japanese-American Citizens League in California and many other organizations. The foundation awarded a grant to Temple University for a project that prepares teachers who speak Asian languages to teach in the Philadelphia public school system.

The company supports many other minority organizations such as the National Council of La Raza; the National Hispanic Scholarship Fund; the National Urban League; the NAACP; the United Negro College Fund; SER—Jobs for Progress; the Cherokee Indian Nation Tribal Complex in Oklahoma; the Opportunities Industrialization Centers of America, which operates a number of Native American job training centers in Minnesota; and many Native American colleges like Navajo Community College in Arizona, Salish Kootenai College in Montana and San Juan College in New Mexico. MetLife has supported Mexican-American cultural programs in San Antonio and San Francisco. The Metropolitan Life Foundation has funded minority business development organizations in Detroit, New York City and other urban areas.

MetLife's Corporate Contributions and Social Responsibility departments manage the company's Targeted Suppliers Program, which was started in 1970 and aimed specifically at purchasing from minority vendors and suppliers. What started as a $50 thousand venture is now an active program whereby the company annually spends more than $50 million with minority contractors.

Besides purchasing supplies from minority vendors, MetLife also does business with minority-owned banks and insurance firms. In 1992, it had deposits exceeding $5 million in twenty-four minority-owned financial institutions. During the year, Treasury, Tax and Loan accounts exceeding $200 million were held in four minority and women-owned banks. The company also ceded $2.5 billion of group life insurance to seven minority reinsurers in 1991.

Office locations: MetLife has its headquarters in New York City. It has offices across the United States and in Canada, Spain, England, Korea and Taiwan.

One Madison Avenue
New York, New York 10010
(212) 578-2211

MORRISON & FOERSTER

This international law firm, founded in 1883, is based in San Francisco and serves many clients in the U.S. and Asia. The firm's practice includes corporate finance, bankruptcy, real estate, institutional lending, union-employer relations, securities litigation, criminal litigation, First Amendment litigation, business tax planning, estate tax planning and trade law, as well as such interdisciplinary legal practices as intellectual property, communications, land use and energy.

1990 revenues: $196,000,000
1991 revenues: $217,000,000

Number of full-time employees: 1,696

Number of partners: 235

Number of these partners who are:
    Black: 5
    Hispanic: 1
    Asian/Pacific Islander: 6

Number of associates: 351

Number of these associates who are:
    Black: 14
    Hispanic: 8
    Asian/Pacific Islander: 25

Number of summer associates employed in 1992: 143

Number of these summer associates who are:
    Black: 18
    Hispanic: 11
    Asian/Pacific Islander: 23
    American Indian: 2

Morrison & Foerster makes no secret of its desire to hire and develop minority attorneys. The firm's aggressive stance on this issue is detailed in the front of the slick and comprehensive fifty-page "Reference Guide," which explains all you could want to know about the firm's practice, approach to attorney development and public service. The guide includes a comprehensive discussion of the firm's commitment to hiring and retaining employees who have been infected with the AIDS virus.

When the American Bar Association created a pilot project to study ways of improving employment opportunities for minority lawyers, Morrison was asked to be a demonstration firm. The firm has developed a comprehensive strategy for improving diversity among the attorney staff, including the creation of a Minority Recruitment Subcommittee. According to Stephen Dunham, Managing Partner for Personnel, the firm's hiring committee includes three minority attorneys—two associates and one partner.

"In our San Francisco office," Dunham explains, "we have a mentor program for minority associates. We pair each of the associates with partners who introduce them to professional development issues and office methods, as well as to the community." The minority mentor program, although most helpful to newly hired attorneys, is also used by more senior minority associates.

Dunham, whose responsibilities include recruiting, diversity training, retention and promotion as well as participation in minority attorney programs, says the firm's San Francisco office began a formal diversity training workshop for attorneys in

1991. "At that time," he says, "we had a daylong session of diversity training. We are now interviewing diversity consultants to develop a program for us because we realize that we can develop greater strength in our firm through improving our communication skills and managing our diversity."

In an infamous scathing letter written anonymously by a Morrison attorney and printed in 1992 in Harvard Law School's newspaper, the firm was accused of laying off associates unfairly. Despite these accusations, the firm is considered among the more politically correct. A more accurate criticism is that the firm is considerably credentials-conscious, with an eye on Harvard and Stanford graduates. Even so, the firm participates in many minority law school student conferences and job fairs and recruits each year at Howard University Law School.

Besides having an excellent reputation for retaining women, in particular those who request part-time status in order to raise children, the firm is well known for its creation of the Upward Evaluation, which allows younger associates to review and grade the more senior associates with whom they have worked.

For the past several years, the firm has participated in three to five job fairs each year for minority law students sponsored by black law students' associations in various parts of the country. In addition, several minority partners participate in the Harvard Law School Alumni Minority Recruitment and Placement Conference, as well as on a panel on diversity issues at the Annual Conference of the National Association for Law Placement.

In 1992, the Los Angeles office received the NAACP Legal Defense and Educational Fund's Pro Bono Legal Services Law Firm of the Year Award in honor of its volunteer work in the community. The Los Angeles and San Francisco offices each have adopted inner-city public schools; staff and attorneys volunteer to take young people on educational trips or coach and sponsor students in academic incentive events. The firm agreed to minority hiring goals set by the Bar Association of San Francisco and the Los Angeles County Bar Association.

Morrison also funds a minority scholarship program at UCLA Law School and matches contributions to fund a minority scholarship at the University of Colorado Law School.

Office locations: Morrison & Foerster has California offices in San Francisco, Los Angeles, Sacramento, Walnut Creek, Palo Alto and Orange County. There are also offices in Seattle, Denver, Washington, D.C., New York, Brussels, Hong Kong, Tokyo and London.

345 California Street
San Francisco, California 94104
(415) 677-7000

MOTOROLA, INC.

Motorola is a leading provider of electronic equipment, systems, components and services for worldwide markets. Products manufactured by the company include two-way radios, pagers, cellular telephones and systems, semiconductors, defense and aerospace electronics, automotive and industrial electronics, computers and information processing equipment.

1990 revenues: $10,880,000,000
1991 revenues: $11,340,000,000
1992 revenues: $13,300,000,000

Number of full-time employees: 54,694

Percentage of these employees who are minorities: 25.1
    Black: 8.2
    Hispanic: 11
    Asian/Pacific Islander: 5.5
    Native American: .4

Number of people in the total management pool: 7,991

Percentage of minorities in the total management pool: 10.5

Percentage of minority managers who comprise each managerial level:
    Vice president: 6.0
    Director: 8.1
    Manager: 9.7

Founded in 1928 by Paul Galvin in Chicago, Motorola was originally known for manufacturing radios for automobiles. Today the company is divided into three business sectors and four business groups. The sectors, which have an average of 20,000 to 30,000 employees, each have annual revenues exceeding $1 billion, while each of the four groups has fewer employees and revenues that account for less than $1 billion. Each group and sector manages its own recruiting and carries out its own diversity activities.

The company recruits at such predominantly black universities as Howard, Florida A&M and Hampton. The company has a unique relationship with Hampton in that Motorola has donated not only money, but also equipment and training to the school's engineering program. A Motorola scientist visits the school four times a year to meet with deans and provide technical advice on expanding the school's engineering program, and the company hosts one of Hampton's engineering professors for an entire summer so that the faculty can be introduced to the latest technology and training methods. Much of the company's recruiting is in the area of engineering and computer science.

According to Roberta Gutman, Director of Human Resources Diversity, "while many of the high-tech companies have not focused on the black schools, we realized that more than eighty percent of all black engineers come out of black colleges. In order to best train the candidates that came out of these engineering schools as well as to create a presence for Motorola, we felt it was wise to first strengthen the programs that these schools were offering. We can help the programs by sending our employees, providing additional funds and by assisting in the training of their faculty."

George Fisher, Motorola's CEO, is not only an outspoken proponent of diversity at Motorola, but he is also a member of the National Urban League's board. Fisher has established a goal that by the end of 1996, Motorola's management will be at parity for minorities—meaning that the representation of minorities in the company's management will mirror the availability of minorities with management qualifications in the population of the United States.

Minorities at Motorola hold such positions as Senior Vice President and General Manager; Vice President of Taxes; Corporate Vice President and Division General Manager and Vice President and General Manager.

There are, however, no minorities on the board of directors. For several years, before he was asked to head the National Science Foundation, the black scientist Dr. Walter Massey served on Motorola's board.

Since each business sector or group is responsible for creating its own diversity program, each has been designed differently. The Land Mobile Products Sector in Chicago uses trainers from the firm J. Howard & Associates. At the Phoenix-based Semiconductor Sector, a diversity program was implemented by Dr. Anthony Itsaro of Denver's Meridien Group. At the corporate headquarters, the diversity initiative is focusing on issues of gender differences and on using professors from a Chicago-area university.

Because Motorola is extremely large and quite decentralized, its various minority employee organizations have different names in different locations. In 1991, in the company's Phoenix Government Electronics Group, black employees established The Network. In Chicago in the Land Mobile Products Sector, black and Hispanic employees established FOCUS, as well as the Land Mobile Products Sector Hispanic Network, a group of professional minority employees which sponsors programs for its members and the community. Other networks and support groups are being formed at other Motorola facilities.

According to Roberta Gutman, in 1989 the company established a goal of naming at least three women and two minority members each year to the vice presidential level through 1996. Thus far, Motorola has lived up to the goal. Gutman says, "It's our belief that attaining this goal will not only increase the representation of minorities in Motorola's executive management, but also provide role models for others within our organization."

The company builds credibility among minority students and potential full-time minority employees through its aggressive Minority Scholarship Internship Investment Program. For the past few years, the company has earmarked more than fifty openings in this summer program for minority students. Besides these internships, partial scholarships of $2,000 are given. The company encourages the students to return each summer until graduation. College seniors who have maintained at least a B-minus cumulative average and who have performed well during the summer internship are offered full-time positions. Gutman says, "We believe that showing this level of confidence in minority students who have worked with us will help ensure their strong performance upon graduation."

Motorola provides financial support and employee volunteers to the National Urban League. Many young minority students are aided through Motorola's various partnerships with the Chicago public school system. Since 1989, the company has been the corporate sponsor for the Chicago Public Schools Science Fair, providing both financial help and employee volunteers. Another school program that Motorola aids each year with both financial and volunteer assistance is the Academic Decathlon, during which fifty employees volunteer over three months to work with and judge students.

In 1992, the company was a major sponsor of the TV broadcast of the Black Engineer of the Year Awards and the Hispanic Engineer of the Year Awards. In 1991, it was a major corporate sponsor of "I Dream a World: Portraits of 75 Black Women Who Changed America," a photographic exhibition brought to Chicago by the Chicago Historical Society. Besides the financial support, twenty African American women employees of Motorola took part in a project called the Sojourner

Program which provided mentors for hundreds of "at risk" African American women in the Chicago area.

At this time, there is no minority supplier-vendor program at Motorola.

Office locations: Headquarters are in Schaumburg, Illinois; the company has offices in other parts of Illinois, as well as in Alabama, Arizona, California, Florida, Iowa, Massachusetts, New Mexico, New York, Texas, Washington State and Puerto Rico. There are also major facilities in Australia, Canada, Costa Rica, France, Germany, Hong Kong, Ireland, Israel, Japan, Korea, Malaysia, Mexico, Taiwan, the United Kingdom, Switzerland, Singapore and the Philippines.

130 East Algonquin Road
Schaumburg, Illinois 60196
(708) 576-5000

THE NEW YORK TIMES COMPANY

The New York Times Company is the parent company of the daily paper of the same name, and of four separate corporate groups. The Newspaper group includes twenty-four daily newspapers and eight nondaily newspapers in eleven states. The Magazine group is responsible for twelve sports and leisure magazines including *Golf Digest* and *Tennis*, and five women's magazines including *Family Circle*. The group also produces marketing services, a golf instruction school, books and videotapes. The Broadcasting/Information Services group includes five network-affiliated TV stations, two radio stations, the Times News Service and Syndication Sales, as well as copyright and trademark licensing services. The Forest Products group includes interests in newsprint mills in the United States and Canada.

1990 revenues: $1,776,761,000
1991 revenues: $1,703,101,000
1992 revenues: $1,773,535,000

Number of full-time employees: 10,316

Percentage of these employees who are minorities: 15.1
    Black: 10.4
    Hispanic: 3.3
    Asian/Pacific Islander: 1.2
    Native American: .2

Number of people in the total management pool: 1,790

Percentage of minorities in the total management pool: 8.5

A well-known liberal institution since the Sulzberger family acquired it in 1896, the New York Times Company has recently begun major efforts to increase its understanding of diversity issues and to increase the focus on attracting and retaining minority employees. Arthur Ochs Sulzberger, Jr., has recently assumed the position of publisher, taking over from his father, Arthur Sr. He has made a personal commitment to improving the company's performance on minority hiring and advancement.

The *Times* recruits for minority newsroom staff primarily through minority journalists' associations, since most positions require prior work experience. According to June Clarke-Doar, Human Resources Manager, the company hires a large number of minority graduates from the University of Miami, Columbia University, New York University and Florida International University.

"Our publisher and senior newsroom staff attend a number of annual conferences and meetings," says Clarke-Doar, "like those sponsored by the National Association of Black Journalists, the National Association of Hispanic Journalists and the National Association of Asian American Journalists. We conduct interviews and build our networks during the conventions. The company also offers minority internships."

In 1992, Arthur Ochs Sulzberger, Jr., established a Diversity Committee with twenty members from across the organization to help define the crucial issues regarding diversity and to begin developing programs to address them.

Lena Williams, Senior Writer in the Style section of *The New York Times*, sits on the Diversity Committee. "Although the paper has always had a progressive reputation," says Williams, "our publisher was particularly interested in gathering recommendations from employees who had suggestions on how we could be more diverse in our hiring, as well as in our editorial coverage."

A black graduate of the Columbia University Graduate School of Journalism, Williams joined the paper in 1974 after her former professor, Charlayne Hunter-Gault, now an anchor on the PBS "MacNeil-Lehrer Newshour," told her about a position in the *Times* sports department. "After being at the paper for just two months," Williams recalls, "they gave me the opportunity to write my own weekly column which appeared each Sunday in the Sports section."

Williams has since worked on the Metro desk, served as a suburban correspondent, covered the New York State legislature in Albany and started up the Washington bureau's civil rights beat. "In 1986," she says, "Abe Rosenthal felt we needed a reporter in Washington to focus on the civil rights issues facing minorities, women, the elderly, gays and other groups that have not received sufficient coverage."

There were approximately ten blacks working in the newsroom when Williams arrived at the paper, but Williams says that management was able to increase that number substantially when it established its minority copy editing training program in 1986.

Sharon Yakata, a Japanese American woman who is Director of Promotions, also sits on the Diversity Committee. "I've been with the company for sixteen years, and at the very beginning, things weren't always that great. I heard a few ethnic jokes from some of the older employees, because that was the only experience these employees had with Japanese people." Yakata adds, "Now I am very happy that our publisher has made a serious effort to create an atmosphere that is welcoming to everyone." The committee, which meets once a month, is headed by Carolyn Lee, an Assistant Managing Editor at the paper. The publisher attends the meetings from time to time and the committee plans to solicit comments on diversity issues from all employees via a company-wide memo.

At WREG-TV in Memphis, Tennessee, Alex Coleman has enjoyed a meteoric career which took him from TV reporter to anchor in less than three years. He joined this New York Times–

owned CBS affiliate at age twenty-two, right after graduating from the University of Alabama.

"I believe that I am the first black male prime-time anchor in this market," Coleman says, "but from the first day I arrived here in 1984, my white and black coworkers and bosses have been supportive and have done everything to make sure I was succeeding at this station. And as many will tell you, broadcast journalism is normally a very competitive business."

Coleman says that although it is highly unusual for a TV news reporter to be hired directly out of college, his two offers came from stations owned by the New York Times Company. Like other stations, WREG works with the local NAACP on fundraising and encourages its 120 employees to volunteer with the Adopt-a-School program that the station supports at the Winchester Elementary School, a largely black school in Memphis. Coleman is often invited to speak about the minority experience in the broadcast business at such schools as Memphis State University, Rust College and LeMoyne-Owen College.

There is currently one minority employee organization at the *Times*, the Black Caucus. Although not as active as it was when first created in the 1970s, the group discusses issues of concern to black employees and keeps senior management informed.

Besides efforts targeted specifically at minority issues, the New York Times Company has established several programs meant to ensure that all employees build the skills needed to advance through the company. Educational assistance is available for all full-time employees who wish to pursue graduate or undergraduate degrees, and for other approved courses which will contribute to their training for future responsibilities within the company.

Minorities at the company hold such positions as General Counsel, Metropolitan Editor of *The New York Times*, Chief Financial Officer of the Regional Newspaper Group, Station

Manager within the Broadcasting Group and Creative Director within the Magazine Group.

There is one minority member on the board of directors, Donald Stewart, president of the College Board. Stewart has been on the board since 1986.

The New York Times Foundation has historically been a generous supporter of minority civic and charitable organizations. In 1991, the foundation's grants were just over $5 million, and went to such organizations as Dance Theater of Harlem, El Museo del Barrio, the Puerto Rican Legal Defense and Education Fund, the Spanish Repertory Theater, the Asia Society, the United Negro College Fund, the Hispanic Women's Center and The Fresh Air Fund, which sends inner-city children on country vacations. Scholarships for minority students were funded at the Columbia Graduate School of Journalism, Memphis Preparatory School, Wellesley College, Andover/Phillips Academy, Fairfield University, the State University of New York at Stony Brook, the Professional Children's School, and the University of Cape Town. Sixty grants totaling almost $700,000 were used to fund efforts to increase minority representation in journalism.

The company belongs to the New York and New Jersey Minority Purchasing Council and the National Minority Development Council. Each year it spends approximately $1 million with minority vendors.

Both the corporate headquarters and The New York Times newspaper are located in New York City. Other offices are in at least twenty states, Canada and a number of countries in Europe, Asia, Africa and South America.

229 West 43rd Street
New York, New York 10036
(212) 556-1234

NYNEX CORPORATION

Through New England Telephone Company, New York Telephone Company and NYNEX Mobile Communications Company, NYNEX Corporation provides wireline and wireless telecommunications services to approximately 12 million customers in the northeastern United States. The company offers these services in selected markets around the world through NYNEX Network Systems Company. The NYNEX companies are also involved in directory publishing, information delivery, data base management, software and consulting services in the United States and abroad.

1990 revenues: $13,582,000,000
1991 revenues: $13,229,000,000
1992 revenues: $13,155,000,000

Number of full-time employees: 87,765

Percentage of these employees who are minorities: 22
    Black: 17.1
    Hispanic: 3.3
    Asian/Pacific Islander: 1.5
    Native American: .1

Number of people in the total management pool: 28,521

Percentage of minorities in the total management pool: 16.4

Percentage of minority managers who comprise each managerial level:

Vice president: 2
Assistant vice president: 6
Managing director: 6
Director: 7
Manager: 17

Salary information:
Vice chairman:	$420,000
Vice president:	$225,000
Department head:	$110,000–$135,000
Division manager:	$80,000–$100,000
District manager:	$63,000–$78,000
Manager:	$40,000–$60,000

Colette Ragin, Staff Manager in NYNEX's Managing Diversity Office, is excited about the opportunities available for minorities at the NYNEX companies. She is particularly proud of the minority support organizations that have helped employees network and build their careers at the company. New York Telephone and New England Telephone both have active minority employee groups, the Minority Management Association (MMA), the Asian Focus Group and the Hispanic Support Organization (HSO).

According to Ragin, the Minority Management Association organizes and conducts seminars to help minority management employees. "The group also aids the minority community," she adds, "by raising money for scholarships, health care programs and employment programs outside of the company." HSO has developed a mentoring program in which Hispanic executives serve as mentor-advisers to minority students in the sixth and seventh grades.

At New York Telephone, Colin Watson, Vice President of Customer Relations, is extremely active in the mostly black group MMA. From the moment he first arrived at the company, he felt comfortable as a minority employee. "When I first began working here in 1972, I already knew that there were black professionals at the company. I was recruited by a black district manager, so I didn't have the concerns that I might have had at a company where I knew no other minority employees." Watson explains that his original recruiter is now a vice president.

Watson holds a master's degree in operations research. He believes strongly in improving the educational goals of young minority children. Like many others at NYNEX, he volunteers through the Adopt-a-School Program, as well as the Executive in the Classroom Program of the New York City Board of Education. Through his involvement with these programs, Watson has the opportunity to serve as a role model for many young minority students.

Janet Humdy, New England Telephone's Managing Director of Human Resources Training, Development and Consulting, was a founding member of MMA in New England in 1980. "Today we have almost one hundred fifty members in New England," she says, "We created the organization as a support group which could network socially and professionally. We also have a banquet each year with prominent minority speakers. In 1992, we had former U.S. Representative William Gray, who recently became the head of the United Negro College Fund. The organization has also raised money for minority scholarships and other aid to the minority community."

Humdy has a master's degree in training and development. She is based in Marlboro, Massachusetts, and has been with the company since 1967. She adds, "Diversity is not new to us here. We've been offering courses for several years. We have a Cross-cultural Seminar, as well as a course called Diversity at Work. We also have a group called the Corporate Committee for Development and Diversity which meets each month and supports our diversity program."

According to Joseph Anderson, director of the company's Managing Diversity Office, NYNEX has established a strong diversity initiative. "Our training is aimed at employees at all levels. It includes our chairman and anyone else working at NYNEX. The program reviews stereotypes, the effects of labeling people by gender, religion, ethnicity, race, education, parental status, sexual orientation, etc. We feel that people can only become productive once they understand how to get beyond stereotypes and biases. My role is to help employees recognize and remove the barriers that they have set up for themselves and others in the workplace."

Anderson adds, "We have a course called Managing Development and Diversity which is for our senior managers. And we also offer a course that is customized for minority professionals which talks about self-esteem, productivity and other issues that are helpful to managers."

NYNEX actively recruits minority interns. Beginning with juniors in high school, the company sponsors a minority internship program called Minority Introduction to Engineering and Science. High school students are given an introduction to engineering, science and mathematics in a six-week summer program at MIT. After the program, NYNEX maintains a relationship with the students.

Since NYNEX sponsors a great deal of university research, it has a program in which it invites college students to work as paid summer interns, continuing the NYNEX-sponsored research. NYNEX also sponsors high school seniors and college students in the INROADS program and the Leadership, Education and Development Program in business in ten graduate business schools.

For several years, NYNEX has had a Minority and Women's Business Program which seeks to expand the amount of business done with minority suppliers. Besides spending approximately $60,000,000 with minority suppliers, NYNEX also uses minority banks and insurance companies. The program offers a twelve-week sales training course to minority business owners as well as a directory of minority suppliers so that all of

NYNEX's purchasing personnel have access to the names and locations of potential vendors.

There is one minority member on the board of directors: Dr. Randolph W. Bromery is a black professor at the University of Massachusetts at Amherst and president of Geoscience Engineering Corporation. Bromery has served as a director since 1986.

The NYNEX Foundation, NYNEX, New England Telephone and New York Telephone Corporate Contributions gave $17 million last year to civic organizations. Many of the programs supported operate in inner-city and minority communities. Organizations that receive support include the National Puerto Rican Forum, the Consortium for Graduate Study in Management and the National Action Council for Minorities in Engineering.

New England Telephone participates in and recruits each year at the three-day Boston Career Expo for minority students. Both NYNEX and New York Telephone recruit from Howard University and participate in the U.S. Minority Career Convention, the national conference of the National Society of Black Engineers and the annual Eastern Technical and Career Conference of the Society of Hispanic Professional Engineers.

Office locations: The corporate headquarters of NYNEX are in New York City. There are many other offices in the northeastern United States, the largest in New York and Massachusetts. NYNEX also has operations in sixty other countries.

335 Madison Avenue
New York, New York 10017
(212) 370-7400

O'MELVENY & MYERS

Founded in 1885, O'Melveny is the oldest law firm in Los Angeles. While most of its U.S. practice is in California, the firm has a well-developed international practice. The firm is organized into seven departments (corporations, litigation, entertainment, real estate and natural resources, labor and employment, bankruptcy and creditors' rights, and tax), and the departments are supplemented with specialized groups of attorneys from interdisciplinary areas.

1991 revenues: $227,000,000 (as reported by *The American Lawyer*)

Salary information:
    First-year associates (New York): $78,000
    First-year associates (elsewhere): $70,000
    The firm also has a profit-sharing plan which associates participate in after two years of employment

Number of partners: 178

Number of these partners who are:
    Black: 3
    Asian/Pacific Islander: 4

Number of associates and special counsel: 360

Number of these associates and special counsel who are:
    Black: 13
    Hispanic: 12
    Asian/Pacific Islander: 19

Number of summer associates employed in 1992: 70

Number of these summer associates who are:
Black: 6
Hispanic: 2
Asian/Pacific Islander: 9

O'Melveny & Myers has a reputation for being progressive in its hiring and in the issues it supports. Many of its attorneys have been involved in public service. Warren Christopher, a long time partner and a recent chairman of the firm, is Secretary of State in the Clinton Administration and was formerly Deputy Attorney General under President Lyndon Johnson and Deputy Secretary of State in President Jimmy Carter's administration. The firm's most prominent black partner, William T. Coleman, Jr., was Secretary of Transportation under President Gerald Ford and is now a litigator and the head of the firm's Washington office. Coleman, a graduate of the University of Pennsylvania and Harvard Law School, has served as president of the NAACP Legal Defense and Educational Fund and on the boards of several corporations.

In a May, 1993, article highlighting the top 10 Asian executives in New York, the Asian American magazine *Transpacific* profiled O'Melveny senior partner Ko-Yung Tung. Tung, who is a native of Beijing, represents such Far East clients as Japan Air Lines and Sunstar.

Recent clients of O'Melveny include Ernest & Julio Gallo Winery, CIGNA Insurance, Tom Werner (cocreator of *The Cosby Show* and *Roseanne*) in his purchase of the San Diego Padres, Security Pacific Bank, Lockheed Corporation and Pacific Gas and Electric Company.

While each of the different offices has its own hiring committee, the main office in downtown Los Angeles has a hiring committee of thirteen attorneys, one of whom is a minority person.

The firm provides diversity training to attorneys who participate in the hiring process and to others who participate in small group discussions led by the firm's Minority Issues Committee and the Management Committee Workshop.

Richard Jones, a partner in the corporations department, is chair of the Minority Issues Committee, which meets monthly and includes sixteen partners and associates from all ethnic groups. Since 1991, the group has identified and addressed issues of special interest to minorities. "We have focused much of our attention on minority retention and recruiting," says Jones. "Although we do not recruit from Howard Law School, we have targeted law schools like U.C. Berkeley, the University of Michigan and Harvard, since they have a large minority makeup. The committee has discussed creating panel presentations whereby our minority attorneys can tell interviewing minority law students what it is like to work in a predominantly white law firm."

The Minority Issues Committee is also responsible for educating the firm's nonminority attorneys on minority issues. Jones says, "We have been conducting small group meetings with our attorneys to discuss the barriers that face our minority coworkers. Specifically, we have examined the work assignment process to ensure that minority attorneys are given the same type of challenging work that nonminorities receive. We've also examined our orientation process to develop methods to make minority attorneys more comfortable when they enter this environment."

According to Jones, the firm has agreed to minority hiring policies recently established by bar associations in New York City, Washington, D.C., and Los Angeles.

Eric Richards is a black corporate attorney who sits on the Minority Issues Committee with Jones. A graduate of Yale College and Harvard Law School, Richards is a fifth-year associate in the downtown Los Angeles office. He says he recognized that the firm had good minority representation while he was working as a summer associate in 1988. "Although I knew that the Los

Angeles office had two black partners," he says, "I didn't realize how important it was to have other senior black attorneys at the firm until I actually began working full-time." Although there is no formal mentor system, Richards says he often talks to the minority partners about his career or minority concerns.

"After being here for four years," Richards admits, "I find that some of the more junior minority attorneys come to me as a type of mentor as well." Richards, who is also a member of the firm's Employment Committee, says the firm has provided diversity training for attorneys by employing the black diversity consultant Jacob Hering of Oakland, California.

Richards adds, "We have also used the instructional videotape, 'A Firm Commitment,' which was created by the San Francisco Bar Association in order to teach attorneys how to interact with minority coworkers." The videotape features typical law firm scenarios that expose subtle discrimination.

After the beating of Rodney King by Los Angeles police in 1991, O'Melveny & Myers took on a prominent role in the investigation of the city's police department. Mayor Tom Bradley created the Independent Commission on the L.A. Police Department to study the department's structure and operation. Of the ten prominent Los Angeles residents appointed to the commission, two were attorneys at O'Melveny. Corporations attorney Gil Ray was appointed the commission's executive director, and Warren Christopher, then chairman, was named chair of the commission. The commission held public meetings around the city and heard speakers from such organizations as the Asian Pacific Legal Center, the Mexican American Legal Defense and Education Fund, the Los Angeles Gay & Lesbian Communities Services Center, the Los Angeles Urban League and the NAACP Legal Defense and Educational Fund.

The firm has created a unique scholarship program administered through the Los Angeles Unified School District. After adopting a largely Hispanic inner-city elementary school several years ago, the firm recently instituted an annual O'Melveny &

Myers Scholarship program through which eight O'Melveny Scholars receive $12,000 scholarships to attend the college of their choice. The students are selected while in elementary school and receive the award upon successful completion of high school. The scholarship program is not only an incentive for young students to stay in school, but it also uses a mentoring component: scholarship recipients are matched with an O'-Melveny employee who acts as a counselor and role model.

O'Melveny attends many minority conferences, programs and job fairs during the year, including the American Bar Association Minority conference, the Black Law Students Association Job Fair, the Mexican American Bar Association's Latino Lawyers Committee programs and Harvard Law School's Minority Recruiting Seminar.

The firm contributes to minority organizations and encourages employee volunterism in minority communities.

Since 1988, the firm has participated in the Mentor Program sponsored by the Constitutional Rights Foundation. Each spring semester, attorneys from the Los Angeles and Century City offices present mock trials for government classes at a Los Angeles public high school.

While the firm does not require attorneys to participate in pro bono work, it has established a goal for each lawyer of offering an average of thirty-five hours of pro bono service in a year. In 1991, 25,000 attorney hours (an average of fifty hours per attorney) were spent on pro bono legal services.

Office locations: Los Angeles, Century City, Newport Beach and San Francisco, California; Washington D.C.; New York; Tokyo; London and Brussels.

400 South Hope Street
Los Angeles, California 90071
(213) 669-6000

PACIFIC GAS AND ELECTRIC COMPANY

PG&E is the nation's largest investor-owned gas and electric utility, serving 12 million people in Northern and Central California. The company's electricity comes from widely diversified resources—fossil fuel plants, hydroelectric plants, a major pumped storage plant, a geothermal complex, the Diablo Canyon Nuclear Power Plant—and from such alternative technologies as wind power, solar power and biomass. PG&E's natural gas comes from Canada, the U.S. Southwest and California.

1990 revenues: $9,470,092,000
1991 revenues: $9,778,119,000

Number of full-time employees: 26,700

Percentage of these employees who are minorities: 28.4
    Black: 6.4
    Hispanic: 10.9
    Asian/Pacific Islander: 9.8
    Native American: 1.3

Number of people in the total management pool: 8,000

Percentage of minorities in the total management pool: 22.6

Percentage of minority managers who comprise each managerial level: Of the top 2% of all jobs (those considered management level and above) at PG&E, 10.9% are held by minorities.

Minorities at PG&E hold many senior positions. There are five vice presidents, two department managers, three division managers, five senior attorneys and many other managers.

According to Bunnie Brown, Director of Affirmative Action Diversity and Employment Services, the company has several minority employee organizations including the PG&E Black Employee Association, the PG&E Asian Employee Association, the PG&E Filipino Employee Association and the PG&E Hispanic Employee Association.

"The Black Employee Association," says Brown, "was organized by black employees in 1970. It has grown to five chapters and serves as a networking group. Each chapter provides college scholarships to students. In 1991, the Bay Area Chapter gave out ten scholarships of one thousand dollars each."

The Hispanic Employee Association has four chapters and sponsors a three-day weekend camp held at company facilities for Hispanic elementary school students from the San Joaquin Valley who are at high risk of dropping out. The camp was honored in 1991 by President George Bush's Points of Light Award. The Asian Employee Association raises money for charities in China through its annual book drive. Besides offering mentoring and networking opportunities for their members, both the Hispanic and Asian employee groups provide college scholarships.

Since PG&E is a public utility with a business that is focused in California, its minority recruiting efforts are aimed at California universities. The company does, however, recruit students at colleges elsewhere such as Howard University, Tuskegee University, Southern University and North Carolina State University. There is also a targeted Hispanic recruiting effort at Texas A&M University and New Mexico State University. The company supports minority engineer societies at many other universities as well.

Brown says her office offers company-sponsored Diversity Awareness Training for all employees. "Our program," she explains, "was announced in 1990, and our goal was to provide all twenty-seven thousand employees with at least four hours of Diversity Awareness training by the end of 1993." While most other companies hire consultants to run a diversity program, PG&E decided to train and certify 110 line and staff employees and then allow those people to implement the training of employees throughout the rest of the company. The American Society for Training and Development's monthly journal cited the benefits of an intensive internal certification process like the one managed by PG&E. In many companies that rely on consultants, the commitment may slacken once the training consultants have left the site. The obvious benefit of PG&E's diversity program is that when the training is complete, the trainers are still with the company.

The diversity trainers are nominated by their business unit/region management and human resource managers. Each nominee completes a questionnaire and is interviewed by the company's diversity planning coordinator, then enters a six-day, sixty-hour course of activities and lectures.

Brown says, "In 1990, our CEO created a Multicultural Task Force, which is headed by a senior vice president and is responsible for making and approving recommendations on diversity to the company's management committee." The task force, which is made up of seven senior managers, meets quarterly.

The company makes charitable contributions to many minority organizations including Chinese for Affirmative Action, the Asian Pacific Youth Leadership Project, the Bay Area Urban League, the Chicano-Latino Youth Project, the United Negro College Fund, Filipinos for Affirmative Action, the NAACP and the National Hispanic Scholarship Fund. Since 1962, the company has awarded a four-year college scholarship through the J. B. Black Scholarship program. Of the thirty-six scholarships awarded each year, two-thirds are reserved for minority students.

PG&E hires minority interns through its support of the INROADS program, and it helped to start the Positive Impact tutorial and mentoring program which provides minority tutors and mentors for Cole Elementary School. The tutors are local high school students and members of the Black Police Association of Oakland.

In 1981, the company established its Equal Opportunity Purchasing Program and spent approximately $26 million with minority- and women-owned vendors. Today the program spends in excess of $300 million with these vendors. The company also invests in the Business Consortium Fund, which provides working capital loans to certified minority businesses.

Office locations: Headquarters are in San Francisco, but the company has offices throughout California.

77 Beale Street
San Francisco, California 94106
(415) 972-7000

J. C. PENNEY COMPANY, INC.

J. C. Penney is a major retailer, with department stores in all fifty states and Puerto Rico. The company markets family apparel, shoes, jewelry, accessories and home furnishings. Besides providing merchandise and services to consumers through its department stores, it also operates a large catalog department.

1990 revenues: $17,410,000,000
1991 revenues: $17,295,000,000
1992 revenues: $19,085,000,000

Number of full-time employees: 194,000

Percentage of these employees who are minorities: 17.2

Number of people in the total management pool: 19,739

Percentage of minorities in the total management pool: 10.7

Salary information:
    Store merchandising managers: $20,000+
    Store managers: $40,000–$170,000+
    Senior executives (excluding
    chairman & vice chairman):   up to $500,000

Founded in 1902 as a small general store in Wyoming, the company was officially named J. C. Penney in 1913 after its founding chairman, James Cash Penney.

    Minorities at J. C. Penney hold such positions as Vice President and Director of Investor Relations, District Manager, Entity Store Manager, Manager of Credit Development, Manager of Retail Accounting Procedures and Manager of Communications Programs and Services. J. C. Penney's board of directors has one minority member, Vernon E. Jordan, Jr., attorney and former head of the National Urban League.

According to Douglas Wolsieffer, Manager of Equal Opportunity Relations, the company established a Minority Advisory Team in 1990 which was comprised of seventeen employees appointed by the chairman from a cross-section of departments within the corporate office. "The team meets regularly," says Wolsieffer, "to make recommendations, and they report their findings to a steering committee that consists of senior management."

The team implemented a Corporate Mentor Program whereby new hires at the management level and transfers to the Corporate Office are assigned mentors. According to Edward T. Howard, director of investor relations and chairman of the Minority Advisory Team, "The mentor program was established for corporate office and nonretail field office associates in order to facilitate the transition of new hires and field transferees into the corporate environment and culture, and to improve retention rates. Special half-day training workshops for both mentors and protégés were developed to answer questions and establish working guidelines for each participant." Howard says the advisory team will also develop a career path process through which the company can inform all minority managers of interdepartmental career opportunities—especially those that will lead to senior management.

Wolsieffer adds that there are also individual affirmative action groups outside the Dallas headquarters. "The company believes that our work force should represent the groups that make up our consumer base," he says. "Diversity is the right thing to do, and it's also beneficial from a business point of view. When you have a diverse work force, you can come up with sensible and sensitive marketing ideas that appeal to our diverse customer base."

After using the three-set videotape series, "Valuing Diversity," developed by consultants Copeland-Griggs, J. C. Penney initiated its own workshop in 1991, "Managing a Diverse Workforce," a one-and-a-half-day workshop available to 18,000 company managers for the purpose of creating an awareness of cultural differences in the work environment. "We conduct a great deal of our training," says Wolsieffer, "at our training center in Dallas, and we encourage employees of every level to learn our diversity strategies."

In 1972, J. C. Penney established the Minority Supplier Development Program in its merchandising department. Within seven years, the company had expanded the program to its other departments and now has relationships with 1,973 minority-owned businesses that act as suppliers. Today the company spends more than $325 million with minority suppliers each year. To publicize its desire to work with minority suppliers, the company publishes a handbook, "Minority Business Opportunities." J. C. Penney also participates actively in the National Minority Supplier Development Council, Inc. In 1990, the Minority Business Development Agency of the U.S. Department of Commerce presented the company with its Director's Appreciation Award.

J. C. Penney interviews at many institutions known for their minority enrollment, including Howard University, Grambling State University, the University of Texas—Pan American, Southern University and Southwest Texas State University. The company supports intern scholarships at Northwestern and the University of Florida, where preference is given to minority students, and makes substantial donations to the United Negro College Fund, the League of United Latin American Citizens and the National Council of La Raza EXCEL Program.

The J. C. Penney Legal Department is active in minority programs that support minorities in the legal profession, including the Hispanic National Bar Association, the American Bar Association Minority Counsel Demonstration Program and the Southern Methodist University School of Law Diversity Clerkship Program.

The company demonstrated its particular strength in targeting the Hispanic consumer market when it introduced its Spanish catalog in 1979 and created the Hispanic Marketing Coordinator Position at the corporate level in 1982. Recognizing the tremendous minority consumer population, Hispanic Marketing evolved into Special Segment Marketing and now also targets African American and Asian American consumers as well.

Office locations: While the company is based in Dallas, there are offices and stores in all fifty states and Puerto Rico.

14841 North Dallas Parkway
Dallas, Texas 75240
(214) 591-1488

PEPSICO, INC.

PepsiCo is an international company most famous for its Pepsi-Cola Company division, which produces and markets such soft drinks as Pepsi, Diet Pepsi, Mug Root Beer, Slice and Mountain Dew. Other divisions of PepsiCo are Frito-Lay, Inc., producer of Fritos, Lay's, Doritos and other snacks; Taco Bell Worldwide Restaurants; Pizza Hut Worldwide Restaurants; and Kentucky Fried Chicken Corporation, operator of KFC Restaurants.

1990 revenues: $17,802,000,000
1991 revenues: $19,608,000,000
1992 revenues: $21,970,000,000

Number of full-time employees: 150,000 PepsiCo, 24,000 Pepsi-Cola division

Although PepsiCo was one of the few companies that would not release statistical information on its overall minority population, its various corporate subsidiaries—particularly Pepsi-Cola Company, Frito-Lay, Inc., and Kentucky Fried Chicken Corporation—have been leaders in their contributions to the minority community, and thus qualified the corporation to be included here.

The company made an important statement on the issue of minority hiring long before it was in vogue. When the company named Harvey C. Russell Vice President in Charge of Special Markets in 1962, Pepsi became the first *Fortune* 500 company to have a black vice president. At Russell's urging, the company went on to hire H. Naylor Fitzhugh, the black Howard University professor, as an executive who helped develop Pepsi-sponsored educational programs.

The corporate parent, now known as PepsiCo, has maintained its great record of contributing to minority causes and organizations. According to Ronnie Miller, Vice President of Corporate Personnel, the PepsiCo parent does not have any minority employee organizations, "but we are currently creating focus groups and launching a diversity scan in order to decide what type of diversity program we would need for executives, middle managers and others at the company." The parent works with minority headhunters to recruit minority professionals. According to Miller, "We are introducing a training course called Interviewing for a Diverse Workforce for our managers who are involved in recruiting." She adds that minorities do hold such management jobs at PepsiCo as Vice President of Community Affairs, Tax Counsel and Director of Project Finance in the treasury department.

PepsiCo actually has a small work force in comparison to its operating units. No true manufacturing, sales or marketing functions are performed by the parent; its employees work primarily in finance, law, public affairs and human resources.

At the Pepsi-Cola division, there are two minority employee organizations—one for blacks and one for Hispanics. Maurice Cox, Pepsi-Cola's Vice President of Corporate Development and Diversity, is a member of the Black Employees Association, formed in the mid-1980s. Cox says the company encouraged the creation of his group and of the Hispanic Employees Association. "The groups meet regularly and have local chapters in other locations," he says, "and they not only encourage diversity and provide networking opportunities, but they also assist in recruiting and give input on business issues that benefit the company's marketing efforts."

In the past, Pepsi-Cola has had a diversity task force made up of senior executives and has offered race relations seminars and diversity training. Now the issue of diversity is worked into the core training program.

The company recruits at such black colleges as Howard University, Morehouse College and Florida A&M University.

Within Pepsi-Cola, minorities hold such positions as Vice President of On-Premise Sales, Vice President of Employee Relations and Director of Ethnic Consumer Marketing. The company also has a Minority Business Enterprise Program, which spent more than $87 million with minority contractors last year. And recognizing that Pepsi bottling franchises also provide jobs in minority communities, the company has one Hispanic-owned bottler in Laredo, Texas, and two black-owned bottlers in Washington, D.C., and Michigan. One of those franchises is run by the former basketball player Magic Johnson and the magazine publisher/entrepreneur Earl Graves.

At the Frito-Lay division, there is a Hispanic Support Group and a Black Professional Association. According to Ed Adams, Director of Diversity and Development at Frito-Lay, the two organizations bring the minority perspective into the business and the marketplace. Adams says the two minority support groups were created in 1990 and have formed local chapters that meet monthly during business hours. Adams, who holds a Ph.D. in industrial organization psychology, has been with PepsiCo since 1987 and has been based at Frito-Lay's Plano, Texas, office since 1990. As a black manager, he is particularly proud of the diversity initiative that has taken shape at Frito-Lay.

"Diversity is our strategic competitive advantage," he says. "Not only is it good for our employees' morale, but it makes good business sense. Our marketplace is made up of diverse cultures, so we need diverse employees who understand that diverse marketplace." Adams had previously spent three years at the Pepsi-Cola division, where he initiated the race relations workshops. At Frito-Lay, he has begun a mentoring initiative whereby senior mentors are matched with minority midlevel managers. Adams explains, "Many minorities in corporate America lack access to nonminority senior executives, so we think that a mentoring program will create an easy way for these groups to meet and learn from each other."

Frito-Lay offers two-day diversity workshops which use similar-race groupings and cross-race groupings. Senior executives at the company have a bonus incentive that takes into account their success in hiring, promoting and mentoring minority employees. Some of the top jobs held by minorities at Frito-Lay include division president and general manager, Vice President of Purchasing, Director of Technology and Director of Packaging.

Frito-Lay has an established Minority Business Development Program which was created in 1983. It provides free business consulting resources to Minority Business Enterprises and has a program which provides scholarships to senior managers of minority businesses so that they can attend the executive program at the Amos Tuck Business School at Dartmouth College. The company also launched the YES for Young Entrepreneurs program, in which minority youth are taught entrepreneurial skills. Specifically, the program awards four-year renewable $10,000 scholarships to students with an interest in attending an entrepreneurial college program.

According to Vince Berkeley, Vice President of Equal Opportunity and Minority Relations at Pizza Hut, the diversity of the company's work force will not only provide opportunities for individuals of all backgrounds, "but it will help us generate new, innovative ideas to meet the demands of our customers. In large metropolitan areas, we will be marketing our products and services to larger numbers of minorities." Recently Pizza Hut implemented three programs to further the company's diversity efforts. The company sponsored a race relations seminar for officers, directors and district managers. A mentor program was designed to help new employees, and an employee Affirmative Action Task Force was established to solve problems and create ways of advancing the diversity initiative.

PepsiCo has contributed a great deal to the minority population through its grants to various schools and universities. The company gave $1 million to Arizona State University's College of Business to fund scholarships for ten students, particularly Hispanic and minority students. Eventually there will be twenty Pepsi Scholars in the program. Another $1-million grant was given to Manhattanville College to support the school's program to promote intercultural understanding and to support the Intercultural House, a dormitory for students interested in diversity awareness. On the high school level, PepsiCo supports the Leadership and Education Development Program, a summer program designed to introduce talented minority students to the world of business. Students are chosen by the nonprofit group A Better Chance, Inc., and attend classes on a college campus and visit local businesses. They are mentored through their high school years and into college.

The Pepsi-Cola division works with inner-city schools through its Pepsi School Challenge in Dallas and Detroit to cut school dropout rates. More than 2,000 students have participated in the program, which Pepsi-Cola financed with a $2-million grant, the largest financial award program ever granted to a public school in the United States.

The Kentucky Fried Chicken division is active in drug prevention programs for young people. It was the first national corporate sponsor of Drug Abuse Resistance Education, which trains local police to discuss the dangers of drug abuse with elementary school students.

Although William T. Coleman, the prominent black attorney and former Secretary of Transportation, was once a member, there are currently no minorities on PepsiCo's board of directors.

Office locations: In separate facilities, PepsiCo's headquarters and Pepsi-Cola's offices are both in suburban Westchester County, approximately thirty-five minutes north of New York City. Frito-Lay is based in Texas, and Kentucky Fried Chicken, Pizza Hut and Taco Bell are in Kentucky, Kansas and California, respectively. The various business divisions have offices and plants throughout the United States and in more than 150 countries.

Purchase, New York 10577
(914) 253-2000

PFIZER INC.

Founded in 1849, Pfizer is a diversified, research-based health care company with sales in more than 140 countries. The company develops, manufactures and markets products in five business segments: health care, consumer products, animal health, specialty chemicals and specialty minerals. Some of Pfizer's brand-name consumer products are Visine, Ben-Gay, Plax dental mouthwash, Coty fragrances and Stetson cologne.

1990 revenues: $6,400,000,000
1991 revenues: $6,950,000,000
1992 revenues: $7,230,200,000

Number of full-time employees: 44,300 worldwide, 17,924 U.S.

Percentage of these employees who are minorities: 21.3
    Black: 8.4
    Hispanic: 6.6
    Asian/Pacific Islander: 6.1
    Native American: .2

Number of people in the total management pool: 8,396

Percentage of minorities in the total management pool: 10.1

Percentage of minority managers who comprise each managerial level:
    Senior management: 5.4
    Middle management: 10.3
    Entry-level management: 11.1

311

Opportunities at Pfizer are organized into the following functional areas: Research and Development, Sales, Marketing, Engineering and Production and Business Support. While there are more opportunities for those with a background in the sciences or engineering, there is also a great need for managers with a business or liberal arts background.

The company recruits at such black universities as Atlanta, Central State, Florida A&M, Hampton, North Carolina A&T, Texas Southern, Wilberforce and Xavier.

The company has had a minority person on its board of directors for more than fifteen years. Currently William J. Kennedy III, chairman of North Carolina Mutual Life Insurance Company, is a director. Some of the highest management positions at Pfizer and its subsidiaries are held by minorities. Titles held by minorities include President of the American Medical Systems subsidiary, Vice President of Employee Resources, Vice President of Clinical Research, Vice President of Marketing U.S. Operations in the Pfizer Oral Care Division, Vice President and General Manager of the Shiley subsidiary, Vice President of Research and Development in the Pfizer Specialty Minerals Group, Director of Finance, Director of Pharmaceuticals Business Development, Assistant General Counsel and Senior Corporate Counsel. Bob Brown, Vice President of Employee Resources at Pfizer, is particularly proud of the company's record of promoting minorities into top management positions.

A black manager himself, Mr. Brown says that more than 20% of the new sales hires at the company's new Pratt Pharmaceuticals Division are members of minority groups. This division used ten minority recruitment agencies and thirteen membership organizations to find minority candidates. Human resources staff called on such organizations as the NAACP, the Urban League and the Hispanic Job Coalition to build a list of job candidates.

To strengthen its minority recruiting effort, Pfizer distributes a manual, "Minority/Female Recruitment Resource

Guide," throughout the company. It provides information on predominantly minority colleges, universities with 20% or more minority enrollment, university placement offices with special programs for minorities, annual career fairs for minorities, minority organizations, minority fraternities and sororities, minority professional associations and minority publications. While a relatively simple concept, this manual keeps the recruiting staff and other company employees up to date on issues of interest to potential minority recruits.

In the late 1970s, Pfizer's Equal Opportunity Affairs and Management Training and Development Departments designed an in-house training program titled Pfizer Equal Opportunity Program: Law & Employment (PEOPLE). The program is periodically updated. According to Marilyn Budzanoski, Supervisor of Equal Opportunity Affairs, participation is not mandatory on a corporate basis, but some facilities require management attendance. The program is used for all levels of management.

According to Budzanoski, the company has no minority employee organizations.

Charitable contributions to outside groups are made through Pfizer Inc. and the Pfizer Foundation, Inc. Funding has been given to the United Negro College Fund, A Better Chance, the National Hispanic Scholarship Fund, the American Indian Science and Engineering Society Scholarship Fund, ASPIRA and many other minority organizations.

Pfizer works with New York City's Metropolitan Transit Authority in its Adopt-A-Station Project, whereby Pfizer has made improvements in a Brooklyn subway station near one of the company's plants. Working with the Enterprise Foundation and New York Equity Fund, the company is helping to develop and rehabilitate 3,415 apartments for low- and moderate-income families in New York. The company has pledged to invest $8.2 million in low-income housing in New York.

The company is also well known for the Employee Volunteer Program, begun in 1968 to encourage employees to use company time to volunteer in constructive community activities. Lillian Fernandez, Director of International Affairs, volunteers with the National Puerto Rican Forum; she serves as chairwoman of the board and oversees a $4-million education and job training organization in five states.

Pfizer has one of the better-established minority vendor programs. Begun in 1967, the Pfizer Supplier Development Program purchased approximately $60 million worth of goods and services from minority-owned companies in 1992.

Office locations: Pfizer has offices and plants in twenty-five states and the District of Columbia. Pfizer has manufacturing facilities in more than sixty-five countries. Headquarters are in New York City.

235 East 42nd Street
New York, New York 10017
(212) 573-2323

PHILIP MORRIS COMPANIES, INC.

Philip Morris Companies is the largest consumer packaged goods company in the world, with major tobacco, food and beer operations. The conglomerate owns: Philip Morris USA, which manufactures Marlboro, Parliament and Benson & Hedges cigarettes; Miller Beer, which Philip Morris acquired in 1969; and JacobsSuchard, which manufactures chocolate candies and Swiss coffees. Philip Morris also owns General Foods and Kraft, acquired through two separate transactions in the 1980s. Philip Morris Capital Corporation is the division which engages in various financing and investment activities including investing in securities of third parties and financing for customers and suppliers of the company's subsidiaries. Many of the activities at the headquarters office are managed by an entity referred to as Philip Morris Management Corp. This profile focuses on the programs sponsored by Philip Morris USA, Philip Morris Management Corp. and Miller Beer.

1990 revenues: $51,000,000,000
1991 revenues: $56,458,000,000
1992 revenues: $59,100,000,000

Number of full-time employees: 105,165

Percentage of these employees who are minorities: 25.4
    Black: 16
    Hispanic: 7
    Asian/Pacific Islander: 2
    Native American: .4

Number of people in the total management pool: 5,044

Percentage of minorities in the total management pool: 15.9

Percentage of minority managers who comprise each managerial level:

Senior vice president:	6.8
Vice president:	8.1
Director:	8.3
Manager:	10.3

Salary information:

Senior management:	$130,000+
Vice president:	$130,000+
Director:	$75,000–$130,000
Manager:	$50,000–$75,000
Professional:	$35,000–$49,000
Entry-level:	$35,000

Minorities at Philip Morris and its operating subsidiaries hold several top positions including Senior Vice President and Chief Administrative Officer at Philip Morris International, Vice President and Treasurer at the Philip Morris Companies parent company, Vice President of Employee Relations at the Philip Morris parent company and Group Director at Philip Morris USA. George Lewis, the parent company's treasurer, is an influential black executive who also sits on the board's Affirmative Action Committee.

There are two minority members on the company's board of directors: Dr. Jose Antonio Cordido-Freytes, president of C. A. Tabacalera Nacional, and Richard Parsons, a prominent black attorney who was an aide to former Vice President Nelson Rockefeller and currently serves as chairman of the Dime Savings Bank of New York.

Although all of Philip Morris's subsidiaries conduct their

own recruiting and community affairs programs (see separate profile on General Foods USA), it is impossible to ignore the overall contributions the parent company has made to the minority work force and the minority community. The Philip Morris name appears on the sponsors' list of just about every major minority fund-raiser, social event or conference. It is particularly well known for its sponsorship and publication of two important biennial books: *The Guide to Black Organizations* and *The Guide to Hispanic Organizations*. Since their initial publication in 1981, these 200-page guides have become important reference books in schools, homes, businesses, government offices and libraries.

The various Philip Morris entities are active recruiters of minority students on college and graduate school campuses. Philip Morris USA recruits many Hispanic students from the University of Texas and the University of New Mexico. Miller Brewing Company is involved with the Business Industry Cluster at Southern University, Grambling State University and North Carolina A&T State University. "We also support the Hispanic Association of Colleges and Universities, in addition to the National Society of Hispanic MBAs," explains Clotilde Dillon, Manager of Workforce Diversity.

Dillon says the companies also recruit at such predominantly black colleges as Howard University, Tuskegee University, Morehouse College, Florida A&M University and Hampton University. Miller Brewing Company was a founding sponsor in 1987 of the Thurgood Marshall Scholarship Fund and continues to sponsor ten other scholarships each year at the National Hispanic University in California.

According to Dillon, Philip Morris has an Affirmative Action Committee composed of senior executives from management and the Philip Morris board of directors. Established in 1976, the committee reviews the company's affirmative action and diversity policies and programs and identifies areas for improvement. Some of the operating companies have created multicultural steering committees to guide company management on the diversity initiative.

There are diversity training programs at several of the companies. Dillon, a Puerto Rican graduate of Fordham University's Graduate School of Social Work, has become an outspoken advocate of diversity both inside and outside the company. As the company's Manager of Workforce Diversity, she has been profiled by *Hispanic* magazine and has given presentations on diversity at Harvard Law School and other schools.

Although it does not have as many employees as the company's other divisions, the Philip Morris Management Corp., the headquarters entity in New York, has done a great deal for the minority community. According to Dillon, this division has helped local communities by sponsoring projects that employ and mentor minority high school students. The division also participates in job fairs sponsored by the National Black MBA Association, National Puerto Rican Forum Inc. and the National Association of Black Accountants.

At Philip Morris USA, approximately 95% of the sales force managers, including the senior vice president of the entire sales organization, have participated in diversity workshops. These workshops have also been implemented in the division's manufacturing facilities. According to Edward Van Dyke, who has been with Philip Morris USA since he joined as a salesman in 1969, "Our factory workers can be working with as many as three thousand fellow employees in a facility, and our sales managers can be managing as many as nine hundred people. It's important for all managers and employees to know how to relate to and manage people from varied backgrounds."

Van Dyke, who has held several Philip Morris sales positions including Director of Regional Sales in Chicago, is now Director of Affirmative Action for the division. "This company has a history of being out front on race and diversity issues," he says. "Our products were boycotted by five Southern states during the 1950s because we hired a black sales representative. Today, minority sales representatives work throughout the country and have the opportunity to mentor each other and to work with such organizations as the Urban League and the NAACP when they organize their conventions." Van Dyke belongs to the Corporate Diversity Council, which meets approximately six times each year and discusses the diversity activities of each of the business units.

The Philip Morris USA division worked with Gordon & Associates, a diversity consultant from Philadelphia, to design the three different workshops used by managers in the New York office, the manufacturing facilities and the sales force.

The division has established scholarships and grants for minority students at such schools as the University of Alabama, Hampton University, Winston-Salem State University, Duke University and the University of Michigan.

Victor Han, Director of Communications at Philip Morris USA, says he has never felt that his ethnicity was an issue at the office. "Since there are so many minorities working for this company," Han explains, "I have never once felt uncomfortable because I am Korean." Han, who has been with the company since 1991, has long been one of the highest-ranking Asian Americans in the public relations field. He first came in contact with Philip Morris in 1984, when he began working with the company as Executive Vice President and Managing Director of the public relations firm Burson-Marsteller in New York. "When I first entered this business in the early 1970s, it was nearly impossible to find another Asian person in the field," says Han, "so I accepted the fact that I would have to network among nonminority professionals. Networking in a multiethnic company like Philip Morris is extremely easy."

Another division of the Philip Morris conglomerate is Miller Brewing Company, which began a diversity program in the fall of 1986 when Miller executives were given diversity training. The division's Workforce Diversity Department presents all new employees with an orientation program on EEO and affirmative action policies.

Philip Morris is a sponsor of the annual Hispanic Achievement Awards and in 1993 was named by *Hispanic* magazine one of the 100 companies providing the most opportunities for Hispanics.

The company hires student interns through the IN-ROADS minority internship program and participates in the National Urban League Black Executive Exchange Program, sponsoring black managers who visit minority colleges and act as instructors and mentors to minority students who want to learn about what it's like being a minority executive in corporate America.

The companies support such minority organizations as the National Urban League, the National Hispanic Scholarship Fund, the Asian Pacific American Legal Consortium, the United Negro College Fund, Dance Theater of Harlem, the Organization of Chinese Americans, the U.S. Hispanic Chamber of Commerce, the National Council of La Raza, the NAACP, the Joint Center for Political and Economic Studies, the Mexican American Legal Defense and Education Fund, the Asian American Journalist Association, Festival Latino and the PanAsian Repertory Theatre. The companies have sponsored a national touring exhibition of African American art by Romare Bearden as well as multicultural programs across the country at universities and libraries.

Through its Minority Vendor Program in 1992, Philip Morris made more than $215 million in purchases from more than 1,500 minority-owned firms, making it one of the largest corporate purchasers from minority businesses. The program, created in 1980, is guided by a group of employees who serve on the Philip Morris Minority Vendor Task Force. Philip Morris also established a Minority Banking Program which currently does business with seventy-four minority-owned banks. In 1991, more than $1.5 billion in tax payments were processed through these minority banks.

Office locations: The parent company, Philip Morris Companies, Inc., is headquartered in midtown Manhattan, along with Philip Morris Incorporated and the domestic cigarette operations, Philip Morris USA. The overseas cigarette operations have offices in Switzerland, Hong Kong and other countries. Miller Brewing Company has main offices in Milwaukee, Wisconsin. The Kraft General Foods, Inc., subsidiary and its various operating units are located throughout the United States, with large offices in Illinois, Tennessee, New York and Wisconsin.

120 Park Avenue
New York, New York 10017
(212) 880-5000

POLAROID CORPORATION

Polaroid designs, manufactures and markets a variety of products in the instant image recording field. These include instant photographic cameras and films, electronic imaging recording devices, conventional films, filters and lenses. The products are used in amateur and professional photography, science, medicine and education.

1990 revenues: $1,970,000,000
1991 revenues: $2,070,600,000
1992 revenues: $2,150,000,000

Number of full-time employees: 8,056

Percentage of these employees who are minorities: 17.5
      Black: 14
      Hispanic: 1.6
      Asian/Pacific Islander: 1.7
      Native American: .2

Number of people in the total management pool: 1,432

Percentage of minorities in the total management pool: 10.1

Percentage of minority managers who comprise each managerial level:
      Senior vice president: 0
      Vice president: 14
      Director: 9
      Senior manager: 10

Manager: 9
Assistant manager: 16

Salary information (all salaries monthly):
Vice president/senior vice president: $10,000–$20,000
Senior manager/director: $6560–$13,000
Managers: $4450–$8000
Senior administrators: $3700–$5400
Administrators: $2800–$4050

"We must become the employer of choice for minorities and women by structuring a work environment that is diverse, by recognizing differences and building upon them, and by providing equal opportunity to all members of the organization." This is what Polaroid's chairman, I. MacAllister Booth, has to say about the direction his company has been taking.

Founded in 1937 by Dr. Edwin Land, Polaroid is a company whose leaders see minority managers as an important segment of their work force.

The company has several management-sanctioned minority employee groups which have made the company extremely popular among minority executives. They include the Asian Leadership Organization, the Hispanics in Polaroid, the Black Salaried Women and the Senior Black Managers. While the Asian and Hispanic organizations have only been in existence since 1988, both of the black employee organizations were established in the 1970s. The Senior Black Managers group meets for two hours every other week. According to Michael LeBlanc, Corporate Vice President of Human Resources, "The purpose of these groups is to improve the work environment of the company." As a member of the Senior Black Managers, LeBlanc says that the organization advises company leaders on such issues as pay and advancement, and contributes to corporate policymaking.

As a means of linking all of the minority employee groups,

an umbrella organization called Polaroid's Diversity Network Alliance was formed in 1989. The alliance meets monthly and provides an opportunity for representatives from each group to collaborate on common goals. LeBlanc, also the first black officer at the company, helped spearhead the alliance and the many race and gender initiatives advanced by the company's chairman. According to LeBlanc, the company is unmatched in establishing groups that support its minority and female employees. Polaroid has established Affirmative Action Committees in most of its business divisions. In the Business and Professional Products Sales group, there is a committee that focuses on race and gender diversity issues. "Many of these committees," says LeBlanc, "have a cross-section of members that represent different racial and ethnic groups. They are not just for people of color."

The company also has a committee called the Team for the Improvement of the Environment for Women and Minorities (the I Team), created in 1989 to develop ways for the company to attract and retain a high-caliber work force. It is a decision-making committee which has the power to set company policy. It is made up of five senior level officers from different departments of the company, as well as representatives from the various minority and women employee organizations. The chair is Vice President of World Manufacturing.

One of the I Team's greatest contributions is bringing diversity training to Polaroid. In 1989, the I Team decided that the company should begin some type of awareness training. This mandate required that each of the company's business divisions hire diversity consultants and perform a needs assessment so that training programs could be designed to suit each division.

According to LeBlanc, each division found it had different issues to tackle. The Manufacturing division has worked with five different consultants in creating a program. The Integral Film Manufacturing division used a series of "Valuing Differences" workshops for all 800 of its employees. Certain other divisions at Polaroid work with J. Howard & Associates, U. T. Saunders Consulting and River Bend Associates. LeBlanc says that, overall, the company has used the Copeland-Griggs videotapes, Rosabeth Moss Kanter's "Tale of O" presentation, outside speakers, case studies, question-and-answer sessions and role-playing.

Under Chairman Booth's urging, the company has sponsored weekend seminars for senior executives called Race and Gender Workshops which discussed the company's progress in hiring, promoting and retaining minorities.

According to Eloise Adamson of Polaroid's Office of Affirmative Action, minorities at Polaroid hold such positions as Corporate Vice President of Human Resources, Director of Manufacturing, Director of Internal Audit, Director of Distribution, Plant Manager and Director of Marketing.

There are two minority individuals on Polaroid's board of directors: Yen-Tsai Fen, a former library administrator at Harvard College, and Frank S. Jones, professor of urban affairs at Massachusetts Institute of Technology.

There is a company-wide Buddy/Mentor Program which was created by the Senior Black Managers and the Black Salaried Women organizations. The program pairs less senior black employees with senior black managers in a six-month buddy/mentor relationship. The pairs meet at least once a month, and mentors are expected to introduce their buddies to at least two people who could be significant in the buddy's career development. LeBlanc says the mentoring program is meant to introduce young employees to the corporate culture, provide a confidant for new hires, integrate out-of-towners into different aspects of the Boston/Cambridge area, improve and inspire the performance of new employees and build a network of contacts. The mentors meet every six months to report to a subcommittee on any new problems or ideas that might help the program.

The company recruits at many universities, including Howard, Florida A&M and Pan American.

It contributes to such organizations as the Mexican American Legal Defense and Education Fund, the National Hispanic Scholarship Fund, the NAACP and the U.S. Hispanic Chamber of Commerce.

There is a minority supplier-vendor program at the company called the Polaroid Minority Business Development Program, which was created in 1978 and spends approximately $30 million each year.

The company is headquartered in Cambridge, Massachusetts, an extremely liberal city, and popular among minority professionals in the Northeast.

Office locations: Polaroid is based in Massachusetts and has offices and plants in Georgia, Illinois, New Jersey, California, Ohio, Texas, Tennessee, Washington and Massachusetts. It also has locations in eighteen other countries including Mexico, England, Japan, Spain, Germany, China and Italy.

549 Technology Square
Cambridge, Massachusetts 02139
(617) 577-2000

PPG INDUSTRIES, INC.

Founded in 1883 as Pittsburgh Plate Glass, PPG is now a diversified global manufacturer and a leading supplier of products for manufacturing, building, processing and other industries. The company makes flat glass and fabricated glass products, continuous-strand fiber-glass, decorative and protective coatings and industrial and specialty chemicals. Each of PPG's divisions, the Glass Group, the Coatings & Resins Group and the Chemicals Group, has its own research and development program and uses its own training programs for new hires.

1990 revenues: $6,021,000,000
1991 revenues: $5,673,000,000
1992 revenues: $5,814,000,000

Number of full-time U.S. employees: 20,976

Percentage of these employees who are minorities: 13.3
    Black: 10.2
    Hispanic: 2.4
    Asian/Pacific Islander: .6
    Native American: .1

Number of people in the total management pool: 2,707

Percentage of minorities in the total management pool: 5.4

PPG's commitment to minority issues begins with its CEO, Vincent Sarni, who has worked to assist many minority organizations including the Negro Emergency Education Drive (NEED), a Pittsburgh-based organization, which he recently served as chairman. NEED provides financial aid to black students for postsecondary education. Other PPG executives like Jeff Gilbert, Director of Human Resources Policy and Practice, take an active role in the organization by serving on the group's board of trustees.

During the past few years, PPG has formed Diversity Teams and Mentoring Teams to improve the quality of life for minority employees. According to George Krock, Manager of Equal Employment Opportunity Programs, the company's Diversity Team has a rotating membership and draws employees who bring different backgrounds and professional skills to the group's activities. The group was responsible for creating the company's diversity training. "Our diversity team worked with a public policy professor from Carnegie-Mellon in order to design a three-day training program we call 'Achieving the Vision Through Valuing Diversity,'" says Krock. "During the first two days of the program, employees learn to become aware of their own feelings about ethnicity, gender, handicap status and other differences. After a few weeks have passed and the employees have thought about these issues with a heightened sensitivity, we take them through the third day, which helps them build skills to both deal with and value the diversity that they face."

During a three-year period, PPG trained all its vice presidents and general managers, then introduced all its other employees to the diversity program.

Another successful program at PPG is its Mentoring Team. Bert Birdsall, Jr., Corporate Manager of Affirmative Action at corporate headquarters and chair of the Mentoring Team, says the company saw that new minority and female employees had not been taught the values and culture of the company as quickly as many white male employees. "To correct this," says Birdsall, "we created a mentoring system so that these new people could be matched with a mentor in the management group. We wanted these managers to provide career direction to the minorities and women who didn't normally forge their own relationships with more senior employees." Birdsall, himself a black manager who has been with PPG since 1973 in several positions in human resources, acknowledges that for minorities to succeed, they must know more than just the formal rules. "They have to understand the culture of the company as well."

Birdsall says that an individual's supervisor is never an assigned mentor because the protégés must have a free-flowing dialogue without having to worry about being evaluated on his or her questions or fears. The Mentoring Team was so successful in helping minorities that it is now used for all new hires at PPG.

At the company's Cleveland plant, a minority employee organization was begun in 1989. Founded by a black manager who now runs PPG's Dover, Delaware, plant, the Minority Focus Group ensures that nonminority managers are aware of the concerns of minorities at the company. The organization is also used for employee networking.

Of PPG's three business groups, the Coatings and Resins Group seems the most progressive with minority issues. A monthly newsletter, *Diversity Dimensions*, is circulated to all associates in Coatings and Resins, as well as to key management personnel. The newsletter presents information and advice on how to apply diversity training skills in the workplace.

There is also a Minority Scholarship Internship Program in the Coatings and Resins Group which selects college students majoring in science or engineering. Winning students receive $5,000 and summer internships at PPG. PPG currently has scholarship winners at Howard University, Carnegie Mellon, Ohio State, Purdue and other schools. As Birdsall explains, since PPG is not a consumer products company that the average student knows by name, the company hopes the scholarships and internships will introduce students to the company so that they will consider returning for full-time employment after graduation.

PPG recruits at such historically black colleges as North

Carolina A&T, North Carolina Central, Hampton University and Morgan State. While most of the positions available at PPG are in engineering and science, the company also recruits in marketing, sales, accounting and finance.

As an additional part of its recruiting effort, the company attends minority-oriented job fairs and advertises in publications aimed at minority students. At a recent job fair sponsored by North Carolina A&T, Birdsall realized how many students simply wanted to know what it's like being a minority employee or minority manager at a *Fortune* 500 company. "We forget that many minority students do not have parents that have this experience, so it's important for minority managers to be actively involved in recruiting and visiting minority students at universities. If they don't have us to answer these questions, there is no one who can advise them on the experience. They need to know that at some of these large companies, a minority person can feel very comfortable and excel in his chosen field. That's what I want them to hear. And that's what I know from my own experience."

Established in 1951, the PPG Industries Foundation contributes to such minority organizations as the National Action Council for Minorities in Engineering and the United Negro College Fund. It also contributes to the minority accounting and minority engineering programs at such universities as Howard, Pennsylvania State, Ohio State, Carnegie Mellon, Northwestern and Purdue. The foundation also sponsors two four-year college minority scholarships through the National Merit Scholarship program.

The corporate headquarters office has adopted Langley High School in inner-city Pittsburgh, where employees tutor students, assist in a speakers' bureau and serve as mentors. The PPG Langley Partnership was created in 1979 and has also provided many summer jobs and college scholarships. The company runs similar programs near its offices in Louisiana and Alabama.

While PPG has three minority members among its twenty-nine top officers, no minority members serve on the board of directors.

Office locations: PPG is headquartered in Pittsburgh and has plants and offices which handle sales, research and development, distribution and manufacturing in most states. The company operates seventy-eight major manufacturing facilities in Canada, France, Germany, Italy, Mexico, the Netherlands, Spain, Taiwan, the United Kingdom and the United States.

One PPG Place
Pittsburgh, Pennsylvania 15272
(412) 434-3131

THE PROCTER & GAMBLE COMPANY

Founded in 1837, Procter & Gamble is an international consumer goods company that manufactures and markets laundry and cleaning products, personal care items and foods and beverages. Its brand-name products include Ivory Snow, Comet, Tide Detergent, Clearasil, Safeguard Soap, Pampers, Crest Toothpaste, Vicks, Bounty Paper Towels, Scope Mouthwash, Jif Peanut Butter, Hawaiian Punch, Duncan Hines Cake Mixes, Citrus Hill Orange Juice and Crisco Oil. In 1989, the Noxell Corporation was merged into Procter & Gamble, adding such brand-name products as Noxzema and Cover Girl.

1990 revenues: $24,100,000,000
1991 revenues: $27,026,000,000
1992 revenues: $29,362,000,000

Number of full-time U.S. employees: 47,868

Percentage of these employees who are minorities: 17.7
    Black: 13.6
    Hispanic: 2.7
    Asian/Pacific Islander: .2
    Native American: 1.2

Number of people in the total management pool: 13,318

Percentage of minorities in the total management pool: 13

Percentage of minority managers who comprise each managerial level:

Vice president: 2 people
Manager: 12.8
Sales force (not necessarily managers):   9.9

If you're looking for a first-class employment opportunity in American consumer marketing, Procter & Gamble is the place to look. While the company's reputation for secrecy does not initially make it seem a welcoming workplace, you should look beyond the facade. More than 25% of all new management hires in 1991 in the U.S. operations were minority members. Although the company has a long way to go before it has substantial minority representation in the highest ranks—there are three minority officers at the vice president level—its current hiring record is impressive.

The company recruits at such historically black universities as Florida A&M, Howard and Tuskegee, as well as from schools with large Hispanic enrollments, including the University of Puerto Rico and the University of Texas at Austin. Procter & Gamble also participates in job fairs sponsored by the Urban League, the National Black MBA Association, the National Hispanic MBA Association and the Boston Career Expo, an annual recruiting fair for minority college students which is organized by several universities in the Northeast.

Each of the separate departments (advertising, finance, research and development, etc.) evaluates its own hiring needs and manages its own recruiting program.

David Clark, who has been with the company since 1985, says P&G is known for its success in training professionals in sales, marketing and advertising. P&G has a reputation for grooming its own—and would rather do this than hire senior managers from competitors. "One of the strengths of P&G," explains Clark, "is that we promote from within. We don't do a lot of hiring from other companies." A black graduate of West Point, Clark is now Personnel Supervisor in the Advertising Department after spending four and a half years in brand management and becoming a Brand Manager for P&G's Duncan Hines division in Canada. "Minority professionals who come here," he says, "know that in addition to getting the best training, they are going to get the best career support through minority mentoring and networking programs."

Clark has had mentors in the Minority Mentoring Program, in addition to serving as a mentor to junior minority managers. "When looking for my own mentors, I found that it was important to select both minority mentors and nonminority mentors," he says, "because you need more than one perspective, and you need access into as many groups as you can find within the company." Clark says the company's Retention Task Force has helped identify other programs and activities that help to retain minority employees and advance their careers.

There are formal and informal minority employee organizations. Within the advertising function, there are several groups, including the Black Advertising Leadership Team, which meets once a month and focuses on training, career planning and social networking.

Lynwood Battle, Manager of Corporate Affirmative Action, says the company has recently created a formal minority mentoring program designed to help new minority managers. "We wanted our junior minority managers to have someone who can teach them the corporate culture, provide career advice and discuss issues that might otherwise be risky to their job advancement," says Battle, who has been with the company since 1970. Each mentor is a senior manager from another department.

Battle acknowledges that diversity is most successful when the line managers are committed to it. "It's not enough for staff managers to advance ethnic and racial diversity," he says. "Line managers have to also be there to serve as role models and provide positive reinforcement for young minority managers." His office has worked with Pope & Associates and developed a two-day diversity training course for staff and line managers as well as other employees. New employee orientation courses and senior management courses all have a diversity component. "Our manufacturing locations are very independent," says Battle, "and they will often supplement the diversity effort with special diversity events that take place on a local level. Our various line divisions are all allowed and encouraged to hire their own diversity consultants in order to design programs that aid their more specific needs."

Procter & Gamble helped to underwrite the Copeland Griggs "Valuing Diversity" videotapes several years ago. Since that time, the company's International Division has also employed consultants from Copeland Griggs to train American employees dealing with businesspeople outside the United States.

The company also sponsors several minority career development programs, including a scholarship program conducted by the Research and Development Division which pays full tuition for the study of chemical technology at the Ohio College of Applied Science. By working with the National Organization for the Professional Advancement of Black Chemists and Chemical Engineers, the company sponsors a fellowship for minorities seeking a Ph.D. in chemistry. The company's research and development department sponsors fellowships for two minority students to obtain their master's degrees and for two minority students to obtain their Ph.D.'s in engineering. Each student receives full tuition, an annual stipend and summer employment at P&G.

Procter & Gamble is also a member of the Advisory Council of Amigos de SER, the nonprofit organization which provides educational and skill training and employment placement to Hispanic Americans. The company participates in, and financially supports, the College/Industry Cluster Program, which brings together administrators of black colleges and representatives of business to assist the colleges in upgrading curricula and increasing the flow of black college graduates into business. They are currently involved with clusters at Jackson State, Howard, Florida A&M, Tennessee State, North Carolina A&T and several other universities.

Several black managers at Procter & Gamble participate in the National Urban League's Black Executive Exchange Program, whereby managers act as "executives in residence" at a black college for several days. They give seminars and talk to students about school and careers. The sales department at the company works with the INROADS minority internship to provide four years of summer work for minority students.

The company has not only been one of the top contributors to the United Negro College Fund, but its chairman has also maintained an active role while sitting on the board of directors of the fund in past years. Durk Jager, an executive vice president at Procter & Gamble, also currently sits on the fund's board. The company supports the American Indian College Fund, through which scholarships are provided to students attending twenty-six different tribal colleges in the United States.

The Procter & Gamble Fund contributes to the National Hispanic Scholarship Fund and to the Society of Professional Engineers Foundation. The fund also supports the Catholic Inner City Schools Education Fund, which provides financial assistance to inner-city elementary schools.

Since 1973, P&G has had an active Minority Business Development program which identifies and works with minority-owned suppliers and vendors.

Office locations: The company has sixty-three plants in twenty-five states. Each plant typically manufactures only one type of product. There are also research, development and engineering facilities in Cincinnati, Ohio; Memphis, Tennessee; Hunt Valley, Maryland; Norwich, New York; Phillipsburg, New Jersey;

and Shelton, Connecticut, as well as in Japan, Venezuela, England, France, Mexico, Canada, Belgium and Germany.

One Procter & Gamble Plaza
Cincinnati, Ohio 45202
(513) 983-1100

THE PRUDENTIAL INSURANCE COMPANY OF AMERICA

Founded in the late 1800s, the Prudential is an insurance and financial services company which provides services to individuals and businesses. Besides offering insurance, annuities, IRAs and mutual funds for individuals, the company also provides residential real estate services through its network of independent real estate offices, credit card services and secured personal loans. Through its subsidiary, The Prudential Investment Corporation, the company advises institutional clients on asset management, specialized investment and various forms of financing. The subsidiary carries out the investment banking and merchant banking activities as well as private debt and equity finance.

1990 revenues: $42,125,000,000
1991 revenues: $50,958,000,000
1992 revenues: $45,000,000,000

Number of full-time employees: 74,637

Percentage of these employees who are minorities: 16.3
    Black: 10.4
    Hispanic: 3.2
    Asian/Pacific Islander: 2.2
    Native American: .5

Number of people in the total management pool: 13,012

Percentage of minorities in the total management pool: 9.6

Percentage of minority managers who comprise each managerial level:

Dept. VP/full VP/senior VP and above:	3.7
Functional and regional VP:	6.5
General manager:	7.3
Manager:	9.3
Associate manager:	10.6

Salary information:

Middle management:	$32,000–$96,000
Upper management:	$75,000–$341,000

The first formal affirmative action program began at Prudential in 1966 with the institution of Plans for Progress. Since that time, minority representation at the company has multiplied fifteen-fold. In 1989, the company launched a Managing Diversity program in response to internal changes and Department of Labor estimates that by the year 2000, 85% of new work force entrants will be women, minorities and foreign-born workers. The two-day training session, designed for all managers, includes one day of awareness-building discussions and one day of skills building.

According to Charles N. Thomas, Vice President of Corporate Human Resources, "We need to teach people with diverse backgrounds how to talk to each other." Thomas, a black manager who has been with Prudential since 1966, developed the Managing Diversity training program while working with the company's personnel training division.

Minorities hold such top management positions as Vice President, Planning and Research; Vice President, Medical Services; Vice President and Career Marketing Development Officer; Vice President of Public Affairs; Director of Real Estate Finance; and Vice President, Human Resources. A black physician, Dr. Harold Davis of New York University Medical Center and Bellevue Hospital in New York, was recently appointed vice president in charge of all employee health programs.

Prudential also has three minority board members: William Gray, the former U.S. Representative and current head of the United Negro College Fund; Lisle C. Carter, Jr., general counsel and senior vice president of United Way of America; and Stanley C. Van Ness, an attorney at the law firm of Picco, Mack, Herbert, Kennedy, Jaffe, Perrella and Yoskin.

Although the company has no separate minority employee organizations, it does have a group called the Minority Interchange, actually a national organization with a chapter made up largely of minority employees from Prudential. Founded in 1975, the nonprofit organization serves as a support group for employees of companies without their own minority employee networks.

Dennis Alvarado, a Prudential Community Relations Consultant who works in the Newark headquarters, says he attends Minority Interchange meetings and is glad to see that many of his fellow minority managers are involved in the group. "The organization promotes minority participation and serves as a networking and support group," says Alvarado, who has been with Prudential since 1987. "We teach each other skills, we develop mentoring relationships and we exchange business ideas that can help us advance in our respective areas." Having received four promotions during his tenure at Prudential, Alvarado believes that the Interchange's support and Prudential's commitment to promoting talented minorities have worked well for his career. Each Interchange chapter elects its own officers, and meetings are held monthly at company offices or local conference facilities. A newsletter is published for members.

Ignace Conic, Manager of College Relations at Prudential, based in Roseland, New Jersey, is also a member of the Minority Interchange. She says the current president of her Interchange chapter is a Prudential employee. "The group is particularly good for junior people who want to network with more senior people at Prudential or at other neighboring companies," she says. "We also sponsor seminars on managing money or buying a house, and we have cultural activities during Black History Month and other times of the year."

Since 1987, Prudential has sponsored the annual Future Leaders Conference in order to educate college juniors on career opportunities. Approximately seventy students participate each year. Two top students from each college or university at which Prudential recruits are selected to attend the conference. In the past, the conference has helped identify outstanding minority students who would make top employees at Prudential.

Prudential recruits at such black colleges as Atlanta University, Bethune-Cookman College, Florida A&M University, Hampton University, Howard University, Morehouse College, Clark University, Spelman College and Xavier University. The company recruits individuals with backgrounds in actuarial science, finance, math, marketing and various liberal arts disciplines.

As Manager of College Relations, Conic has been very involved in the minority recruiting program. She says the company once had a minority recruiting unit which was separate from general college recruiting. Today it has been merged so that minority students will sometimes be interviewed by minority employees and sometimes by nonminority employees. "When we recruit from largely minority colleges," says Conic, "we bring minority and nonminority managers because our new recruits have to be introduced to the diverse atmosphere that they will find on the job."

Conic and her department attend conventions sponsored by such groups as the National Association for Equal Opportunity in Higher Education, where she meets minority administrators from the black colleges; the National Association of Black

Accountants; the National Council of La Raza; the National Urban League and the NAACP.

Prudential is the largest employer for the INROADS program in the state of New Jersey. It also hires minority interns from the Sponsors for Educational Opportunities (SEO) program, which provides college internships for minority students interested in banking, accounting and the insurance professions.

The Prudential Foundation, formed by the company in 1977, funds many minority-based urban development and youth development programs. It donates approximately $16 million each year. Organizations supported by the foundation include the National Puerto Rican Coalition, which received a grant to increase the involvement of community development corporations in Hispanic neighborhoods; the Latino Resource Organization, where funding was used to promote the dissemination of educational resources to the Latino community in East Los Angeles; the National Consortium for Education Access, where a grant is being used to increase the pool of black faculty Ph.D.s at universities; and the Asian Pacific American Legal Center of Southern California, where funding is being used to produce and distribute Asian-language immigration materials. The Prudential also supports the NAACP, the National Council of La Raza, the National Urban League and many other minority organizations.

In 1974, the company established a minority purchasing program that seeks out minority vendors and contractors. In conjunction with this effort, in 1991 Prudential and the New York–New Jersey Minority Purchasing Council sponsored the area's largest minority purchasing convention.

Through its Minority Banking Program, established in 1968, Prudential maintains a credit line of more than $50 million with fifty-two minority-owned or operated banks. The company also makes its federal tax payments through minority banks.

Office locations: The Prudential has its headquarters in Newark, New Jersey. It has other offices across the United States and in Canada, Mexico, Europe, South America and Southeast Asia.

751 Broad Street
Newark, New Jersey 07101
(201) 802-6000

THE QUAKER OATS COMPANY

Quaker Oats is a worldwide producer and marketer of consumer grocery products. It sells cereals, mixes, grain-based snacks, syrup, corn products, rice and pasta products, chocolates, canned beans, edible oils, beverages and pet foods. The company is responsible for such brand names as Rice-A-Roni, Aunt Jemima breakfast products, Quaker Oatmeal, Quaker Chewy Granola, Life Cereal, Cap'n Crunch Cereal, Ken-L Ration and Gaines Pet Foods, Gatorade Drinks, Van Camp's Pork and Beans and Celeste Pizza.

1990 revenues: $5,030,600,000
1991 revenues: $5,491,200,000
1992 revenues: $5,576,400,000

Number of full-time U.S. employees: 11,567

Percentage of these employees who are minorities: 21
    Black: 12.4
    Hispanic: 6.7
    Asian/Pacific Islander: 1.8
    Native American: .1

Number of people in the total management pool: 1,943

Percentage of minorities in the total management pool: 9.8

Quaker Oats was founded in 1886 as the American Cereal Company. Most of its business is in its domestic grocery products operations. That business is divided into six groups: Breakfast

Foods, Frozen Foods, Pet Foods, Food Service, Golden Grain and Grocery Specialties.

In 1990, Quaker made a serious commitment to the minority community when its chairman, William Smithburg, signed a Fair Share Agreement with the NAACP. At the time, only fifty or so companies had signed the agreement, which ensures that a percentage of business is conducted with minority contractors.

Minorities at Quaker Oats hold such positions as President of the Breakfast Division, Vice President of Financial Services, Vice President of Corporate Programs, Senior Vice President of the North American Foods Group and Regional Director of Grocery Product Sales. The company has one minority board member, William J. Kennedy III, chairman of the board of the North Carolina Mutual Life Insurance Company.

Besides recruiting at many schools with large minority populations like Hampton University, Morgan State University and Morehouse College, Quaker endows minority scholarships at such schools as the University of Tennessee, Loyola University in Chicago, Depaul University, Fisk University and Atlanta University.

The company sponsors Ethnic Open Houses for minority MBA students which include bringing students to the Chicago headquarters for a two-and-a-half-day weekend visit. In 1991, the open house included a speech by Chairman Smithburg, presentations by brand management and marketing research, dinners, breakfasts, tours of the offices and the Chicago community and visits to dance clubs.

The company typically hires four minority interns each year through the INROADS program, and also sponsors interns through the Spanish Coalition for Jobs Internship Program.

In 1993, twenty-two minority professionals from the company participated in the National Urban League's Black Executive Exchange Program, whereby minority managers volunteered to spend several days at a historically black college to teach seminars in their area of expertise and serve as mentors to students who wanted to learn about the experiences of minorities in corporate America.

According to Joan S. Green, Quaker's Director of Affirmative Action, the company has a Diversity Council which consists of twenty employees representing a cross-section of the company's work force. "The purpose of the council," says Green, "is to provide a forum for minorities and nonminorities to share concerns relating to the workplace and to provide management with input on ways to improve recruitment, cultural practices, role models and mentoring."

The company began working with diversity consultant R. Roosevelt Thomas, director of the American Institute for Managing Diversity, in 1988 to develop strategies to enhance diversity at the company. Thomas performed a cultural audit of the company before helping to design a training program for employees.

Quaker has already dealt with the needs of its diverse work force in two of its plants which have a large minority population. In 1989, at its Bridgeview, Illinois, pasta production plant, where 40% of the employees are Hispanic, the company began offering courses in English as a Second Language. Going back to the early 1970s, after Quaker's acquisition of the Celeste Italian Foods division, supervisors at the Rosemont, Illinois, plant were given training in Spanish language and culture in order to better manage the largely Hispanic work force in that division.

Green, who also serves on the board of the Hispanic Alliance for Career Enhancement, a networking and placement organization in Chicago, introduces Quaker's human resource managers to various minority headhunters and placement firms to make sure the company meets job hunters it might not normally reach.

One organizer of the Quaker Hispanic employee organization was Julie Ramos. Because of her work on behalf of minority issues, she was recently selected as a Quaker representative to receive the YMCA's Black and Hispanic Achievers Award. A member of the Quaker Oats Diversity Council, Ramos works in the company's BBC Division, in Chicago.

An employee group called the Ethnic Issues Task Force had been responsible for recommending diversity projects to Quaker's senior management. The company has a Black History Committee which schedules speakers to make presentations focusing on issues of interest to black employees and others during February.

Quaker sponsors important presentations made by groups like the League of United Latin American Citizens (LULAC). Last year, Quaker helped underwrite the organization's Political Education Forum, which invited U.S. Congressional and State Representative candidates to discuss the redistricting of Hispanic communities and the growing Hispanic population in the Chicago area.

The company hires employees with background in finance, marketing, accounting, business administration, industrial engineering, operations management and many liberal arts fields.

Besides making product donations to many groups, Quaker Oats contributes to such minority organizations as the National Hispanic Scholarship Fund, the National Urban League and the NAACP. The company is a partner in the Chicago Equity Fund, formed by Chicago companies to finance housing rehabilitation projects for low-income neighborhoods in the city. It is also a partner in a similar project in Oakland, California. The Quaker Oats Foundation, established in 1947, contributed $3 million to several hundred organizations in 1991, including the Corporate/Community Schools of America and the American Institute for Managing Diversity.

The company continues to invest in the Chicago-based Minority Venture Capital Fund, a limited partnership that provides venture capital to minority-owned and -operated businesses in the Chicago area.

The company recently received the Minority Enterprise Development Award from the United States Small Business

Administration and the Minority Counsel Demonstration Award, given by the American Bar Association to companies that promise to help improve opportunities for minority law firms and minority attorneys who work in nonminority law firms.

In 1992, the company was honored by Cosmopolitan, the black chamber of commerce in Chicago, as Corporation of the Year for its support of local minority businesses and for helping to prepare minority individuals for careers in retail food store management.

Office locations: The company is headquartered in Chicago. There are offices and plants in twenty-three states and in Argentina, Belgium, Brazil, Canada, England, France, Germany, Italy, Malaysia, Mexico, Spain and Venezuela.

321 North Clark Street
Chicago, Illinois 60610
(312) 222-7111

RYDER SYSTEM, INC.

Founded in 1933, Ryder is an international company providing services to the highway transportation and aviation industries. Besides being the world's largest full-service truck leasing and rental company, it is a provider of school buses, a manager of public transit systems and a distributor of parts for commercial and business aircraft.

1990 revenues: $5,162,000,000
1991 revenues: $5,061,000,000

Number of full-time employees: 30,721

Percentage of these employees who are minorities: 16.9
    Black: 9.2
    Hispanic: 6.2
    Asian/Pacific Islander: 1.1
    Native American: .4

Number of people in the total management pool: 2,064

Percentage of minorities in the total management pool: 10.8

Percentage of minority managers who comprise each managerial level:
    Vice president: 2
    Director: 8
    Manager: 15

Salary information:
    Vice president: $84,000+
    Group director: $70,600–$122,200

Director:	$54,600–$103,300
Senior manager:	$51,400–$79,300
Manager:	$46,600–$75,400
Consultant:	$42,400–$68,200

"What does a white male CEO know about diversity?" This is the provocative headline that runs across a recent Ryder advertisement. The ad refers to the company's CEO, Tony Burns. The ad and the company are as honest and progressive as Burns, himself a former chairman of the National Urban League and an organizer of many community-based activities.

While many major corporations somehow fail to carry the same values as their top management, this is not so with Ryder. There are progressive managers here as well as progressive programs for minority employees who are looking for minority employee networks, training programs and minority scholarships.

Minorities at Ryder hold such positions as Senior Vice President of the ATE Management and Services Company Division, Vice President of the General Aviation Services Division, Vice President of Corporate Tax, and Central Region Vice President of Ryder Student Transportation.

Vernon E. Jordan, Jr., former head of the National Urban League and partner at the law firm of Akin, Gump, Strauss, Hauer and Feld, is a member of Ryder's board of directors.

The company recruits at such black universities as Tuskegee, Alabama A&M, Florida A&M and Hampton. It is a member of the Florida A&M University Cluster, a consortium of companies that serves in an advisory and financial assistance capacity. Ryder sponsors minority scholarships at, and recruits many Hispanic students from, the University of Miami, Florida Memorial College and other colleges in Florida.

Because Ryder is a government contractor and therefore monitored with regard to minority hiring and retention, the company is particularly sensitive to the need for programs that help minority and nonminority employees deal with diversity issues. Its training program, "Valuing Diversity," is a daylong workshop which addresses an individual's biases and explains how those biases can slow productivity and affect employees in the workplace. "Before we designed the current diversity workshop," explains James Champion, Director of Corporate Human Resources, "we had worked with the firm Harbridge House and created an affirmative action program where we trained more than two thousand managers to become aware of issues that affect minorities and women."

Champion says that along with "Valuing Diversity," the company uses a program called "Managing Differences" to train all employees who fall between supervisor and senior management. "We train fifteen to twenty-five managers at a time," says Champion, "by using videotapes, flip charts and lectures. Our chairman will frequently join these sessions and speak with the managers as well."

According to Gerri Rocker, Corporate Manager of Human Resources, the company's diversity efforts have been advanced by the minority network organizations at Ryder. There is a Ryder Hispanic Council and a Ryder Black Employee Network, as well as a group that represents female managers. Periodically, the CEO asks the organizations to address special meetings of the Ryder System Executive Committee.

George Perera, Group Director of Information Systems Operations and Technology, is president of the Hispanic Council, the newest of the employee networks. "The council," Perera says, "is working on ways to raise Ryder's profile within the Hispanic community and to attract Hispanic employees to come work for the company."

The Hispanic Council targets Hispanic communities in Miami, Los Angeles, San Antonio, Houston and New York to aid recruiting efforts, besides advising senior management on Hispanic issues and providing internal role models and mentors for its newer Hispanic members and employees. It has supported the National Hispanic MBA Association, the José Martí Scholarship Fund, the Coalition of Hispanic American Women and many other organizations.

Champion says the employee networks are strengthened because they have the full support of the company's top management. As president of the Black Employee Network, formed in 1987, Champion is aware that both Ryder and the minority employees benefit from these employee groups. "Our company realizes that blacks and Hispanics face certain barriers when trying to fit into a corporate environment," says Champion, "and we know that employee organizations can create a friendlier environment."

The Black Employee Network meets monthly and publishes a quarterly newsletter for its members called *Network News*. Besides providing information on recent promotions of black employees, the newsletter reports on internal management issues of importance to members, as well as fund-raising requests for such organizations as the United Negro College Fund. The Network operates at the Miami headquarters and in six other regions. The seven regional groups get together at an annual meeting in Miami and will frequently invite training consultants to address issues of concern to the network's membership.

Perera, who holds a master's degree in linguistics, has been with Ryder since 1967, though he had considered entering the teaching profession. "My Ryder career grew so quickly as I was given promotions," he explains. "I was taking on more and more responsibility as I was promoted. It was attractive to be in a company that recognized my skills. And it was even more gratifying to work with people who were sensitive to ethnic differences." Perera tells of a performance appraisal several years ago at which a white manager complained about a Hispanic employee who would not make sufficient eye contact with the manager. Perera explained to the manager that some people in the Hispanic culture consider it an act of defiance to make bold eye contact with a supervisor. "We have the type of ethnic and racial climate here," says Perera, "that encourages employees to discuss their ethnic and racial differences."

As head of the Hispanic Council, Perera has a lot of advice for the Hispanic job applicant who is considering Ryder or any other company. "I think it's important for Hispanic job hunters to meet other Hispanic employees during the interviewing process," he says. "An interviewee should ask to meet at least one Hispanic employee. If the employer is not receptive to this request, then that tells you something about the company. I don't think there is anything unreasonable about that type of request, and I am glad that Ryder is eager to accommodate interviewees who raise this issue." Perera points out that Hispanic job hunters should also realize that every Hispanic community is different. His experience at Ryder has told him that while the Miami Hispanic community is politically active, it is not as economically vibrant as the Los Angeles Hispanic community.

The company has a minority supplier-vendor program begun in 1983 and supports such organizations as the National Council of La Raza, the NAACP, SER—Jobs for Progress and the Cuban American National Council. Because of the chairman's long-standing relationship with the National Urban League, the company has created strong partnerships with that organization in Kansas City, Atlanta and Los Angeles. The Partnership for Employment and Training allows Ryder to work with Urban League chapters in various cities and hire and train minority individuals whom the Urban League has identified.

Office locations: The company is headquartered in Miami, Florida, and has operations in every state except Alaska and Hawaii. It also has offices in Canada, Great Britain and Germany.

3600 NW 82 Avenue
Miami, Florida 33166
(305) 593-3726

SARA LEE CORPORATION

Sara Lee is an international manufacturer and marketer of brand-name consumer packaged goods. While the company is best known in the United States for its baked goods, Sara Lee sells packaged meats under the Hillshire Farm, Jimmy Dean and Ball Park labels, as well as coffee under the Omnia and Karavan brands and shoe care products under the Kiwi label. Sara Lee is also the largest hosiery manufacturer in the United States and Europe, with brand-name products including L'Eggs, Hanes, Liz Claiborne and Donna Karan. Hanes underwear for men is the fastest-growing underwear brand in the country.

1990 revenues: $11,605,934,000
1991 revenues: $12,381,483,000
1992 revenues: $13,200,000,000

Number of full-time employees: 62,783

Percentage of these employees who are minorities: 30
    Black: 22.2
    Hispanic: 5.2
    Asian/Pacific Islander: 1.4
    Native American: 1.2

Number of people in the total management pool: 6,028

Percentage of minorities in the total management pool: 9.8

Percentage of minority managers who comprise each managerial level:

Officers and managers: 9.9
Professionals: 8.8

Founded in 1939 as a small wholesale sugar, coffee and tea distributor, the company did not get its Sara Lee name until 1954, after it had already introduced various other foods and grocery products. Today it is also a leading producer of household and personal products.

Minorities at Sara Lee hold such positions as Vice President and General Manager of a division, Director of Corporate Information Security, Executive Director of Business Development, Director of Marketing for L'Eggs, Director of Marketing for Hanes, Director of Sales for L'Eggs and Vice President of Human Resources.

There are two black members of Sara Lee's board of directors: Vernon E. Jordan, Jr., former head of the National Urban League and a current partner in the law firm of Akin, Gump, Strauss, Hauer and Feld; and Willie D. Davis, president of All-Pro Broadcasting.

Sara Lee recruits at such black universities as Clark, Atlanta and Florida A&M. The company also recruits from Winston-Salem State University, a predominantly black school on whose board Sara Lee president Paul Fulton currently sits. According to Janice Fenn, Senior Manager for Organization Development and Planning, Sara Lee also has a strong minority recruiting effort targeted at such universities as Michigan, Chicago and UCLA. "We have worked to develop strong relationships with campus minority organizations," says Fenn, "so that we can expand our minority recruiting effort to the large non-minority universities as well."

Fenn is proud of the Sara Lee Fellows Program, which sponsors scholarships for students at such schools as Duke University, the University of Chicago, Wake Forest, Northwestern, the University of North Carolina and Clark-Atlanta. At least one fellow at each school is a minority student. Currently

Northwestern has three minority fellows and Clark-Atlanta has six minority fellows. The company also sponsors minority interns through the INROADS program.

A diversity training course called "Strategic Diversity Program" was created in 1990. According to Eva Chess, Manager of Public Responsibility, one of the first steps in the company's diversity initiative was the board's election of a black woman to head the company's public responsibility activity in the role of a corporate vice president. A diversity development team outlined several planned diversity activities, which included the following: (1) creating a comprehensive training and development program and setting diversity hiring goals which move accountability from human resources to line management; (2) adopting specific recruiting policies for hiring minorities in executive, management and professional positions, and (3) assessing minority representation in corporate business ventures and community support programs.

Although it is up to each business division to implement its own training methods in a way that fits the culture of its work force, the primary initiative is developed at headquarters. According to Fenn, the initiative focused on making the company a place where minorities could advance in the same manner as nonminorities. At headquarters, there is a diversity steering committee made up of senior executives in human resources, corporate affairs and public responsibility, as well as Fenn. "Each spring we update the board of directors on what diversity activities are taking place at each of the various divisions," says Fenn. Recently Elynor Williams, Vice President of Public Responsibility, presented Sara Lee's accomplishments in this area to the Joint Center for Political and Economic Studies in Washington, D.C. Fenn says the Sara Lee Knit Products and Sara Lee Hosiery divisions have begun their training programs.

There are no formal minority employee organizations at the company.

The company contributes to such organizations as the

NAACP, the U.S. Hispanic Chamber of Commerce, the Latino Institute, Operation PUSH, the Chinese American Service League, the Jackie Robinson Foundation, the NAACP Legal Defense and Educational Fund, the National Urban League and Korean American Women in Need. In 1992, it contributed more than $11 million to charitable organizations. Its Sara Lee Foundation, established in 1981, makes an annual Leadership Award of $100,000 to organizations that aid disadvantaged inner-city communities. The foundation has also honored such minority professional women as Lena Horne and Marian Wright Edelman through its Frontrunner Awards.

Besides working with several minority-owned public relations companies, Sara Lee has a purchasing steering committee which spends 20% of its total purchasing budget with minority contractors. In 1992, the company spent $30 million with minority vendors.

Office locations: The company has offices and plants in twenty-seven states and overseas locations in more than thirty countries.

Three First National Plaza
Chicago, Illinois 60602
(312) 726-2600

SIDLEY & AUSTIN

Founded in 1866, this Chicago-based law firm has an international practice with four offices in the United States and two offices overseas. The practice at Sidley is broken into seventeen groups. Some of the larger practice groups are Corporate and Securities Law, Bankruptcy, Antitrust Litigation, Banking, Environmental, Estate Planning, Government Regulation, Labor, Intellectual Property, Health Care, Medical Malpractice, Taxation and Real Estate.

1992 revenues: $230,000,000 (as reported by *The American Lawyer*)

Number of full-time employees: 1,002

Percentage of these (U.S.) employees who are minorities: 36.8
Black:	28.3
Hispanic:	5.0
Asian/Pacific Islander:	3.1
American Indian:	.1
Other Minority:	.3

Number of partners: 267

Number of these partners who are:
Black:	4
Hispanic:	1
Asian/Pacific Islander:	1

Number of "of counsel" attorneys: 26

Number of "of counsel" attorneys who are:
  Asian/Pacific Islander: 1

Number of associates: 365

Number of these associates who are:
  Black: 11
  Hispanic: 7
  Asian/Pacific Islander: 20

Number of summer associates employed in 1991: 91

Number of these summer associates who are:
  Black: 6
  Hispanic: 4
  Asian/Pacific Islander: 7

Salary information:
  First-year attorneys: $70,000

Besides representing AT&T in its recent $7.4-billion acquisition of NCR Corporation, Sidley & Austin works with such other clients as Sara Lee Corporation, Baxter International Inc., Borden Inc., Kimberly-Clark Corporation, R. R. Donnelley & Sons Co. and the Maytag Corporation. Sidley & Austin's pro bono legal practice has handled matters for the Midwest Immigrant Rights Center, the Lawyers' Committee for Civil Rights Under Law, the American Civil Liberties Union and other nonprofit organizations.

Over the past few years, the firm has employed such prominent minority attorneys as Sharon Pratt Kelly, mayor of Washington, D.C., and the late Wiley Branton, former dean of Howard University Law School. The hiring committee includes a minority attorney, and the firm holds meetings with attorneys to discuss strategies and issues that relate to minority recruiting.

According to Linzey D. Jones, a black partner in Sidley's Chicago office, the firm has a Minority Task Force which aids the diversity effort. "It was created in 1987," says Jones, "as an internal resource group to augment the firm's efforts to identify and attract minority law students." The Task Force is chaired by one of Sidley's minority partners and includes a member of the firm's Management Committee and minority and nonminority attorneys from the recruiting teams for several law schools.

Task Force members maintain contacts with law professors and minority law student groups for the referral of minority law students, and members attend minority law student job fairs. The Task Force also organizes social activities for minority law students.

The firm has a mentoring program that pairs minority associates with partners in their particular practice group. The mentor assists the associate in the assignment of work and in the development of client relations.

Jones says the firm contributes to or participates in several law-related groups that support minority attorneys and law students, including the American Bar Association's Commission on Opportunities for Minorities in the Legal Profession, the American Bar Association's Minority Counsel Demonstration Program, the Chicago Committee on Minorities in Large Law Firms, the Asian-American Bar Association and the National Black Law Students Association. Sidley also pays the annual dues for its minority attorneys who belong to minority bar associations.

At Howard University Law School, the firm sponsors the Wiley A. Branton Scholarship, awarded to the top-ranking first-year student. Branton, who had been a dean at Howard, was a partner at Sidley, practicing in the areas of antitrust and civil rights litigation before he died in 1988. The firm also contributes to the Ronald Kennedy Fellowship program at the Northwestern University School of Law by providing financial support to minority law students and an opportunity to work for the firm during the summer.

Besides hiring several minority undergraduate students who have expressed an interest in law, the firm participates in the University of Illinois Minority Access Program, whereby minority college students at the school spend four weeks at the university's law school, participating in a simulated law school classroom experience and a legal writing program. The students then intern for four weeks at the law firm.

The firm also provides financial support to such groups as the Chicago Urban League, the United Negro College Fund and the NAACP Legal Defense Fund. The firm participates in the Chicago Board of Education's Adopt-a-School Program, whereby several of its attorneys work directly with the predominantly Hispanic student population at the Kanoon Magnet School, teaching classes on law-related subjects and hosting the students on visits to the firm's offices. The firm supports the Chicago Coalition for Law Related Education, which conducts a mock trial litigation program in local high schools. In 1991, the firm provided financial support, and more than twenty-five of its attorneys coached mock trial teams at mostly black high schools in the Chicago area.

Minority attorneys at the firm have become involved in bringing the subject of diversity to both Sidley and other local firms. Recently Jones moderated a diversity training program for twenty-four major Chicago firms. A chairperson of the Chicago Committee on Minorities in Large Law Firms and Chairperson of the Chicago Bar Association's Coordinating Council for Minority Affairs, Jones, along with black Sidley partners Stephen Hill, George Jones and R. Merinda Wilson, has participated in panel discussions on minority issues during American Bar Association conferences. Members of the Management Committee and Recruiting Committee recently participated in a diversity training program sponsored by the Chicago Bar Association.

Evaluation of associates takes place twice a year. After the first two years, associates' salaries and bonuses vary based upon individual performance. Although many firms have extended the period to eight years, associates at Sidley are considered for partnership after about seven years. New associates do not rotate among practice groups at the firm. They are assigned based on their interests and the firm's needs.

The firm recruits at Howard University Law School.

Office locations: The firm's main office is in Chicago. There are also offices in Los Angeles, Washington D.C., New York, London, Singapore and Tokyo.

One First National Plaza
Chicago, Illinois 60603
(312) 853-7000

SIMPSON THACHER & BARTLETT

Founded in 1884, this international law firm is one of the few old-line New York firms which has been able to maintain its "white shoe" reputation while also advancing some visible, progressive, outspoken attorneys in its partnership. The firm is organized under the following department titles: Corporate (which includes general corporate, commercial banking, capital markets, mergers and acquisitions, specialized financing); litigation; bankruptcy; real estate; tax; employee benefits; personal planning and insurance.

1991 revenues: $195,000,000 (as reported by *The American Lawyer*)

Number of partners: 101

Number of these partners who are:
    Black: 2

Number of associates and senior attorneys: 339

Number of these associates and senior attorneys who are:
    Black: 8
    Hispanic: 3
    Asian/Pacific Islander: 12

Number of summer associates employed in 1991: 44

Number of these summer associates who are:
    Black: 4
    Asian/Pacific Islander: 3

Salary information:

First-year associate (New York):	$83,000
Fourth-year associate (New York):	$102,000–$132,200
Seventh-year associate (New York):	$128,000–$178,800

It is no surprise that Simpson is progressive on issues involving minorities. The firm has produced three New York City Bar Association presidents, and many of its partners have played prominent roles in public service. Among the partners are Cyrus Vance, former Secretary of the Army under President Lyndon Johnson and Secretary of State under President Jimmy Carter; Conrad Harper, counsel to the Secretary of State under President Bill Clinton and president of the prestigious City Bar Association of the City of New York; and John Carr, who caught the attention of many in the legal community when he testified on behalf of Professor Anita Hill during the Clarence Thomas–Anita Hill U.S. Senate hearings. Both Harper and Carr are black partners at the firm.

Vance, a partner in the New York office, serves as chair of the New York City Bar Association's Committee to Enhance Professional Opportunities for Minorities. He is also currently Envoy of the Secretary General of the United Nations for the recent crisis in Yugoslavia.

Richard Beattie, chairman of the firm's Executive Committee, has also been extremely active in government. Besides working for the Department of Health, Education and Welfare in the Carter administration, he has served on the New York City Board of Education and is chairman of the Fund for New York City Public Education.

According to Carr, who has been with the firm since 1983, Simpson works pro bono for the Dance Theater of Harlem, the Lawyers Committee for Civil Rights and various Haitian refugee litigants. Simpson also worked pro bono to protect a large African American cemetery site from being developed into a federal office building complex in lower Manhattan. Because of its record, the firm was awarded the Presidents' Pro Bono Award by the New York State Lawyers Association in 1992.

A graduate of Harvard Business School and Harvard Law School, Carr began his legal career in Simpson's corporate department. He says Simpson's Wall Street image does not get in the way of its progressive attitude on diversity in the workplace. "I have always been comforted," he says, "by the long-term commitment to diversity at the firm. Conrad Harper is the most senior black partner at a major New York law firm and has been a partner since 1974. Despite the firm's old-line, Wall Street image, the makeup of the attorneys here reflects a great deal of variation in ethnic, religious and economic backgrounds. Moreover, I also know that racial diversity is a goal maintained at the most senior levels of the firm."

Litigation partner Harper agrees. He believes that all firms must do more than just hire minority attorneys. "Our obligation," he says, "includes developing that person's skills, making him feel welcome and giving him encouragement."

The firm recruits at such minority law student functions as the Black Law Student Association Mideast and Northeast regional job fairs and the Tulane University regional job fair.

Simpson gives to such organizations as the Puerto Rican Legal Defense Fund, the Mexican American Legal Defense and Education Fund, the NAACP Legal Defense and Educational Fund and the City Bar Association Committee on Minorities, and hires minority college interns through the Sponsor for Educational Opportunities (SEO) Program.

The firm represented the bank Manufacturers Hanover Trust in its merger with Chemical Bank, as well as Matsushita in its purchase of the MCA entertainment conglomerate, which includes MCA Records and Universal Studios. Several years ago, Simpson represented Kohlberg, Kravis and Roberts in the purchase of the cigarette and food company RJR Nabisco.

Although originally a Wall Street firm, Simpson has

moved to a 1980s midtown Manhattan skyscraper across the street from Grand Central Station. As at other big-city law firms, the hours here are long.

Associates who join the firm are not required to rotate through different departments.

Office locations: The firm's main office is in New York City. There are offices in Columbus, Ohio; London and Tokyo.

425 Lexington Avenue
New York, New York 10017
(212) 455-2000

SONY MUSIC ENTERTAINMENT INC.

Sony Music Entertainment Inc. is a division of the Japan-based electronics and entertainment company Sony Corporation. The division was created when the Sony parent purchased CBS Records in 1988 and renamed it as a Sony entity. The company produces, manufactures and sells records, tapes, compact discs and video software. Artists who perform on the Sony Music label include Mariah Carey, Gloria Estefan, New Kids on the Block and Michael Bolton. Record labels distributed by the company include Columbia, Epic and Def Jam.

1990 revenues: $3,228,553,991
1991 revenues: $3,361,553,000

Number of employees: 3,000+

Percentage of these employees who are minorities: 20%+

Number of people in the total management pool: almost 1,000

Percentage of minorities in the total management pool: 15%+

Since Sony Music is a division of the Japan-based Sony Corporation, it has no separate board of directors. Founded in 1946, the parent company has a board which has been made up of Japanese executives based in Japan.

Minorities at Sony Music hold such positions as Senior Vice President of Sony Music International, Vice President of Strategic Planning, Senior Vice President of the Epic Black

Music Division, Senior Vice President of Corporate Affairs, Vice President of Sony Software Corp., Vice President and Senior Counsel, Deputy Managing Director and Senior Vice President of Black Music Promotion.

The company established a Minority Development Department in 1989. Donna Pedro Bradford, Director of Diversity and Staffing Development, heads this department. "My role is to assist minority employees who are seeking advancement within the company," she says. "This includes career planning and implementing policies and programs to enhance minority retention."

Adrian White, Senior Legal Counsel in Sony's West Coast office, says one-quarter of her department is made up of minority attorneys. "When I was interviewing for a position with Sony Music," White says, "the race issue had not crossed my mind except for the fact that I realized that blacks and other minorities make up an important part of the profit margin in a company like this." White, who is a graduate of Stanford Law School, came to Sony Music in 1986 after working as a litigation associate in the New York firm of Breed, Abbott & Morgan.

Such departments as business affairs or A&R (artists & repertoire) are particularly attractive positions for minorities interested in music companies like Sony because of the large number of black and Hispanic artists and the large minority audiences. "Those who want to break into entertainment law," White warns, "should realize that, like other music companies, we almost never hire students directly out of law school. We prefer to hire attorneys who have spent at least a few years at a large corporate firm where they have received quality training."

Sony Music departments offer internships for minority youths, attend minority-oriented job fairs and have recruited minority employees from such universities as Howard, New York, Columbia and Xavier.

Since 1979, the company has had a Summer Minority Internship Program for college students. In 1991, twenty-seven minority students were employed as paid interns in a ten-week program. In 1990, a Minority Engineering Internship Program was established, and students were hired to work in Georgia, New Jersey and Connecticut offices of the company.

Sony Music is a major contributor to National Council of La Raza, the Martin Luther King, Jr., Center for Nonviolent Social Change, the Thurgood Marshall Scholarship Fund, the Schomburg Center for Research in Black Culture, the NAACP, the Alvin Ailey Foundation, the 21st Century Commission on African-American Males and many other organizations.

The company has sponsored Lisette Melendez's benefit concerts as well as rap artist L. L. Cool J.'s "It's Cool to Stay in School" lectures to inner-city students and singer Peabo Bryson's performance at the annual Delta Epsilon fund-raiser in Philadelphia. The event raised funds to assist the organization in scholarship aid, tutoring and cultural enrichment of young black Americans.

Still in its infancy, the diversity initiative at Sony Music began in 1991. According to Bradford, thus far the company has conducted focus groups and senior management meetings to identify the type of training program which will be designed for the company.

Sony's Minority Purchasing Program was created in 1990 and helps identify minority- and women-owned vendors and suppliers. The program supports the National Minority Supplier Development Council.

Office locations: The company has offices in New York; Los Angeles; Carrollton, Georgia; Pitman, New Jersey; and Terre Haute, Indiana. There are subsidiary offices in Taiwan, Germany, Japan, Austria and the Republic of Korea.

51 West 52nd Street
New York, New York 10019
(212) 445-4321

SPRINT CORPORATION

Sprint is a diversified telecommunications company providing global voice, data and videoconferencing services and related products. Besides being one of the country's three major long-distance companies, serving 6 million customers, Sprint also owns local telephone companies, a subsidiary which sells security systems and a publishing and advertising business.

1990 revenues: $8,400,000,000
1991 revenues: $8,900,000,000
1992 revenues: $9,230,400,000

Number of full-time employees: 43,099

Percentage of these (U.S.) employees who are minorities: 16.7

Black:	12
Hispanic:	2.4
Asian/Pacific Islander:	1.9
Native American:	.4

Number of people in the total management pool: 18,017

Percentage of minorities in the total management pool: 11

Percentage of minority managers who comprise each managerial level:

Vice president:	7.8
Assistant vice president:	6.8
Director:	7.3

Group manager: 6.6
Manager: 8.5

Salary information:

There are about sixteen different salary grades for non-sales positions at Sprint. The minimum salary for the lowest-grade position is $21,525. The minimum salary for the eighth-highest-grade position is $42,556. The minimum salary for the highest-grade position is $120,320.

Sprint was previously known as United Telecommunications. Founded in 1899, the company in 1986 combined its US Telecom communications operations with those of GTE Sprint to form Sprint, a partnership then owned equally by the company and GTE Corporation. The company subsequently acquired 100% of the partnership and renamed all of its operations Sprint Corporation.

Minorities at Sprint hold such positions as Vice President of Marketing/Advertising, Vice President of Government Affairs, Vice President of Human Resources, Regional Director of Human Resources and Community Affairs Officer. James I. Cash, Jr., a black professor at Harvard Business School, sits on the board of Sprint.

The company has recruited minority students from South Carolina State University and North Carolina State University, as well as from such nonminority colleges as the University of Missouri at Columbia and the University of Pennsylvania.

According to Kay Brown, Director of Fair Employment Practices, the company is training all employees through its diversity programs. In 1991, a one-day training program called "Valuing Diversity" was developed in-house. Approximately sixty trainers and selected managers were certified to facilitate the program. More than 700 supervisors and managers have attended. The program is offered through the company's training department, which is known as the University of Excellence. Special requests for additional training programs are handled by the Fair Employment Practices Department.

In 1991, an expanded module on diversity was developed for National Management Practices, a mandatory training program for all supervisors in the Long Distance Division. "Additionally," says Brown, "the University of Excellence is developing an executive overview which will introduce senior management to a new two-day program called 'Managing Diversity.' This enhanced program will include skills-building techniques." The company also has a mandatory training program for supervisors in its Local Telephone Division, called Affirmative Action—Next Phase.

In the Kansas City offices, black employees in July 1991 established a minority support organization called Building Employee Success Together (BEST). In the Dallas region, black employees in 1992 created another group called Sprint Employees Embellishing Diversity (SEED). The group offers employee development and training programs and seminars for its members.

In 1990 and 1991, Sprint received awards and honors recognizing its record on minority affairs from *Hispanic* magazine, the Southern Christian Leadership Conference, the IN-ROADS minority internship program, the Kansas City Chapter of the National Black MBA Association and the National Council of La Raza.

The company participates in the Adopt-a-School program and INROADS. Sprint cosponsors the Hispanic Excellence Series and the Black Excellence Series videotape and guidebook learning program for junior high and high school students. The company also participated in the first annual Asian Pacific American Heritage Conference in Virginia and the Southern Christian Leadership Conference's Black Achievers in Business and Industry Program. Sprint representatives attend conventions sponsored by the Urban League and other civil rights groups.

Sprint has a Minority Purchasing Program which in 1992 spent approximately $20 million with minority-owned suppliers, compared to $2 million spent in 1988.

Office locations: Sprint maintains offices in almost every state of the United States. Their overseas business operates from offices in such countries as Mexico, Argentina, Canada, Germany, Finland, Korea, Kenya, Japan, Peru, Israel and Spain.

2330 Shawnee Mission Parkway
Westwood, Kansas 66205
(913) 624-3000

3M [MINNESOTA MINING AND MANUFACTURING COMPANY]

Although officially incorporated under the name Minnesota Mining and Manufacturing Company, 3M operates as a global leader in industrial, commercial, health care and consumer products. The company's four business sectors are Industrial and Electronic, Information and Imaging Technologies, Life Sciences, and Commercial and Consumer. 3M is responsible for such brand names as Scotch Tape, Post-it Notes and Scotchgard fluorochemical protectors, in addition to computer discs, fire extinguishers, sandpaper, camera film, household cleaners, putties for automobiles, videotapes and laser imagers.

1990 revenues: $13,021,000,000
1991 revenues: $13,340,000,000
1992 revenues: $13,883,000,000

Number of full-time U.S. employees: 48,666

Percentage of these employees who are minorities: 11
    Black: 4.2
    Hispanic: 3.6
    Asian/Pacific Islander: 2.7
    Native American: .5

Number of people in the total management pool: 6,922

Percentage of minorities in the total management pool: 5

Percentage of minority managers who comprise each managerial level:

Senior vice president: 3.7
Vice president: 1.6
Director: 4.2
Manager: 4.7

3M was founded in 1902. The company can be a little overwhelming to the newcomer who tries to get a grasp on all of the products it produces. Although there are four major business sectors, at least two dozen business groups operate within those sectors. Most of 3M's business comes from sales of industrial, electronic and imaging products.

Minorities at 3M hold such positions as Division Vice President of Consumer Audio and Video Division, Division Vice President of Identification and Converter Systems Division, General Manager of Office Documentation Systems, Manager of New Business Development, Senior Research Chemist, Technical Director of Industrial Chemicals, Technical Director of Industrial Abrasives and Plant Supervisor. The company has one black board member, Aulana L. Peters, a partner at the Los Angeles law firm of Gibson, Dunn & Crutcher.

The company recruits at such black universities as Florida A&M, Howard, Tuskegee, Prairie View A&M and North Carolina A&T State. There is a targeted effort to recruit Hispanic students from the University of Texas, the University of California at Berkeley, Texas A&M University and UCLA. 3M also recruits many American Indian students from the University of Oklahoma, Oklahoma State University, Montana State University and Oregon State University.

Employees are hired in chemistry, chemical engineering, sales, pharmaceuticals, electrical engineering, advertising and finance.

3M sponsors a program called "Working with Diversity" to train its managers and other employees on the importance of welcoming cultural and ethnic diversity into the work force. The program requires that all managers attend or lead diversity meetings, and that all other employees attend. The "Working with Diversity" program was created by the company's Workforce Diversity Task Force and was reviewed by the company's human resource managers and 3M's Multicultural Advisory Committee. The program includes a videotape presentation, as well as lecture and question-and-answer sessions. Employees are typically trained in groups of fifteen to twenty. The training programs are surprisingly short—only forty-five minutes to an hour, but the videotape is a provocative film which features 3M employees of all backgrounds discussing their own first impressions in dealing with minorities and nonminorities in the workplace.

Ajit Rao, who works in Administration in 3M's Camarillo, California, office, says he used humor to get beyond the naivete that some coworkers expressed about his Indian background. He says that certain employees assumed that all of the foreigners at the company knew each other. "People would ask me, 'Do you know so and so?' and I'd say no. And they'd say, 'Why not, you know, he's from India.' Well, we've got eight hundred fifty million people in India."

3M's Multi-Cultural Advisory Group seeks better ways to promote minorities to positions of higher responsibility. It consists of twenty-five employees, of different racial, ethnic, age, gender and physical handicap status; supervisors, professionals and technicians, selected to serve three-year terms. Both the Multi-Cultural Advisory Group and the Women's Advisory Committee are subcommittees of the Human Relations Advisory Committee on Diversity.

There are also several minority employee organizations that employees can join for networking, mentoring and overall information gathering. One such organization is the 3M Chinese Fellowship, which conducts meetings and lunches for Chinese employees. The group was formed to improve networking, but also invites outside speakers to discuss business issues with its members. Another minority employee organization is the 3M Native American Council, whose goals are as follows: "To increase cultural understanding between 3M and the Native American population; to aid the company in recruitment, retention and promotion of Native Americans; to participate in Native American community outreach; and to provide support to student and professional Native American organizations." The group supports the American Indian Science and Engineering Society and the American Indian Centers in Minneapolis and St. Paul and provides assigned mentors for new hires at the company.

Jimmee Gaulden, Human Resources Supervisor, has been with 3M company since 1979. Although he now enjoys the Twin Cities community, he recalls that his first years were "utter culture shock." Gaulden and many other minority employees first came to 3M at a time when the surrounding community was almost uniformly white. Although the outlying suburbs still have few minorities, the Twin Cities have growing minority populations, especially because of the presence of such other major corporations as Honeywell, General Mills and Pillsbury.

3M typically gives more than $30 million each year to charitable causes. It offers minority engineering scholarships at Purdue University, Northwestern University, the University of Michigan, University of Illinois and other schools. Among the many groups 3M supports are the National Society of Black Engineers, the Society of Hispanic Professional Engineers and the National Action Council for Minorities in Engineering. In 1972, 3M created the Science Training Encouragement Program (STEP) to bring minority high school students into 3M labs and other technical environments. The students selected for STEP show a strong potential for future careers in math and science. Today a number of former STEP students hold management jobs at 3M.

3M's Minority Supplier Program, started in 1972, now spends more than $30 million each year with minority vendors. The company supports the Minnesota Minority Purchasing

Council, which sponsors the Corporate Minority Business Exchange.

Office locations: Headquarters are in St. Paul, Minneapolis. 3M has offices and plants across the United States, in such states as Illinois, Iowa, California and Wisconsin. The overseas business works out of manufacturing operations in more than forty countries.

3M Center
St. Paul, Minnesota 55144
(612) 733-1110

TIME WARNER INC.

Time Warner is an international media and entertainment company that was formed through the mega-merger of Time Inc. and Warner Communications. Included within the Time Warner conglomerate are four divisions: publishing, music, film and TV, and cable. The publishing group includes such magazines as *Time*, *People* and *Sports Illustrated*. Other businesses in the publishing group are the Book-of-the-Month Club, Warner Books, Time Inc. Books and Little, Brown. The music group includes Warner Bros. Records, Atlantic Recording and Elektra. Recording artists performing on these labels include Madonna, Anita Baker, Quincy Jones, Paula Abdul and Phil Collins. The film group has released such movies as *Malcolm X*, *JFK* and *Batman*. The TV group includes Warner Bros. Television and Lorimar. These companies are responsible for *Murphy Brown*, *Family Matters*, *Full House* and other shows. The cable group includes Home Box Office Inc. Time Warner also has an interest in Black Entertainmeainment Television (BET) and Whittle Communications.

1990 revenues: $11,517,000,000
1991 revenues: $12,021,000,000
1992 revenues: $13,070,000,000

Number of full-time U.S. employees: 33,378

Percentage of these employees who are minorities: 23
    Black: 14.2
    Hispanic: 5.8

Asian/Pacific Islander: 2.8
Native American: .2

Number of people in the total management pool: 5,734

Percentage of minorities in the total management pool: 12.2

Recognizing that a large percentage of its consumer base comes from the minority community, Time Warner has committed millions of dollars to minority organizations and educational projects that aid minority children across the country. Its record on social responsibility is so comprehensive that it is hard to find an organization or a progressive cause that the company has not contributed to with money, equipment or the volunteered time of its employees or performers.

As Audit Manager in the company's corporate audit department, J. Edward Robinson is responsible for the audits of the book publishing, retail stores and international theater businesses owned by Time Warner. Robinson, a black CPA and a board member of the New York Urban League, says he has never had any difficulty networking with other minority professionals at the company. "Although we have no formal minority organizations here," he says, "my seven years of experience at the company have shown me that networking is a rather simple activity for all of us."

After graduating from Queens College with a bachelor's degree in accounting and economics, Robinson worked for two major accounting firms and then a petroleum company, where he served as audit manager. Time Warner is currently paying for Robinson to attend New York University in the school's two-year Executive MBA program. Robinson, who works in an office that overlooks Manhattan's Rockefeller Center, says he has always felt comfortable as a minority at the company. "Since I had come from accounting firms where the staff was predominantly white and since there was already another black manager in my department when I got to Time Warner," he says, "I was certain that I would have no problem as a black manager here."

Before the merger of Time and Warner, both had been known as progressive companies that gave generously to the minority community, but Time was known as a company whose upper ranks were very male, very Ivy League and very white. The combined cultures of Time and Warner have created a much more progressive environment in which both minority hiring and promotion are taken seriously.

Today minorities at Time Warner hold such positions as Executive Vice President and Group President of Warner Music Group, Vice President of Corporate Human Resources, Senior Vice President and Chief Financial Officer of Time Warner Cable, Chairman of East/West Records and General Counsel of Warner Cable. Richard D. Parsons, the black chairman and CEO of the Dime Savings Bank of New York, sits on the board of Time Warner.

While there is currently no diversity training program, Alvin Washington, Vice President of Human Resources, says the company is investigating strategies. According to Washington, "The company realizes that creating diversity in our work force is important not just because it is a moral objective, but also because it allows us to better understand our diverse consumers and their needs." Washington, who is one of the most influential *Fortune* 500 human resources executives, had worked with Warner Communications for several years before the merger with Time Inc.

Because this company is made up of such large business divisions, community affairs, college recruiting and employee development activities are decentralized. Overall, however, the company recruits at such black colleges as Clark Atlanta University, Morehouse College, Spelman College and Howard University.

The Time Warner Publishing Group has a particularly active minority recruiting program. It sponsors a Minority Scholars Program which recruits at Clark-Atlanta University, Harvard and Wharton for minority students who work with the magazine's management for ten weeks during the summer. Besides providing competitive salaries, the company pays for each student's transportation and housing. Also, the company sponsors summer interns for editorial positions through the National Association of Black Journalists.

According to Washington, "Time Warner's Music Group offers an executive management training program through which black participants are trained to become senior managers in the sales, distribution and manufacturing sections of the organization." The program consists of training in branch management, sales management, marketing, distribution, development of financial projections, budgeting and leadership training.

What is most impressive about Time Warner is its record in minority community outreach. Not only does it give large financial contributions to minority organizations, but it helps develop and fund creative and educational programs of particular importance to minority youth. Besides being a primary sponsor of the black photo exhibit and related book *Songs of My People*, the company supports the Institute for Black Parenting, the National Urban League, the Puerto Rican Legal Defense and Educational Fund and the Children's Defense Fund. Through the Thurgood Marshall Scholarship Fund, Time Warner provides full four-year scholarships to minority college students. In 1992, as a Black Music Month contribution, the Music Group awarded two academic scholarships to the United Negro College Fund.

The company has working relationships with the National Association of Black Owned Broadcasters. At Howard University's School of Communications, Time Warner has provided funding for the development of a student-produced weekly TV news magazine called *Howard NewsVision*, broadcast throughout the Washington, D.C. area. The program is the only student-produced news show in the country to be broadcast in a major market.

As the largest private supporter, Time Warner helps the Police Athletic League run sixty-three recreational and educational centers for children in New York. Fifteen New York employees are regular volunteers at Covenant House. The company also runs the Time to Read literacy program in Charlotte and San Diego, which uses volunteer tutors from the company and elsewhere. In addition, Time Warner executives serve on many nonprofit boards including those of the National Council of La Raza, the NAACP Legal Defense and Educational Fund and Howard University. Reginald Brack, the highest-ranking publishing executive at Time Warner, is a well-respected contributor to civil rights causes in his position as chairman of the board of the National Urban League.

The Time Warner Minority Vendor Program spends more than $60 million each year with minority- and female-owned businesses.

Office locations: Time Warner is based in New York City. The company's divisions have operations in most of the fifty states including New York, California, Tennessee, Florida and Illinois. There are also offices in Europe, Japan, Venezuela and other overseas locations.

75 Rockefeller Plaza
New York, New York 10019
(212) 484-8000

TRW INC.

Founded in 1901, TRW is an international company which provides products and services with a high technology or engineering content to the automotive, space and defense, and information systems markets. Specific products include steering gear assemblies, valves and aerospace satellites. TRW is also the world's largest producer of air bags for automobiles.

1990 revenues: $8,100,000,000
1991 revenues: $7,900,000,000
1992 revenues: $8,300,000,000

Number of full-time U.S. employees: 45,496

Percentage of these employees who are minorities: 23.5
    Black: 8.8
    Hispanic: 6.8
    Asian/Pacific Islander: 7.4
    Native American: .5

Number of people in the total management pool: 7,285

Percentage of minorities in the total management pool: 14

Percentage of minority managers who comprise each managerial level:
    Senior executives: 2.8
    Official managers: 14.0

TRW responds quickly to the needs of its minority employees and of the minority community around it. It demonstrated its commitment to the minority community that was devastated by the Los Angeles riots in April 1992. Six days after the civil unrest and destruction began, TRW's board of directors had already voted to contribute more than $100,000 to civic and minority organizations working to repair the lives of those in the South-Central Los Angeles area.

TRW's business is divided into three major industry segments. Its Automotive Segment manufactures steering systems, seat belts, air bags and engine valves. The Space and Defense Segment designs and manufactures military and civilian spacecraft equipment, lasers, antisubmarine warfare technology and propulsion subsystems. The Information Systems and Services Segment is responsible for providing financial institutions, businesses and individual consumers with credit information, direct marketing, real estate information and related services. Not included in any of these segments is the company's business in environmental waste cleanup services.

Minorities at TRW hold such positions as Deputy General Manager in the Command Support Division, Vice President and General Manager in the Defense Communications Division, Vice President of Operations in the Koyo Steering Systems Company, Vice President and General Manager of Support Services and Vice President in the Systems Integration Group. Charles T. Duncan, a black partner in the New York law firm of Reid & Priest, is a member of the board of directors.

The company recruits at such black colleges as Howard University and Tuskegee University and at universities with large Hispanic enrollments such as the University of New Mexico, California State University at Los Angeles and New Mexico State University.

The TRW Minority Scholarship Program supports scholarships for minorities seeking math or science degrees at Howard, the University of Tennessee, Morgan State, Wilberforce University, Ohio Wesleyan, Tennessee Tech and Tuskegee.

The Space and Defense Division is particularly supportive of Minority Engineering Programs, and members serve on program advisory boards at such schools as UCLA, UC Santa Barbara, UC San Diego, the University of Southern California and California Polytechnic Institute in Pomona. The division hosts student mixers and sponsors student groups like the Society of Latino Engineering Students, the National Society of Black Engineers and the Society of Hispanic Professional Engineers. The company participates in the INROADS program by providing internships for minority students. TRW also participates in the Adopt-a-School program through the National Action Council for Minorities in Engineering.

At the Space and Defense Division, headquartered in Redondo Beach, California, with nearly 15,000 employees, Bill Izabal spearheads the affirmative action and college relations program. He believes that when American companies set up facilities in neighboring countries like Mexico, they must do more than just send American managers to crash courses in Mexican culture. These companies should, he says, "recruit some Mexican American engineers who already speak the language and understand the culture."

Izabal may be more sensitive to issues of diversity because he grew up in South-Central Los Angeles speaking only Spanish until the first grade. But he has put his own diverse background and master's degree in human resource management to good use as he guides TRW further into affirmative action programs that attract and retain minorities. "We want to be the preferred employer for minorities," he says. "It makes good business sense." The company's goal is to have 5% African Americans and 5% Hispanics representing its new college hires—twice the present availability in the labor market. TRW has been able to meet this goal because it not only works to recruit minorities, but also works to build up minority engineering programs at several universities.

The company also monitors the attitudes of minority members it hires, in order to make sure barriers are identified before they begin to discourage success. To evaluate employee satisfaction among minorities, TRW uses a computer-based, twenty-five-item questionnaire which assesses the quality of working relationships among various ethnic groups at the company.

Laura Colflesh, Director of Employee Relations and Workforce Diversity at the Space and Defense Division, is particularly proud of the Division's Workforce Diversity Steering Committee. As vice chairperson of the committee, she works with the division's senior executive officer and fourteen other committee representatives who come from staff and line jobs to improve diversity-related activities and attitudes. "We meet once a month," says Colflesh, "and we look at the training and mentoring that minority employees are receiving or are in need of receiving. We use internal resources as well as outside consultants." Colflesh says the committee discusses the division's performance appraisal process and tries to make sure that all employees are being considered equally for promotions into management.

Colflesh says the company has a six-hour management development training program that is an important component of the initiative to value and manage diversity. Her office also offers a two-hour program which uses case studies and discussion to train people in diversity awareness.

TRW also has an Affirmative Action Advisory Committee which Colflesh says was a grass-roots employee organization that evaluated the ethnic diversity program. Although the employees began the group on their own, Colflesh says the company benefits from its input.

Several minority employee organizations aid the diversity initiative at other divisions within TRW. Since 1990, the Asian

American Upward Mobility group has analyzed and encouraged the managerial and executive development of Asian American employees. There is also a Space and Technology task force of African American employees which has focused its attention on scholarships for black students. Beginning in 1990, a Diversity Panel was created to respond to issues raised by black, Hispanic and Asian American employees who shared their views during a series of focus group meetings that took place in early 1991.

According to Isaac Brooks, Director of Employee Relations at corporate headquarters in Cleveland, the overall diversity effort is important for employees and for management. "If we're going to get any competitive advantage today," he explains, "we are going to get it from managing and understanding people from different cultures. We recognize that the demographics are changing—and that includes both our employees and our consumers. We need to be sensitive to both groups."

The TRW Foundation provides funding to many minority organizations. Formed in 1953, it gives more than $8 million dollars each year to civic organizations and schools. Most recently it has given to the Greater Cleveland Roundtable to support the organization's efforts to improve race relations in Cleveland, as well as to Karamu House, the oldest black theater in the United States, and to Volunteers of America of Los Angeles to help create an entrepreneurial video for African American youth.

Along with other TRW employees in Cleveland, Brooks volunteers his time with the Western Reserve Historical Society to help build and maintain its African American Archives Collection. The company also gives financial support to the Urban League, the NAACP, the National Hispanic Scholarship Fund and the Society of Mexican American Engineers and Scientists to benefit a special SAT preparation program for students.

TRW has a minority supplier-vendor program, and because of its great support of Hispanic suppliers, it was awarded the Congressional Hispanic Aerospace Award in 1990.

Office locations: TRW has offices in thirty-four states, as well as in Australia, Austria, Belgium, Canada, China, Hong Kong, India, Japan, Mexico, Thailand, the United Kingdom and several other countries.

1900 Richmond Road
Cleveland, Ohio 44124
(216) 291-7000

TURNER BROADCASTING SYSTEM, INC.

Founded by cable TV entrepreneur Ted Turner in 1970, Turner Broadcasting is now the largest supplier of entertainment, news and information programming for the basic cable industry. Its operations include U.S. and international program syndication and licensing, sports and real estate. Some of Turner's entities are Cable News Network, TBS Superstation, Headline News and Hanna-Barbera Productions, as well as the Atlanta Hawks and Atlanta Braves sports teams. Turner Broadcasting also owns World Championship Wrestling, Inc., a producer of live and taped wrestling events.

1990 revenues: $1,437,536,000
1991 revenues: $1,552,438,000

Number of full-time employees: 5,500

Percentage of these employees who are minorities: 29

Number of people in the total management pool: 558

Percentage of minorities in the total management pool: 25.9

Turner Broadcasting is an extremely youthful, entrepreneurial and aggressive company. It is run by its founder, Ted Turner, *Time* magazine's "Man of the Year" in 1991. After Turner first purchased WTCG, a small independent TV station in Atlanta, he created WTBS, a "Super Station" that would develop original programming. It was the eventual creation of Cable News

Network (CNN) in the early 1980s that really made the company known. It has since become a major entertainment company—one of the few to thrive outside Hollywood and New York.

One of the driving forces behind the company's support of minority causes and organizations is Xernona Clayton, Turner's Corporate Vice President of Urban Affairs. One of the first black women to have her own TV interview program, Clayton originally came to the company to produce documentaries. Clayton says, "When Ted Turner sees talent out there that can add value to the company, he hires them—regardless of ethnicity, race or gender. He convinced me that I could contribute a lot to the company and the community through my position here."

Turner was right. While many executives at other companies remained quiet in the face of the 1992 Los Angeles racial confrontations that followed the verdict in the Rodney King beating trial, Clayton brought the issue right to the company. She arranged a Unity Day Rally for company employees at the Omni Hotel in Atlanta; well over 1,000 people attended. "It was obvious that people were privately discussing their feelings about racism and all the violence that was shown on TV during the riots," Clayton explains. "I wanted to create a forum where the employees could all discuss the Rodney King verdict, the lootings and the rioting. We need to be responsive to issues like this." Clayton invited riot victims and others to speak at the presentation.

Although Turner Broadcasting has no minority employee organizations, the company has always hired minority managers. When the company hired Bill Lucas to manage the Atlanta Braves baseball team, he became the first black general manager in the business. Clayton has been with the company since 1980. There are many other minority managers at the company, in such positions as Vice President of Programming, General Manager, Senior Producer, Department Head in Marketing, Sales Manager and Research Supervisor. Almost 25% of the company's managers are minorities.

There are two minority members on the Turner board of directors: the former baseball player Henry L. Aaron, currently Vice President of Community Relations for the company and Senior Vice President of the Atlanta Braves Baseball Team, and Rubye Lucas, a former educator and currently Manager of Employee Training at the company.

The company recruits at such black universities as Howard, Clark, Jackson State, Norfolk State and Atlanta. The company also networks through the League of United Latin American Citizens (LULAC) and the U.S. Hispanic Chamber of Commerce to recruit Hispanic graduates. By working with the Walter Kaitz Foundation, Turner Broadcasting also hires black college graduates into management positions.

Turner's Atlanta Braves baseball team contributes more than just money to minority programs in the community. Working with the Atlanta Housing Authority and U.S. Department of Housing and Urban Development to provide inner-city housing communities with youth sports programs, the Atlanta Braves are developing a baseball field in the John Hope–University Homes housing community. They are also providing uniforms, bats, balls, pitching machines, coaches, volunteers for educational activities and a staff person to work with the resident leaders of the community.

Working with Henry Aaron, Turner has designed and implemented an internship program to provide business training for minorities in baseball. The ten-week program focuses on marketing and other practical business issues valuable to those in sports management.

In May 1992, Turner Broadcasting teamed up with the Atlanta City Public Schools for a monthlong educational project, "No Drugs, No Way," to teach third-, fourth- and fifth-grade children about the danger of drugs. The program included assemblies and educational material, as well as poster and essay contests.

As a major media company, Turner Broadcasting recognizes that it can also alter the biases the public holds against minorities. As a part of its diversity effort, it has created a Minority Resource Guide which is used by editors and producers at the Cable News Network. When an expert opinion is needed to support an on-air news story, CNN editors can refer to the guide for potential minority interviewees.

On a corporate level, Turner Broadcasting supports such organizations as the Urban League, the NAACP, the U.S. Hispanic Chamber of Commerce, Operation PUSH and the National Association of Black Journalists.

The company belongs to the National Minority Supplier Development Council and frequently schedules breakfast or luncheon events to host the minority vendors that offer supplies and services to the various business divisions.

Office locations: The company has its headquarters in Atlanta and has offices and news bureaus in many other cities across the United States, and in India, Japan, France, Germany, Latin America and other countries around the world.

One CNN Center
100 International Boulevard
Atlanta, Georgia 30303
(404) 827-1700

UNITED PARCEL SERVICE, INC.

UPS is the world's largest package delivery company, providing ground and air service in the United States, as well as service to more than 180 countries and territories. The company operates aircraft fleets as well as three related businesses: Martrac, which transports produce by rail; UPS Truck Leasing; and UPS Properties, which develops facilities for leasing on sites close to UPS operations.

1990 revenues: $13,606,344,000
1991 revenues: $15,019,830,000
1992 revenues: $16,500,000,000

Number of employees: 245,470

Percentage of these employees who are minorities: 25
    Black: 15.3
    Hispanic: 7.4
    Asian/Pacific Islander: 2
    Native American: .3

Number of people in the total management pool: 39,559

Percentage of minorities in the total management pool: 18.4

Percentage of minority managers who comprise each managerial level:
    Staff executive managers: 9.8
    Midmanagers: 12.5
    Supervisors: 20.1

Founded in 1907 in Seattle, Washington, UPS remains a major employer of minorities across the country. As a great contributor to the minority community, the company has recently received several awards including the National Urban League's Equal Opportunity Award and the annual Social Responsibility Award from the Martin Luther King, Jr., Center for Nonviolent Social Change. Every year since 1985, *Fortune* magazine has named UPS the most admired company in the transportation industry.

The company's commitment to minority representation is evident in the composition of its board. On a relatively small board, there are only five outside directors; two are minorities: William H. Brown III, partner in the law firm of Schnader, Harrison, Segal & Lewis, and Calvin E. Tyler, Jr., Senior Vice President of Operations at UPS.

Tyler, who has been on the board since 1991 and has worked with the company since 1964, says UPS is a company that believes in diversity at every level of its work force. "I first joined the company when I was in college in Baltimore," says Tyler, "and as I advanced into management positions, I saw minority employees in many of our other cities who were advancing into management jobs as well. We are known for promoting from within, so it's a good place to be if you are willing to work hard and aim for the opportunities that are here."

Tyler says that at age twenty-three, he was training drivers. As he moved into higher management jobs, he had the opportunity to mentor other minority employees. Before moving with the company to Atlanta in 1991, he had been based at its former headquarters in Greenwich, Connecticut, where he had worked in human resources.

The diversity of the work force also left an impression on Luis Hernandez when he first interviewed with the company. Now a District Manager in the Metro Dallas District Southwest Region in Texas, Hernandez says he clearly remembers meeting Filipinos, blacks and Hawaiians when he was first recruited in

Los Angeles. "I immediately knew UPS would be a place where minorities would be comfortable," he says. "Once I became a supervisor, of my twelve employees, eight were minorities. You meet managers of all backgrounds in this company. They are simply looking for people who will work hard."

What frustrated Hernandez, however, was the lack of esteem of some of the younger minority employees who were starting off in entry-level jobs. "When I became a division manager, fifty percent of my employees were minority, but almost none were holding management jobs or had considered applying for management jobs, but that's why there are minority managers here—so we can talk to these people and tell them that this company will give them the opportunity if they show the initiative." Hernandez began a crusade to encourage his most talented employees to apply for management positions.

"I had black and Hispanic college graduates who were very bright," he says, "but they were satisfied with their income. Even my secretary, a very bright, hardworking Mexican woman, had talked herself out of applying for a management position." Hernandez started talking to these employees, taking them to lunch—convincing them that supervisory jobs were open to them. His former secretary is now a human resources supervisor, and many of his former employees have also moved into management.

Not surprisingly, Hernandez does a lot of recruiting of minority graduates. He worked with Congressman Matthew Martinez in Los Angeles to attract members of the Hispanic community into the company.

The company also actively recruits at such black colleges as Fisk University, Hampton University, Morehouse College, Howard University, Cheyney State College, Medgar Evers College, Virginia State College, Virginia Union University and Tennessee State University, and at schools with large Hispanic enrollments such as the University of Texas at El Paso and East Los Angeles College.

The company's minority recruiting program offers full-time, summer and semester internship positions.

UPS has a Valuing Diversity Workshop which was first presented in 1989 and was designed by both the company and outside consultants. Using videos, other visual material, "break-out" groups, question-and-answer sessions, role-playing and discussion, the workshop avoids long lectures. According to Fred Fernandez, Affirmative Action Manager, "You can't simply lecture to people about the importance of diversity. They have to become involved and learn it for themselves through planned exercises. And the experience must be enjoyable in addition to being educational." The workshops are kept to twenty people and use discussion leaders who come from line jobs or from the human resources office.

According to Fernandez, "Meeting the challenge and successfully incorporating diversity into our workplace is key to our roles as supervisors and managers here. It is essential that our management team have the skills and abilities to effectively cope with the changing work force."

Besides using the Copeland Griggs videotapes, Fernandez says the company has another program that also aids the diversity effort. Known as the People Workshop, this program was developed in the early 1980s and is designed to encourage managers to treat coworkers and subordinates with sensitivity and compassion while still being productive. The three-day workshop uses videotapes and debates. All managers and supervisors have been trained at least once in the workshop.

The company also has two other videos. One features the CEO, who discusses the importance of diversity, and the other features line managers and function managers discussing how diversity affects their jobs. Through all of its diversity efforts, the company has worked with such consultants as Aileen Hernandez, a former president of the National Organization of Women; Jaime Canton; and Russell Spector, former counsel with the Equal Employment Opportunity Commission.

UPS participates in the Urban League's Black Executive Exchange Program by sending black managers from the company to colleges where minority students can gain from meeting role models and learning about the experiences of minority members in corporate America.

Since 1968, the company has sponsored a unique community-based project for its employees and inner-city communities called the UPS Urban Internship Program. Each year, the company selects about twenty-five UPS managers and sends them to an inner-city community, where they volunteer full-time at a civic organization. The UPS "interns" stay with the organization for several weeks and do everything from dishing out food in soup kitchens to reading stories to children of migrant workers.

According to Fernandez, the purpose of the Urban Internship Program is to teach UPS managers about the cultures of the country's diverse population and help them gain insight and understanding that can be applied on the job and in their communities. Interns have worked with such organizations as the Mexican-American Cultural Center in San Antonio, Texas; the Southern Christian Leadership Conference in Atlanta; Henry Street Settlement on New York City's Lower East Side; and the Congress of Racial Equality in New York. More than 700 UPS managers have participated in these programs.

The company contributes large sums to minority organizations. In 1991, the UPS Foundation gave $75,000 to the National Council of La Raza, $250,000 to the National Urban League, $10,000 to the United States Hispanic Chamber of Commerce, $50,000 to the National Catholic Conference for Interracial Justice, $15,000 to the Mexican-American Cultural Center, $10,000 to Little Big Horn College, $20,000 to the NAACP and $40,000 to the National Hispanic Scholarship Fund. It also established an endowment of $683,000 for the United Negro College Fund. This is just a fraction of the financial assistance that the company provides each year to groups that focus on minority issues.

UPS is a member of the National Minority Supplier Development Council and has a minority supplier-vendor program which spends approximately $10 million each year with minority contractors.

Office locations: UPS headquarters are in Atlanta. It has offices in all fifty states, as well as locations in more than 180 foreign countries and territories.

400 Perimeter Center—Terraces North
Atlanta, Georgia 30346
(404) 913-6000

THE UPJOHN COMPANY

Founded in the late 1800s, Upjohn serves the world's health and nutritional needs by researching, developing, manufacturing and marketing human pharmaceuticals, pharmaceutical and specialty chemicals, animal pharmaceuticals and vegetable and agronomic seeds. It markets such products as Rogaine (to treat thinning hair) and Micronase (an antidiabetes agent) and such over-the-counter brands as Kaopectate and Cortaid. The company is also concentrating a great deal of its research efforts in the area of cancer and infectious diseases, including AIDS.

1990 revenues: $3,020,868,000
1991 revenues: $3,401,799,000
1992 revenues: $3,638,925,000

Number of full-time U.S. employees: 9,885

Percentage of these employees who are minorities: 11.8
        Black: 6.8
        Hispanic: 1.8
        Asian/Pacific Islander: 2.4
        Native American: .8

Number of people in the total management pool: 961

Percentage of minorities in the total management pool: 9.3

Percentage of minority managers who comprise each managerial level:
        Executives (Executive directors, VP): 7.8
        Directors: 5.8

Associate directors: 10.9
Managers: 7.5
Supervisors: 10.3

Salary information:

Salaries are competitive with other companies in the industry. As an example, an engineer with a master's degree
and three years of experience would be considered a grade 86
and would be paid between $3,033 and $4,549 per month.
An employee working in accounting and finance with a master's degree and eight years of experience would be a grade
89 employee and would receive between $4,281 and $6,421
per month. Professional and supervisory salaries can range as
high as $10,785 per month. Executive salaries can well ex-
ceed this amount.

Although the pharmaceutical industry would like to see a lot
more minority Ph.D. candidates graduating from universities,
Upjohn has aggressively reached out to recruit those they can
find, as well as encourage minority students to pursue graduate
degrees in the sciences. Because of this, minority managers can
be found at every level at Upjohn. There are at least three minority corporate vice presidents, two vice presidents and several
executive directors of divisions. There are many more minority
scientists and researchers in the company's divisions. The company also has one minority board member, Daryl F. Grisham,
president and CEO of Parker House Sausage Company.

Upjohn recruits at such black schools as Spelman College,
Tuskegee University, Meharry Medical College, Morris Brown
College, Clark College, Morehouse College and Fisk University. The company develops special relationships with its "Core
Schools" and also recruits at minority job fairs sponsored by minority professional associations. An Affirmative Action Committee was established to develop ideas and programs that aid in

recruiting blacks and other minorities with doctoral degrees. In 1989, Upjohn's CEO appointed several employees to the Black Advisory Group to advise the company on increasing the representation of minorities and to advise on career development and community affairs issues that affect minorities.

According to Denise Todd, Upjohn's EEO Administrator, the Black Advisory Group has been very successful at helping to mentor new hires at the company. Todd says its members have also volunteered to teach science seminars for young people at local community centers. She has been a member since the group's founding.

Upjohn also has a program whereby it brings faculty members from historically black colleges to its facilities to introduce them to new research techniques and discoveries. "We have worked very closely with Jackson State University," says Todd, "and we can help them improve their science programs by not just providing them with the latest research equipment, but by also introducing their professors to ideas and methods that can benefit their curriculum and their students." Upjohn scientists also visit the campuses to discuss the latest technology with professors and students.

At the Upjohn Laboratories division, the Affirmative Action Committee tries to identify core schools with talented minority students who should be encouraged to pursue doctoral programs. The committee then recommends that the company make financial contributions to these schools so that scholarships can be provided for these high-potential students.

While there is no current mentoring program, the company is considering implementing one for minority employees who are new to the Kalamazoo area.

According to Todd, Upjohn's EEO Administrator, diversity training has been, and continues to be, implemented in several divisions. "We have been working with Harbridge House out of Northbrook, Illinois, and Pope & Associates from Cincinnati, Ohio," says Todd, "for several of our divisions. The

North American Pharmaceuticals Division's sales group has been trained already, and so have all managers in the Human Resources and Engineering divisions. It's brought so much value to the company that we are expanding the programs for our other divisions."

As a further part of the diversity initiative, upper-level supervisors are evaluated each year with regard to their success at increasing the representation of minorities within their departments.

Leon Clark, Manager of Assay Service Spectroscopy in the company's Quality Control Division, believes in Upjohn's commitment to increasing minority representation in the industry. When he came to interview with the company in 1978 he was impressed when he had the opportunity to talk to three black managers in his division. As a black manager with a graduate degree in analytical chemistry, he says he can appreciate what the company has done to find minority employees interested in science and health careers. "The core school concept that we have applied at Jackson State University is remarkable," says Clark. "Two years ago, we approached the entire junior year chemistry class and made each one of them a summer job offer. We want them here for the summer so that they will think about us when they are ready to graduate." In Clark's division last summer there were twenty-five student interns. Twenty were minority members.

As a black person who had his own reservations about western Michigan many years ago, Clark says Upjohn has to sell both the company and the community to minority job hunters. "When you bring an entire junior chemistry class for the summer," he says, "you have a much better opportunity of showing them that the community is hospitable and welcoming to minority citizens."

Upjohn contributes to many minority organizations: the National Action Council for Minorities in Engineering; the Michigan Educational Opportunity Fund, which provides scholarships for Hispanic students in Michigan; the Council for Career Development of Minorities; the NAACP; the National Urban League; the United Negro College Fund; the YMCA Black Achievers Program; the National Hispanic Scholarship Fund; and the Youth Opportunities Foundation, which provides educational assistance for Mexican American students. Since 1976, Upjohn's Minority Vendor Program has developed and purchased goods and services from minority contractors.

Upjohn also sponsors scholarships for minority students through the American Fund for Dental Health, nursing services on American Indian reservations, and a role model program for minority elementary students through the Hands-On Science Training Program at Western Michigan University.

As a chemist who is well aware of the percentages of minority students who are seeking careers in science and health, Leon Clark says he and many others at Upjohn visit local elementary schools to introduce math and science to the students. "We realize that fear of math is what keeps many minority students from pursuing careers in science," he says. "By having minority scientists from the company talk to these minority children at an early age, they can develop an awareness and an attraction for the subject."

Office locations: Upjohn is based in Kalamazoo, Michigan, and has offices and plants in twenty-seven other states and Puerto Rico. Its international locations include approximately forty-four countries, among them Australia, Belgium, Brazil, Canada, Chile, Colombia, France, Hong Kong, Iran, Italy, Japan, Kenya, Korea, Lebanon, Nigeria, Spain, Switzerland and the United Kingdom. The company has a location in South Africa.

7000 Portage Road
Kalamazoo, Michigan 49001-0199
(616) 323-4000

US WEST, INC.

US West is a diversified, global communications company which provides communications services and data solutions to more than 25 million residential and business customers in fourteen Western and Midwestern states. The company, which was formed at the time of the 1984 breakup of the Bell System, is also involved in directory publishing and direct-mail lists, cellular mobile communications, cable television and financial services.

1990 revenues: $9,900,000,000
1991 revenues: $10,000,000,000
1992 revenues: $10,300,000,000

Number of full-time employees: 65,981

Percentage of these employees who are minorities: 15.1
    Black: 4.78
    Hispanic: 7.90
    Asian/Pacific Islander: 1.46
    Native American: .96

Number of people in the total management pool: 21,334

Percentage of minorities in the total management pool: 13.36

Percentage of minority managers who comprise each managerial level:
    Top 1%:   7.34
    Directors and above: 11.2

While many minority professionals would tend to shy away from certain regions of the country, US West is one employer that has provided several reasons for minority professionals to consider exploring the Mountain States and the American Northwest, which this company has served so well. This is a company that is particularly committed to helping minority employees build networking and career support groups.

The first minority employee resource groups at the company were formed in the late 1970s. Today there are eight organizations, including the Alliance of Black Professionals, an American Indian group called Voice of Many Feathers, a Hispanic group called SOMOS and the Pacific Asian American Network. There are also employee organizations that focus on women, veterans, the disabled, gays and lesbians.

According to Darlene Siedschlaw, US West's Director of Equal Employment Opportunity and Affirmative Action, each of these employee resource organizations has chapters in every state. "These organizations are important to the company," says Siedschlaw, "because they support our vision of pluralism and nondiscrimination. The groups not only provide networking and professional mentoring for members who are just joining the company, but they also contribute a great deal to the community through fund-raisers and volunteer programs." Recently SOMOS gave several thousand dollars to create college scholarships for Hispanic high school students.

Each of the groups meets with Siedschlaw and other senior executives six times a year to discuss topics that are of interest to both employees and management.

Minority women are particularly active in speaking out and creating career development programs at US West. The company features a Women of Color Project, a leadership development program that targets minority women with high potential. The minority women selected by the program have special networking meetings with corporate officers, one-week survival training workshops and special skills-assessment and goal-setting lessons. The women who participate in this program range in age from twenty-nine to fifty-nine.

It is probably because of these many groups and programs that minorities have captured so many top positions at US West. They hold such jobs as President of a Marketing Resource Group, Vice President of Network and Technology Services and Vice President of Marketing, as well as several vice presidential positions in the New Mexico, Minnesota and Nebraska companies.

US West has two minority board members. Remedios Diaz-Oliver, a Hispanic woman who has been on the board since 1988, is president and CEO of American International Container, Inc. Jerry O. Williams, a black businessman who is managing director of the Monotype Corporation Plc., has also been a board member since 1988.

According to Siedschlaw, the company put its employees through an awareness training in 1974. "At the time," she says, "we were using a five-day high-impact workshop that focused on racism and sexism. Over time, we reworked the program so that we could deal with other biases that might exist in the workplace." Since 1989, US West has been using two workshops: a single-day workshop designed for all employees which uses two facilitators and helps explain people's cultural differences, and a second which takes place over three days and is designed for leaders at the company. Besides explaining cultural differences, it teaches the employee to manage his or her work force while appreciating these differences.

In 1989, the company set a goal of having all of its employees in each of its offices trained on these diversity issues within five years.

Perhaps because the American Indian employee is not well represented in many major companies, US West has dedicated itself to what it calls an "American Indian Leadership Initiative." It contributes money to and helps develop the curriculum at such schools as Nebraska Indian Community College in Win-

nebago, Nebraska; Little Big Horn Community College in Little
Big Horn, Montana; Navajo Community College in Arizona;
Fort Berthold College in Fort Berthold, North Dakota; Sinte
Gleska University in Mission, South Dakota; and Oglala Lakota
Community College in Kyle, South Dakota. The company cur-
rently employs ten interns from these tribal colleges.

The company recruits at such black colleges as Atlanta
University and Southern University and at universities with
large Hispanic enrollments like the University of Arizona and
the University of New Mexico.

The company supports such minority organizations as the
U.S. Hispanic Chamber of Commerce, the Colorado American
Indian Chamber of Commerce, the Urban League, the National
Society of Black Engineers, the Society of Hispanic Profession-
als and the Mexican Engineering Students Association.

It offers internships to minority youth and encourages employee volunteerism in minority communities. The US West
Foundation, one of the largest corporate foundations based west
of the Mississippi River, is responsible for the charitable contributions and grants of all US West companies. The foundation
has a special grant program aimed at increasing the number of
minority teachers and administrators in Western states. The
Access for Minorities to Careers in Education Project is conducted jointly by the University of Northern Iowa and five Iowa
school districts with substantial numbers of black, Hispanic,
Asian and Native American students. Funding is used to identify future teachers, support them during their college years and
prepare them for teaching careers in their communities.

In 1991, the company's new hires out of college were 43%
minority. The percentage of summer interns was even higher—
54%.

Since 89% of all American Indians living on reservations
are within the fourteen-state US West territory, the foundation
has directed a great deal of money to tribal colleges and the
American Indian College Fund. A large amount of funding has

gone to the United Sioux Tribes to increase economic development on reservations. The Council on Economic Priorities named the company a winner of the 1992 Corporate Conscience Award because of its support of socially responsible programs.

Many employees at US West participate in a company-sponsored program established in 1983 called Choices. The employees volunteer their time to present seminars to high school students on such issues as job hunting, career development and the importance of staying in school. Governors of at least four states have commended the Choices program and its contributions to young people.

Besides being a member of the National Minority Supplier Development Council, the company makes sure that its Minority/Women Business Enterprise Program spends at least 10% of its purchasing budget with minority contractors. In addition to this program, the company has assigned a manager to specifically target and develop American Indian entrepreneurs.

Office locations: US West is headquartered in Englewood, Colorado, and provides local telephone service to Arizona, Colorado, Idaho, Iowa, Minnesota, Montana, Nebraska, New Mexico, North Dakota, Oregon, South Dakota, Utah, Washington and Wyoming. The company also has offices in Stamford, Connecticut; San Diego, California; and Washington, D.C. There are also overseas offices in several countries.

7800 East Orchard Road
Englewood, Colorado 80111
(303) 793-6500

WARNER-LAMBERT COMPANY

Warner-Lambert is a worldwide company in the business of developing, manufacturing and marketing health care and consumer products. Its products include pharmaceuticals, chewing gums, breath mints, candies, shaving products and home aquarium products. The brand names associated with Warner-Lambert are Parke-Davis, Dentyne, Clorets, Trident, Bubblicious, Listerine, Rolaids, Benadryl, Halls, Lubriderm, Schick and Cognex, a drug used by Alzheimer patients.

1990 revenues: $4,700,000,000
1991 revenues: $5,100,000,000
1992 revenues: $5,598,000,000

Number of full-time employees: 10,379

Percentage of these employees who are minorities: 19.3
Black: 10.5
Hispanic: 4.5
Asian/Pacific Islander: 4.0
Native American: .3

Number of people in the total management pool: 2,016

Percentage of minorities in the total management pool: 10

Percentage of minority managers who comprise each managerial level:
Vice president and above: 5
Manager and above: 11

The company has four primary business segments, which include ethical (prescription) products, nonprescription items, gums and mints, as well as a segment that consists of products outside these categories. Each business segment has its own management staff.

Minorities at Warner-Lambert hold such positions as President of the Canada and Latin America Group, Vice President of Research, and numerous plant and senior managers. The company has two minority board members: Dr. LaSalle D. Leffall, chairman of the department of surgery at Howard Medical School, and William Gray, former U.S. congressman and current head of the United Negro College Fund.

Warner-Lambert recruits at many colleges and graduate schools with predominantly minority student populations. Included among this group are Florida A&M University and Atlanta University. The company provides minority scholarships at both Xavier University and Florida A&M. The company also provides graduate business school scholarships for minorities through the Consortium for Graduate Study in Management. Each summer, approximately ten of these scholarship recipients are hired for summer positions. The company currently has three full-time employees who had received scholarships through the consortium.

Lawana Dumas, Senior Product Manager for oral hygiene products, has been active in recruiting minority and other students to Warner-Lambert. A 1985 MBA graduate of the Wharton School, Dumas says that her division, Consumer Health Products, has identified certain colleges as well as business schools on which to focus the minority recruiting effort. "When we go to large business schools like Columbia University, Northwestern and the University of Chicago," she says, "we work with the campus minority organizations to both get names of students and develop a rapport with the minority population."

According to Maria Gagnier, Director of Equal Opportunities at Warner-Lambert, the company has a minority employee organization called the Black Caucus, as well as an Equal Employment Advisory Committee created in 1988. The eighteen-person committee includes representatives of different divisions, management levels and ethnic groups. The committee focuses on upward mobility for minority employees and holds bimonthly luncheons at which members advise company managers on affirmative action issues, and review policies on recruiting, training, compensation and career planning for minority employees. The committee has also revised the job posting system, instituted a sexual harassment seminar and arranged annual diversity days which celebrate different ethnic backgrounds.

Gagnier says there is a full-day diversity training program called "Participating in a Diverse Workforce." "In 1990, we worked with the consulting group Harbridge House," she says, "and we developed a program which uses videos and discussion sessions." The program talks about legal rights, stereotypes and other issues that apply to minorities and women in the workplace. Gagnier adds, "This is a required program for all of our employees. Thus far, all senior managers and supervisors have received the training. We feel that white managers in corporate America have to understand that helping minorities over hurdles is not special treatment. It's just necessary in order to build a stronger work force."

Dumas agrees. After being with the company since 1987 and serving on the Equal Employment Advisory Committee, she sees that senior management has taken a greater role in developing minority managers like her. "Although I had worked in marketing at Playtex for about a year before I came here," she says, "I have risen to senior product manager in a very short time. And what's helped me is my ability to find mentors in the company. While it's also helpful to find other minorities to mentor you, I've been fortunate because I've had nonminority bosses who were also very excited about me." Dumas adds that minority managers should also consider finding mentors and support groups from organizations like the National Black MBA Association.

The company hires in finance, marketing, chemistry and many other areas on both the graduate and undergraduate level.

Warner-Lambert contributes to such minority organizations as Native American Media, the National Hispanic Council, SER—Jobs for Progress, the NAACP, the League of United Latin American Citizens, the United Negro College Fund and the National Puerto Rican Coalition. The company has worked with the Adopt-a-School program and adopted three inner-city schools. More than 120 Warner-Lambert employees volunteer to work with and serve as role models for the school children.

Each year, the company also awards inner-city students scholarships to attend academically challenging private schools in the community. The company also hires minority interns through the INROADS program. The Warner-Lambert Foundation contributes approximately $9 million each year to charitable causes.

For several years, the company has had a minority supplier-vendor program which currently spends more than $25 million each year with minority contractors.

Office locations: Warner-Lambert is headquartered in Morris Plains, New Jersey. It has plants and offices across the United States and in Canada, Asia, Australia, Africa, Europe, Latin America and the Middle East.

201 Tabor Road
Morris Plains, New Jersey 07950
(201) 540-2000

THE WASHINGTON POST COMPANY

The Washington Post Company is an international media company that owns such daily newspapers as *The Washington Post* in Washington, D.C., and the *Herald* in Everett, Washington. It also owns *Newsweek* magazine, several television stations, cable systems and a syndicated news service. The company owns Stanley H. Kaplan Educational Center, a tutoring service that prepares students for college and graduate school entrance tests, and Legi-Slate, Inc., an on-line information service that covers congressional legislation and other government-related matters.

1990 revenues: $1,438,640,000
1991 revenues: 1,380,261,000

Number of full-time U.S. employees: 6,625

Percentage of these employees who are minorities: 26
    Black: 18.6
    Hispanic: 4.2
    Asian/Pacific Islander: 3.0
    Native American: .2

Number of people in the total management pool: 1,172

Percentage of minorities in the total management pool: 19

Percentage of minority managers who comprise each managerial level:
    Vice president, director or equivalent: 10.0
    Department head or equivalent: 33.7
    Supervisor or equivalent: 13.8

Under the leadership of former CEO Katharine Graham, and most recently during the tenure of CEO Donald Graham, the Washington Post Company has built a solid reputation within the media industry for its commitment to attracting and developing minority employees.

Leonade Jones, a black woman who is treasurer of the corporation, is one of the highest-ranking African Americans in corporate America. A graduate of Stanford University's law and business schools, Jones came to the Washington Post Company in 1975. "As you can imagine," she says, "at that time there were very few companies that would hire a black female manager, even one from Stanford. The Post was one of the few that would not only hire me, but that would allow me to progress upward through the company." Jones started as a financial analyst at corporate headquarters, and later moved to one of the broadcasting divisions as Director of Financial Services. She was named Vice President of Business Affairs for the division, then returned to corporate headquarters as Assistant Treasurer. She assumed her current position shortly thereafter.

The Washington Post is still carrying out the kind of activities that made Jones's progress possible. It starts with the recruiting process. The *Post* newspaper recruits for newsroom positions at such traditionally black universities as Hampton and Howard. The paper also participates in INROADS, the national internship program for minority students. Each year the paper sponsors a high school senior in one of its departments. Past interns have worked in advertising, personnel, accounting and the newsroom. The paper also has a general internship in its newsroom, open to college students and people making mid-career moves into journalism. Two of the twelve to eighteen slots are generally held by minorities.

The broadcast division does much of its hiring through industry associations, and sends representatives to interview at the annual conventions of the National Association of Hispanic Journalists, the National Association of Black Journalists and the Asian American Journalists Association. In addition, it sends out job postings to colleges and universities with high minority enrollment, and attends career fairs at local schools to identify attractive minority candidates. There are internships in almost every department at the television stations, and minority students are recruited for those positions at the career fairs. Similarly, *Newsweek* has an editorial internship program and actively encourages applications from minorities.

The company makes a concerted effort to ensure that it creates an environment in which minorities can advance through the organization. The *Post* newspaper conducts a one-day diversity training program called "Valuing Diversity in the Workplace," designed by the paper's human resources professionals; every manager at the company has been through the program.

All of the broadcast group's stations have minority training programs designed to teach minority candidates skills they will need to move through the organization. For example, WFSB in Baltimore sponsored a twelve-month "hands-on" training program to train minorities to assume producers' positions at the network. During the course of the year, participants learned as well as actually worked in the positions, and received the same benefits as full-time employees.

There are no formal minority employee organizations in any of the Post company's divisions, but there is a strong informal network among the minorities at the company, according to Leonade Jones. "There are minority men and women in positions of influence throughout the corporation," she notes, "and we all know each other and help each other out. A young person entering the company would have many role models to emulate." Minorities have successfully moved into several high-ranking management positions within the newspaper organization, attaining such positions as Vice President and General Counsel; Vice President, Communications; Corporate Treasurer; Director, National Advertising; Assistant Comptroller; Budget Manager; Director, Classified Advertising; Assistant Managing Editor; Editor and Director of Recruitment.

Minorities have also attained high-level positions in other divisions within the corporation. At Stanley Kaplan, these positions include Regional Operations Director; National Director, Campus Programs; National Director of Instructor Development; Director of Production; Corporate Counsel and Director of Marketing. The broadcast group's television stations also have significant minority representation at senior levels: WFSB in Hartford has a black program manager, a black urban affairs director, a Hispanic local sales manager, and four black anchors. At *Newsweek* magazine, an assistant managing editor, various bureau chiefs, and staff photographers are minorities; on the business side of the magazine, minority managers can be found in marketing, information systems, customer service, manufacturing and finance. Barbara Scott Preiskel, a black attorney in New York, sits on the board of directors.

Besides this informal network within the Washington Post organization, the National Association of Minority Media Executives serves as a forum for discussing issues of interest to minority employees. "The group started in 1990," says Jones, "and the D.C. chapter has attracted a good cross-section of people from newspapers, magazines, television and cable companies. It's a way of getting minorities from various parts of the entertainment industry together to increase our presence in the industry." In addition, Washington Post employees are active in other minority organizations. The program manager at WFSB is active in the Urban League; a reporter there is president of the National Association of Hispanic Journalists.

The Washington Post Company has no formal minority vendor program, but does include as a purchasing goal the identification and development of minority- and women-owned businesses.

The corporation has made several generous donations to minority organizations, including the United Negro College

Fund, the Congressional Black Caucus and the Asia Society. In addition, the various divisions sponsor programs tailored to their areas of expertise. Stanley Kaplan provides special pricing and scholarships to disadvantaged students through organizations like the Urban League, ASPIRA and the Children's Aid Society, and schools like New York Technical College, Marquette University in Madison, Wisconsin, the University of Illinois and Truman High School in New York City. The broadcast division has contributed to the Urban League, the San Juan Center, the Hispanic Community Center, El Hogar Del Futuro Inc., and the Hartford Street Youth Project. *Newsweek* has contributed to the Asia Society, the Associated Black Charities, Dow Jones High School Journalism for Minorities, Howard University, the Japan Society and the National Association of Hispanic Journalists. *The Washington Post* has been a generous contributor to the African Continuum Theater Coalition; Asian American Arts & Media; the Latin American Festival; and the National Caucus and Center on Black Aged.

The journalism profession has traditionally been a tough field for minorities to enter, but Leonade Jones believes that companies like the Post are committed to changing the industry's image. "Donald Graham has stated his commitment to diversity—to continuing the work of Katharine Graham in this area. That, to me, is a crucial factor for success in changing things. Without the CEO's commitment, it's impossible."

Office locations: The company is headquartered in Washington, D.C. There are major offices in New York, Miami, Jacksonville, Detroit, Hartford, Seattle, and other cities across the United States.

1150 15th Street, N.W.
Washington, D.C. 20071
(202) 334-6600

WEIL, GOTSHAL & MANGES

This international law firm is based in New York City and ranks among the ten largest firms in the United States. Weil, Gotshal has a broad-based practice with attorneys in the following departments: corporate; litigation; business reorganization (bankruptcy); trade practices and regulatory law (incorporating intellectual property and high technology); employment law and ERISA; business and securities litigation; real estate; tax; and trusts and estates.

1991 revenues: $252,000,000 (as reported by *The American Lawyer*)

Number of partners: 147

Number of these partners who are:
Black: 2
Hispanic: 1
Asian/Pacific Islander: 2

Number of associates: 456

Number of these associates who are:
Black: 14
Hispanic: 6
Asian/Pacific Islander: 13

Number of summer associates employed in 1992: 62

Number of these summer associates who are:
    Black: 5
    Hispanic: 4
    Asian/Pacific Islander: 7

Salary information:
    First-year associates (New York): $83,000

Attorneys at Weil, Gotshal & Manges are in an enviable position these days. While many other major law firms are downsizing, this firm, founded in 1931, continues to enlarge its partnership and increase the size of its incoming classes and summer associate program. The firm has even picked up partners who were already successful at other well-established firms in New York and other cities.

Weil, Gotshal has one of the best records of any law firm in the country in the area of hiring and committing resources to minority employees and minority issues. "We hope that we can serve as a model for other firms who are attempting to address diversity issues in a responsible manner," explains Managing Partner Stephen Dannhauser. He says that the firm has already brought in an outside consultant to interview the partners and associates in focus groups as well as on an individual basis, in order to design a training program that addresses diversity issues.

Weil, Gotshal was one of the first law firms to put a partner in charge of minority recruiting. That partner, Mary Jean Potenzone, also a member of the firm's employment law and ERISA department, works in conjunction with the recruiting office. She says, "Bringing more talented minority attorneys into the firm is the right thing to do. And as a partner, I have the attention of the firm's Management Committee, and am in the position to advise them on the direction that needs to be taken in order to best attract and retain minority attorneys. The Management Committee is totally behind me on this, and that's what makes the difference."

Potenzone attends minority conferences and job fairs at law schools and often underwrites programs that are sponsored by minority law student organizations. Besides sitting on the firm's Diversity Committee and Hiring Committee, she attends the Minority Roundtable, a monthly meeting of minority law students, minority attorneys and hiring partners from major New York firms, to learn what strategies are succeeding at other firms with regard to minority retention and diversity.

The firm received a great deal of attention when it began working with the Harlem-based Boys Harbor, which aids several thousand inner-city minority young people each year with its recreational and educational programs. Ira Millstein, senior partner at Weil, Gotshal, decided not only to fund the Boys Harbor Midnight Basketball Program, but also to provide free legal counseling to the young people and families who participate in Boys Harbor activities. As a part of the program, Weil Gotshal employees also volunteer to help the young men and women who come to Boys Harbor as they prepare for the General Equivalency Diploma (GED) exam. The firm trains each of the volunteer tutors.

Millstein, an antitrust attorney who also serves as chairman of New York's Central Park Conservancy, is active in liberal causes that affect minorities both inside and outside the legal profession. He is a member of the New York City Bar Association committee that studied minority retention in New York law firms.

With regard to practice, Weil, Gotshal distinguished itself by becoming one of the first major law firms to develop a bankruptcy department, and it continues to have the largest bankruptcy practice in the United States. It has handled such recent bankruptcies or restructurings as Drexel Burnham Lambert, Federated Department Stores, Eastern Airlines and Macy's. Its mammoth corporate department is still performing the kind of merger and takeover deals that disappeared from most other firms after the 1980s.

Four minority partners sit on the firm's hiring committee. One of the two hiring partners is a Japanese woman, Akiko Mikumo, who has also been a corporate partner since 1989. The firm has a Diversity Committee which consists of partners, support staff supervisors and associates. The committee discusses diversity issues that arise at the firm. According to Madeline Lacovara, Consultant for Program Development, the firm works with Freada Klein & Associates, a diversity training consulting group in Boston, to develop a training program that will assist attorneys and staff members on managing diversity. Lacovara says, "As the attorney population becomes increasingly diverse and as our support staff grows, we want to create a climate for positive development for everyone." Lacovara points out that 50% of the support staff is minority.

To address some of the support staff's needs, Lacovara has helped implement a program called "Skills for the Future," a mini-school for support staffers within the firm. Realizing that some staff members are currently returning to college or are simply interested in self-improvement, the firm hires adjunct professors from New York area colleges to visit the firm and teach three-week or ten-week courses on such topics as critical thinking and problem solving, writing skills and reading for pleasure.

Although Weil, Gotshal ranks in the country's top ten revenue-grossing firms, it is not an old-line law firm where one finds 200-year-old portraits of the Founding Fathers or gets a shoeshine from a little old man who moves from office to office. This is a place where black, Hispanic, Asian and white secretaries call black, Hispanic, Asian and white attorneys by their first names and where people hang whatever they want on their office walls. The firm uses Upward Evaluations, a unique system whereby junior associates have the opportunity to anonymously critique senior associates, and it has also created a Firm Committee, which is made up of partners, associates and staff who meet monthly to discuss quality of life issues.

Although most other major firms hire only second-year

law students, Weil, Gotshal recruits both first-year and second-year students into its summer associate program. Each summer associate is given a permanent associate "sibling" who helps the student get adjusted to the firm's culture. Similarly, each new full-time associate is given a partner "mentor" once he or she joins the firm. The partner is typically in the new associate's department.

The firm contributes to such organizations as the NAACP Legal Defense and Educational Fund, as well as to minority law student conferences sponsored by Harvard, the University of Pennsylvania and other major law schools. It also sends representatives to minority job fairs at such universities as Tulane and Rutgers.

Office locations: Offices are in New York, Washington, D.C., Houston, Dallas, Miami, Menlo Park (Silicon Valley, California), London, Budapest, Warsaw and Brussels.

767 Fifth Avenue
New York, New York 10153
(212) 310-8000

XEROX CORPORATION

Xerox is a multinational company in the document processing and financial services markets. Founded in 1906, Xerox is best known for its photocopy equipment. Its business products and systems activities encompass the designing, manufacturing, marketing and servicing of a complete range of document processing products and systems. These products include copiers, electronic printers, typewriters, optical scanners, publishing machines, software and workstations. Xerox also has a financial services division which offers insurance, investments, investment banking services, commercial and industrial finance. In addition to its manufacturing, sales and marketing locations in 130 countries, the company also has research facilities in the United States and abroad. These research facilities identify new technologies and document-related business opportunities for Xerox.

1990 revenues: $17,900,000,000
1991 revenues: $17,830,000,000
1992 revenues: $18,300,000,000

Number of full-time U.S. employees: 66,529

Percentage of these employees who are minorities: 24.7
- Black: 13.5
- Hispanic: 6.1
- Asian/Pacific Islander: 4.6
- Native American: .5

Number of people in the total management pool: 9,520

Percentage of minorities in the total management pool: 17.3

Given its commitment to minority hiring and minority causes, it is no surprise that Xerox employs one of the highest-ranked and best-respected minority executives in corporate America. Barry Rand has served as President of U.S. Marketing and is now Executive Vice President of Operations for the company. Many minority MBA graduates speak of him as a role model and an inspiration because he is candid enough to talk about the barriers that have faced minority managers in corporate America.

Minority caucus groups and the changes they have brought to Xerox and its minority work force have been the subject of several case studies used at Harvard Business School. As a leader in creating a diverse workplace, Xerox and its unique organizations and programs can serve as a model for any company seeking to implement an environment supportive of the minority professional.

The Xerox Minority Advisory Committee was first established by the company's president in 1972, two years after independent black caucus groups began forming within the company across the country.

Mignon Williams, Vice President and National Sales Manager, has been with Xerox since 1978 and believes that she and other black women have been given strength through the minority employee groups at the company. "When I first came to Xerox," Williams says, "I was worried about how I could sell to others who are not black when I'm a black salesperson. I wondered why they would buy from me. It was during the minority caucus meetings and conventions that I learned that other minority professionals had these same concerns. But they also had solutions for my worries." Williams says the most important career decision she made after coming to Xerox was attending her first minority caucus group convention in Philadelphia.

One unique contribution Xerox has made to its employees' quality of life is the development in 1971 of a program called the Social Service Leave. Since that time, several hundred Xerox employees have taken fully paid leaves of absence from their jobs—ranging from a month to a year—to work full-time on social action projects of their own design.

Minorities at Xerox hold powerful positions, beginning with Barry Rand's as Executive Vice President of Operations. Other jobs held by minority managers are Vice President of Corporate Affairs, President of the Engineering Group, President of Canada Operations, President of the Systems Group, Vice President of Personnel, and Vice President and General Manager of the Southwest Region.

The company has two minority board members: Yotaro Kobayashi, chairman of Fuji Xerox Co., Ltd., in Tokyo, and Vernon E. Jordan, former head of the National Urban League and partner at the law firm of Akin, Gump, Strauss, Hauer and Feld in Washington, D.C.

Xerox recruits at such schools as Howard University, Florida A&M, Morehouse College and North Carolina State University.

After working at Xerox since 1974, Al Martins, Vice President of Public Affairs, believes minority graduates should remember to ask the hard questions when they talk to prospective employers. He says students who are honest and discuss their concerns about minority advancement will be able to detect which companies are truly committed to hiring and retaining minority managers. "When I first came to Xerox," says Martins, "the people here knew what I stood for. I did not try to hide my black culture and identity. I wanted them to know that it was important to me. In an environment like this, people will respect your differences if you respect yourself."

Martins, who has held a number of management positions at Xerox, including Vice President of Strategic Planning and Vice President of Independent Business Operations, also applauds the company for its support of diversity and its endorsement of the minority caucus groups. He believes that some companies put a limit on the number of minority professionals they will hire or support. "When I was working for another *Fortune* 500 company," he says, "I was up for a management position, and I was told that the company already had a black manager. And that was only twenty-one years ago—in the early 1970s."

The many minority employee caucus groups at Xerox include Bay Area Black Employees in San Francisco; the Hispanic Association for Professional Advancement in Irving, Texas; the Corporate Few in Washington, D.C., and Philadelphia; Metropolitan Area Minority Employees in New York City; the Concerned Association of Rochester, Inc.; Los Angeles Area Black Employees; Minorities United in the Southern Region in Irving, Texas; and Midwest Concerned Black Employees. Each group offers networking, mentoring and other activities that provide career support to new and existing minority employees. Mignon Williams says many companies have asked Xerox to help them establish caucus groups in their own workplaces.

The company's "Managing Diversity" program includes an unusual component that has been reported on by virtually every human resources journal in the country. Besides using instructional lectures and videotapes, Xerox goes one step further by working with actors to dramatize everyday situations that encourage discrimination in the office. By working with Theatre Outreach, a Cornell University program which uses interactive theater to teach diversity sensitivity skills to business managers and employees, Xerox addresses the nuances of prejudice. The short skits re-create business scenarios like meetings, annual reviews and other interactions that take place between minorities and nonminorities in the office.

The Xerox Foundation contributes more than $15 million each year. It supports such minority organizations as the United Negro College Fund, the National Action Council for Minorities in Education and the National Hispanic University. The foundation's Engineering Awards Program provided scholarships to seven predominantly black colleges in 1991. In addition, the company sponsors the Xerox Community Involvement Program, which funds teams of Xerox employees who want to work on special community projects. Since its creation in 1974, more than 100,000 employees have worked on projects in 140 cities.

Office locations: Xerox has its corporate headquarters in Stamford, Connecticut. Research plants and additional administrative offices are in California and New York. There are domestic marketing offices in forty-eight states, and manufacturing and engineering offices in California, Illinois, New York and Oklahoma. Financial services offices are in eleven states. Outside the United States, there are marketing, research, administrative and manufacturing locations in Japan, Canada, United Kingdom, France, Poland, Haiti, Italy, Mexico, Germany and Nigeria.

P.O. Box 1600
800 Long Ridge Road
Stamford, Connecticut 06904
(203) 968-3000

CONVERSATIONS WITH BUSINESS LEADERS

During several conversations, the following experts on minority issues responded to some key questions regarding the status of minorities in corporate America: John Jacob, Executive Director, National Urban League; Dr. William F. Gibson, President, NAACP; Hazel Dukes, President, New York State Conference of NAACP Branches; Louis Nuñez, President, National Puerto Rican Coalition, Inc.; Ernest Prince, President, Urban League of Westchester; Dr. Setsuko Matsunaga Nishi, President, Asian American Federation of New York; Conrad Harper, President, Association of the Bar of the City of New York; Cau O, Executive Director, Asian American Federation of New York; Sharon McPhail, President, National Bar Association; José Niño, President, U.S. Hispanic Chamber of Commerce; Derryl Reed, President, National Black MBA Association; Howard Mills, Director of Conferences, National Urban League; and Henry Der, Executive Director, Chinese for Affirmative Action.

Do you have a theory that explains why there are so few minority executives in our country's major corporations?

William Gibson: Part of the problem stems from the fact that employers promote those people who make them feel most comfortable. White male executives will often disregard qualifications and choose to promote fewer minorities and women because they feel less comfortable around these individuals than they do with other white males. The minority person's problem is not so great in the competition for entry-level positions. The greater problem lies in gaining the promotions. And that's because the more senior positions are decided by the old-boy network, which most minorities are not a part of.

John Jacob: It all comes from a misperception that American business holds about the abilities of minorities. There are actually some companies that assume that there are no qualified minorities out there. One mistake they make is to overlook the very places where they will find large numbers of talented minority students. For example, I recently spoke with a corporation president who said that he was looking to hire more black college graduates, but he admitted that he had never considered recruiting at Howard University—one of the most competitive black colleges!

Cau O: When considering Asian applicants, employers assume that we are best suited for positions that involve math and science, so they rarely consider us for jobs that involve creativity or "people skills." The other problem is that we are always perceived as foreigners—even when we are born here.

Louis Nuñez: Although discrimination is still a major factor, another reason why many companies do not have Latino executives is that 70% of the American Latino population is concentrated in just six or seven states. Since we don't reach a critical mass in most states, we are even more likely to be absent from companies that are headquartered in those locations.

Some employers say that they are hiring minorities, but the minority employees choose to leave before gaining senior positions. Why does this happen?

José Niño: First of all, we are not being hired. I cannot point to a single industry that has been successful at hiring large numbers of Hispanics into important management positions. Of course we are hired in the entry-level jobs, but that's not enough. And when we are hired, it is with the expectation that we will be satisfied with that entry-level job. No one is mentoring us and no one is encouraging our development. That's why Hispanic employees leave before reaching management positions.

William Gibson: This comment is just a sham. There are

many minority managers who have the qualifications and the intellect to advance, but discriminatory attitudes prevent them from receiving the promotions that their white counterparts are receiving. Typically, we get stopped at the vice president level. After four or five years of being passed over, and after seeing our white coworkers pass us by, we naturally get frustrated. Who can stay in a job when you've been stripped of your self-esteem? Who wants to settle for that?

Hazel Dukes: If an employer truly wants a minority employee to stay in a company and to advance, he needs to address the fact that there may be white coworkers who do not want the minority to be there. Instead of simply hiring the minority person, the employer has to alter the bigoted views of coworkers. The employer has to work at bringing the minority person into the company's political network. This requires making use of sensitivity training, assigning a mentor and monitoring the treatment of the employee. These are very simple steps.

Is there something that minority managers can do to improve the future of incoming minority employees?

John Jacob: Too many of us congratulate ourselves when we finally get accepted into these positions. Even worse, some black managers are in the position of hiring other blacks, but they try not to because they are afraid that their white bosses will become suspicious. Minorities have to mentor each other, build informal networks and give professional support to minority employees who lack the many support systems that white males have.

Henry Der: Because Asian Americans were particularly late when it came to organizing ourselves into networking groups at companies, we have to introduce each other to the organizations that focus on Asians in business—groups like the Asian Business League, Organization of Chinese Americans, Chinese for Affirmative Action and the Council of Asian American Employee Associations.

Derryl Reed: They can create minority employee organizations that offer mentoring programs for incoming employees. And they can urge their companies to bring in a diversity consultant who will sensitize employees to the different cultures in their workplace.

What can companies do to foster diversity and create greater opportunities for minorities?

Hazel Dukes: If companies really want to foster diversity, they need to put more minority directors on their boards. Board members give direction to the company in the areas of hiring, promotion, community involvement, the creation of scholarships, et cetera. It's a simple step, and more companies should be seeking out some of the talented black executives who can bring a lot to their corporate board.

Setsuko Matsunaga Nishi: Company personnel officers should stop demanding that minority candidates have better credentials than white job applicants. Traditionally, Asians and other minorities are expected to have more education at a higher-quality school in order to be taken as seriously as a white candidate who is applying for the same position.

Ernest Prince: When employers are dismissing a white employee who is not fulfilling his responsibilities, the employers should not mislead the employee or other staff members. Oftentimes, talented blacks are hired to replace a fired white employee, and employers lead others to believe that "affirmative action" was the reason for the personnel change. This causes undue resentment.

Conrad Harper: Employers can establish regular review periods and other objective checks on employee performance. We discovered that minority employees succeed more often in firms that have frequent reviews. Whites benefit more often when there is little regulation and where informal friendships and cliques are created.

Derryl Reed: Employers should be ready to answer questions about their diversity efforts and to explain the lack of minority managers in their company. Minority job applicants are going to look at these issues, and they will appreciate employers who are willing to address these issues.

There has been a lot of talk about the "glass ceiling," a level beyond which minorities cannot rise in the typical corporation. At what level does the glass ceiling exist?

Setsuko Matsunaga Nishi: Minorities are often segregated in staff jobs where they have no one to supervise and where they plateau early and are never given the skills or the opportunity to run a division or the company. Very few minorities are being prepared to run their companies because they are never given line jobs. A line job is a position which is connected to the company's revenue building, which would include the head of sales or head of manufacturing. These are the people who are groomed to lead a company. The highest jobs minorities are allowed to attain are Vice President of Community Affairs or Director of Human Relations.

Louis Nuñez: When I look at the statistics gathered by the Hispanic Association for Corporate Responsibility, it is obvious that although Latinos make up 8% of the U.S. population, they rarely ever reach the level of vice president or board director.

Ernest Prince: At some companies, there are positions that are known as "black jobs," like the titles that relate to community relations. But, in many cases, blacks don't even reach the glass ceiling.

What are some of the negative stereotypes that keep minorities from being judged fairly?

Sharon McPhail: The stereotype that I deal with is that we are not "qualified" unless we are "overqualified." In my position, I am often approached by law firms who are looking to be referred to talented black law school graduates. Then I get the firm's prerequisites: "He or she has to be a summa cum laude graduate from Harvard or Yale Law School, who served on Law Review and who went to an Ivy League college and who has twelve years of experience in this particular specialty." These firms would never ask for a white person to be this qualified.

Setsuko Matsunaga Nishi: The biggest stereotype about Asians is that we have poor interpersonal relations. What is so insulting about this stereotype is that it is even applied to Asian people who were born in America. Employers should stop labeling us as "foreigners." This even happens to second- or third-generation Asian Americans who have never been outside of the U.S. Another mistake that employers make with regard to Asians and certain other minority employees is to assume that a non-English accent suggests a lack of intelligence.

José Niño: Of course every ethnic group has its own issues to deal with. Hispanic Americans have to deal with English as a second language and the fact that even when we are bilingual, we may have an accent. We are the fastest-growing population in this country, and we are an important consumer base. Employers will lose their Hispanic customer base if they insist on holding on to myths that suggest we are inferior to others. An accent is no reflection on one's ability to be a good manager.

Do you have any advice for the minority job hunter or employee?

Howard Mills: Minority job hunters and employees should be joining minority organizations and business associations. By attending conferences, they can network with others who can help them in their careers. National organizations like the Urban League have local chapters that receive job postings and interview requests, but the applicant needs to contact us or try to attend our job fairs.

Henry Der: I have noticed a disturbing trend about which I'd like to warn Asian American employees. I want to discourage in-house Asian American employee groups from telling their non-Asian employers that the company should hire and promote more Asians in order to create business contacts in Asian and Pacific Rim countries. Asians should not have to sell their case in this way; white employees don't promise their bosses new contacts to foreign countries.

Derryl Reed: We have to recognize that job performance is not enough to gain us promotions in corporate America. Minorities have to spend more time establishing networks with coworkers, associations, alumni and anyone who can provide contacts and advice. It's not that you are brownnosing, but you have to learn your company's culture and contribute to it so that the people in power see that you are contributing.

Ernest Prince: Black job applicants should not be afraid to be the first black employee in a company or department. We have an obligation not to let any company escape from dealing with African Americans.

ELEVEN PRINCIPLES FOR RESPONSIBLE CORPORATE DIVERSITY

For companies that recognize the value of fostering diversity in the workplace yet are unsure about how to demonstrate this commitment to employees, I present eleven simple principles:

1. Create an office or appoint a staff manager responsible for diversity issues.
2. Set annual diversity goals in hiring and promotion for each of your company's divisions—in both staff and line jobs.
3. For each division head responsible for hiring and promotion, tie that person's bonus compensation to his or her success at meeting annual diversity hiring and promotion goals.
4. Hire a diversity training consultant to present at least six hours of ethnic and racial sensitivity training to all managers each year.
5. Incorporate a diversity training component into the orientation sessions for all new employees.
6. If you have a college recruiting program, 10% of those universities should be schools with at least a 50% minority enrollment.
7. Create a minority vendor-supplier program and use minority contractors, minority-owned banks, law firms and other minority-owned service businesses for at least 5 to 10% of your annual purchasing budget.
8. To include a wide range of views, make sure that your company's board of directors includes at least one woman and one ethnic minority person.
9. Encourage minority employees or lead the effort in creating

company-sanctioned minority support groups, networks and mentoring programs.

10. Establish a task force or committee that addresses minority-related issues.

11. Establish a relationship with at least two minority organizations in the community that would make job referrals as well as post your job openings for their minority members or constituents.

APPENDIX

CORPORATE HEADQUARTERS BY LOCATION (NOTE
THAT MANY COMPANIES HAVE OFFICES IN MORE THAN
ONE STATE)

NORTHEAST

Connecticut: Champion International, General Electric, Xerox
Massachusetts: Polaroid
New Jersey: Campbell Soup Company, Hoechst Celanese,
Johnson & Johnson, Merck, Prudential Insurance, Warner
Lambert
New York: American Express, American Telephone & Tele-
graph, Avis, Avon, Bristol-Myers Squibb, Colgate-Palmolive,
Corning, Equitable, Ernst & Young, General Foods, IBM, East-
man Kodak, Merrill Lynch, Metropolitan Life Insurance,
NYNEX, The New York Times Corporation, PepsiCo, Pfizer,
Philip Morris, Simpson Thacher & Bartlett, Sony Music Enter-
tainment, Time Warner, Weil, Gotshal & Manges

MIDDLE ATLANTIC

Delaware: E. I. Du Pont de Nemours and Company
Pennsylvania: Bell Atlantic, PPG Industries
Washington, D.C.: Amtrak, Hogan & Hartson, MCI, Marriott,
The Washington Post Company

SOUTH

Florida: Burger King, Ryder System, Inc.
Georgia: Coca-Cola, Turner Broadcasting System, Inc., United Parcel Service, Inc.
Tennessee: Federal Express
Virginia: Gannett

WEST

California: Atlantic Richfield, Chevron, Clorox, Hewlett-Packard, Levi Strauss, Morrison & Foerster, O'Melveny & Myers, Pacific Gas & Electric
Colorado: Adolph Coors, US West
Texas: American Airlines, Exxon, J. C. Penney

MIDWEST

Illinois: Allstate Insurance, Ameritech, Leo Burnett Advertising, McDonald's, Motorola, Quaker Oats, Sara Lee, Sidley & Austin
Kansas: Sprint Corporation
Michigan: Chrysler, *Detroit Free Press*, Dow Chemical, General Motors, Kellogg, Upjohn
Minnesota: Dayton Hudson, General Mills, Honeywell, 3M
Missouri: Anheuser-Busch, Hallmark
Ohio: Borden, Procter & Gamble, TRW

APPENDIX

CORPORATIONS LISTED BY INDUSTRY

ACCOUNTING

Ernst & Young

ADVERTISING

Leo Burnett Company, Inc.

AIRLINE AND AVIATION

American Airlines
Federal Express Corporation
General Motors Corporation
TRW Inc.
United Parcel Service, Inc.

APPAREL AND ACCESSORIES

Levi Strauss & Co.
Sara Lee Corporation

AUTOMOTIVE

Avis Rent-A-Car System, Inc.
Chrysler Corporation
General Motors Corporation
Ryder System, Inc.
TRW Inc.

CHEMICALS AND OIL

Atlantic Richfield Company
Chevron Corporation
Corning Incorporated
Dow Chemical Company
E. I. Du Pont de Nemours and Company.
Exxon Corporation
Hoechst Celanese Corporation
Merck & Co., Inc.
PPG Industries, Inc.
The Upjohn Company

COMPUTERS, ELECTRONICS AND OFFICE EQUIPMENT

General Electric Company
Hewlett-Packard Company
Honeywell Inc.
IBM
Eastman Kodak Company
Motorola, Inc.
3M
Xerox Corporation

CONSUMER PRODUCTS

Avon Products, Inc.
Borden, Inc.
Bristol-Myers Squibb Company
Clorox Company
Colgate-Palmolive Company
Corning Incorporated
Dow Chemical Company
General Electric Company
Hallmark Cards Incorporated

Johnson & Johnson
Eastman Kodak Company
Pfizer Inc.
Procter & Gamble Company
Sara Lee Corporation
3M

COSMETICS

Avon Products, Inc.
Procter & Gamble Company

ENTERTAINMENT

Anheuser-Busch Companies, Inc.
Sony Music Entertainment, Inc.
Time Warner Inc.
Turner Broadcasting System, Inc.

FINANCIAL SERVICES

American Express Company
The Equitable Life Assurance Society of the United States
General Electric Company
Merrill Lynch & Co., Inc.
Metropolitan Life Insurance Company
The Prudential Insurance Company of America

FOOD AND BEVERAGES

Anheuser-Busch Companies, Inc.
Borden, Inc.
Burger King Corporation
Campbell Soup Company
Clorox Company

Coca-Cola Company
Adolph Coors Company
General Foods U.S.A.
General Mills, Inc.
Kellogg Company
McDonald's Corporation
PepsiCo, Inc.
Philip Morris Companies, Inc.
Procter & Gamble Company
The Quaker Oats Company
Sara Lee Corporation

HIGH TECHNOLOGY

Ameritech
General Electric Company
Hewlett-Packard Company
Honeywell Inc.
IBM
Motorola, Inc.
TRW Inc.
Xerox Corporation

INSURANCE

Allstate Insurance Company
The Equitable Life Assurance Society
Merrill Lynch & Co., Inc.
Metropolitan Life Insurance Company
The Prudential Insurance Company of America

LAW

Hogan & Hartson
Morrison & Foerster

O'Melveny & Myers
Sidley & Austin
Simpson Thacher & Bartlett
Weil, Gotshal & Manges

MEDIA

Detroit Free Press
Gannett Co., Inc.
General Electric Company
The New York Times Company
Time Warner Inc.
Turner Broadcasting System, Inc.
The Washington Post Company

PAPER PRODUCTS

Borden, Inc.
Champion International
Hallmark Cards, Inc.
3M

PHARMACEUTICAL

Bristol-Myers Squibb Company
Dow Chemical Company
Hoechst Celanese Corporation
Johnson & Johnson
Merck & Co., Inc.
Pfizer Inc.
The Upjohn Company

PHOTOGRAPHIC AND FILM PRODUCTS

Eastman Kodak Company
Polaroid Corporation
3M

RESTAURANT AND HOTEL

Burger King Corporation
General Mills, Inc.
Marriott Corporation
McDonald's Corporation
PepsiCo, Inc.

RETAIL

Dayton Hudson Corporation
Hallmark Cards, Inc.
J. C. Penney Company, Inc.

TELECOMMUNICATIONS

American Telephone and Telegraph
Ameritech
Bell Atlantic Corporation
MCI Communications Corporation
NYNEX Corporation
Sprint Corporation
US West, Inc.

TRANSPORTATION

American Airlines
Amtrak
Federal Express Corporation

Ryder System, Inc.
United Parcel Service, Inc.

UTILITIES

Pacific Gas & Electric Company

RECOMMENDED READING

BOOKS:

DICKENS, FLOYD, JR. AND JACQUELINE B. DICKENS. *The Black Manager: Making it in the Corporate World*, New York: AMACOM, 1991.

KANTER, ROSABETH MOSS AND BARRY STEIN. *A Tale of "O": On Being Different in an Organization*, Cambridge, Massachusetts: Goodmeasure, Inc. (video).

LODEN, MARILYN AND JUDY B. ROSENER. *Workforce America: Managing Employee Diversity as a Vital Resource*, Homewood, Illinois: Business One Irwin, 1992.

THOMAS, R. ROOSEVELT, JR. *Beyond Race and Gender: Unleashing the Power of Your Total Work Force*, New York: AMACOM, 1991.

MAGAZINES:

A. Magazine (*Incorporating ASIAM*) (Metro East Publications, Inc., 296 Elizabeth Street, New York, New York) Asian American

The Black Collegian (Black Collegiate Services, Inc., 1240 South Broad Avenue, New Orleans, Louisiana) African American

Black Enterprise (Earl G. Graves Ltd., 130 Fifth Avenue, New York, New York) African American

Ebony (Johnson Publishing Co., Inc., 820 S. Michigan Avenue, Chicago, Illinois) African American

Emerge (Emerge Communications, Inc., 170 Varick Street, New York, New York) African American

Essence (Essence Communications, Inc., 1500 Broadway, New York, New York) African American

Filipinas (Filipinas Publishing, Inc., 5222 Diamond Heights Blvd., San Francisco, California) Filipino

Hispanic (Hispanic Publishing Corporation, 111 Massachusetts Avenue, N.W., Washington, DC) Hispanic

Hispanic Business (Hispanic Business Inc., 360 S. Hope Avenue, Suite 300 C, Santa Barbara, California) Hispanic

Indian Life, (Intertribal Christian Communications, Box 3765 Station B, Winnipeg, Canada) Native American

Interrace (Interrace, Inc., P.O. Box 15566, Beverly Hills, California) interracial

Jet (Johnson Publishing Co., Inc., 820 S. Michigan Avenue, Chicago, Illinois) African American

Minorities and Women in Business (Venture X, Inc., PO Drawer 210, Burlington, North Carolina) all minorities

Native Peoples Magazine (Media Concepts Group, Inc., 5333 North Seventh Street, C-224, Phoenix, Arizona) Native American

The Second Generation (New York Asian News, Inc., 145 West 28th Street, 11th floor, New York, New York) Asian American

Transpacific (Transpacific Media Inc., 23715 W. Malibu Road, Malibu, California) Asian American